T0301280

AMERICAN DEADLINE

COLUMBIA JOURNALISM REVIEW BOOKS

COLUMBIA JOURNALISM REVIEW BOOKS

For more than fifty years, the *Columbia Journalism Review* has been the gold standard for media criticism, holding the profession to the highest standards and exploring where journalism is headed, for good and for ill.

Columbia Journalism Review Books expands upon this mission, seeking to publish titles that allow for greater depth in exploring key issues confronting journalism, both past and present, and pointing to new ways of thinking about the field's impact and potential.

Drawing on the expertise of the editorial staff at the *Columbia Journalism Review* as well as the Columbia Journalism School, the series of books will seek out innovative voices and reclaim important works, traditions, and standards. In doing this, the series will also incorporate new ways of publishing made available by the Web and e-books.

For a complete list of titles, see page 303

AMERICAN DEADLINE

REPORTING FROM FOUR
NEWS-STARVED TOWNS IN
THE TRUMP ERA

GREG GLASSNER,
CHARLES RICHARDSON,
SANDRA SANCHEZ, AND
JASON TOGYER

Columbia University Press   *New York*

Columbia University Press
Publishers Since 1893
New York   Chichester, West Sussex
cup.columbia.edu

Library of Congress Cataloging-in-Publication Data
Names: Glassner, Greg, author. | Richardson, Charles (Journalist) author. |
Sanchez, Sandra (Journalist) author. | Togyer, Jason, author.
Title: American deadline : reporting from four news-starved towns in the
Trump era / Greg Glassner, Charles Richardson, Sandra Sanchez,
and Jason Togyer.
Description: New York : Columbia University Press, 2023. | Series: Columbia
journalism review books | Includes index.
Identifiers: LCCN 2022044121 (print) | LCCN 2022044122 (ebook) |
ISBN 9780231208406 (hardback) | ISBN 9780231208413 (trade paperback) |
ISBN 9780231557412 (ebook)
Subjects: LCSH: Rural journalism—United States. | Trump, Donald,
1946– —Press coverage. | COVID-19 Pandemic, 2020– —Press coverage. |
Press and politics—United States. | Reportage literature, American.
Classification: LCC PN4888.C7 G53 2023 (print) | LCC PN4888.C7 (ebook) |
DDC 071/.3—dc23/eng/20221121
LC record available at https://lccn.loc.gov/2022044121
LC ebook record available at https://lccn.loc.gov/2022044122

Columbia University Press books are printed on permanent
and durable acid-free paper.
Printed and bound by CPI Group (UK) Ltd, Croydon, CR0 4YY

Cover design: Milenda Nan Ok Lee
Cover image: Mega Pixel © Shutterstock

CONTENTS

ACKNOWLEDGMENTS

This book began as a collaborative effort, and that spirit has been its guiding force. The collaboration began with two publications—*Columbia Journalism Review* and the *Delacorte Review*—that took the form of a newsletter, *The Year of Fear*, which appeared weekly over the course of 2020. That project was made possible by the generous support of the New York Community Trust.

The remarkable journalists whose work brought that newsletter and this book to life—Greg Glassner, Charles Richardson, Sandra Sanchez, and Jason Togyer—worked with a team of terrific editors: Cissi Falligant, Mike Hoyt, and Natasha Rodriguez of the *Delacorte Review* as well as Brendan Fitzgerald and Savannah Jacobson of *Columbia Journalism Review*.

Thanks as well to the project's illustrator, Eleonore Hamelin.

And special thanks to Philip Leventhal of Columbia University Press for his wise editing and stewardship of this book.

AMERICAN
DEADLINE

INTRODUCTION

T his is the story of four towns in 2020 that had little in common but the loss of the newspapers they once knew. Two saw their newspapers die. Two watched as papers that were once thick and thriving struggled to survive. This story unfolds at a time when those communities and the nation could ill afford the loss of the stories those newspapers once told.

Conversations don't die when newspapers disappear or wither. They instead get shorter and less urgent because it is hard to ask, "Did you hear?" when no one has and when no one can reply, "Yes, I read about it this morning in the paper." Gone are seemingly mundane but often illuminating stories about town councils, school boards, mayors, city managers, budget hearings, high school football games, libraries, church events, start-ups, shutdowns, layoffs, arrests, trials, fires, deaths, births, elections. Even as the newspapers disappeared, however, the stories were still there, waiting to be discovered and told.

Since 2005, according to a study at the University of North Carolina at Chapel Hill, 2,100 American newspapers have vanished,[1] transforming many of those communities into what are now called "news deserts." Many of the surviving 6,700 weeklies and dailies, the study went on to report, became newspapers in name only, "ghost" papers with vastly reduced staffs and readership.

The loss of those newspapers has been felt most acutely in the communities they once served, many of them too poor and aging to support a paper. It has also been felt more widely in ways that are not necessarily apparent. News spreads not only to local readers but up the journalism food chain, from local weeklies that pride themselves on covering *everything* to local dailies that have to fill a paper every day, to larger dailies, to regional papers, and on to the national media reporters eager to learn what is taking place *out there*, in the hinterlands, "flyover country," the "real" America.

The disappearance of those stories has created a dangerous void in understanding the issues, mood, and outlook that animate the many parts of the country less accessible to the national news media. That is what happened in 2016, when many Americans woke up on the morning after Donald Trump's election asking, "How did that happen?" It became clear almost overnight not only that many had missed the story but also that one important reason why they missed it was that too few reporters were deployed locally to report on it.

What happened in 2016, however, was not merely about a missed story or slashed local journalism payrolls. That election revealed a divide that Americans assumed existed but whose depth was not fully appreciated. In the four years that followed, that divide only deepened, even as understanding it did not. How could it be otherwise when the papers that might illuminate what was taking place in hundreds of towns and villages and cities across the country were no more?

The powerful and inexorable force of digital disruption had by 2020 exacted a profound toll on journalism, both national and local. As is so often the case with disruptive technology,

wrote the Harvard Business School professor Clayton Christiansen, its impact is felt most acutely by legacy businesses, for
whom all the ways they have achieved success are suddenly rendered obsolete.[2] For newspapers, that meant their reliance on
print advertising—in particular its most profitable form, classified advertising—became an unsustainable business model.
Ads once made newspapers so profitable that margins of more
than 20 percent were not unusual. Now the advertisers were
going to free websites, such as craigslist. News organizations
shifted from print to online only to discover that the digital
giants Facebook and Google were devouring advertising dollars
that had for decades sustained newsrooms.

Because so many newspapers had gone public when business
was thriving—and investor money poured in—they were now
vulnerable to the demands of shareholders, who, rather than seeing newspapers as a source of ever-increasing quarterly earn-
ings, were now looking at shrinking profits. The response was
to cut and, when that didn't stanch the losses, to cut more. The
maxim in newsrooms became "doing more with less," a propo-
sition that defied the laws of mathematics. Local reporters who
had been covering, say, three or four towns, now found themselves covering upward of ten because their once crowded newsrooms were now filled with empty desks. There were few more
dispiriting experiences in journalism than to walk into a once-
thriving paper and be greeted not by the din of a pulsing newsroom as deadline approached but by silence.

At the same time, newsrooms both large and small fell prey
to corporate raiders who bought up news properties by the
dozen, having calculated that by shrinking already decimated
newsrooms to the barest essentials, they could siphon off what
profits remained. Then they could sell off the real estate. And
even as new models emerged—nonprofit news organizations,

4 ∞ INTRODUCTION

online-only start-ups—the void left by the demise and disappearance of what until recently had been thriving newspapers
was felt not only by their remaining loyal readers but also by
those who had reported the news. To talk to women and men
who had felt a deep connection to the communities they covered was to hear a lament that began with anger and ended in
heartbreak. That's where our newsroom once stood, they would
say, after the wrecking crew had come and gone.

In the early winter of 2020, when this account begins, it was reasonable to believe that the drama that would overwhelm all
others in the months to come would be the presidential election,
arguably the most fraught in memory, with each side convinced
of not only the urgent need for victory but also the terror of
defeat. That relentless narrative was propelled into motion on
January 16 with the opening of the third presidential impeachment trial in the nation's history. Just three weeks later, on February 4, the day the Senate acquitted President Trump, Pete Buttigieg, the former mayor of South Bend, Indiana, and Senator
Bernie Sanders of Vermont emerged the winners in a virtual tie
in the Iowa Democratic caucuses, outpacing ten other rivals in
the race to unseat the president. A week later in New Hampshire, Sanders won again. Former vice president Joe Biden, who
finished a disappointing fifth, left early for South Carolina in
the hope of reviving his moribund campaign.

There were, of course, other stories, among them a dispatch
from Washington State on January 20—a year to the day before
the next presidential inauguration—when doctors in Snohom-
ish County alerted local and state health officials that a thirty-
five-year-old man who had recently returned with his family
from Wuhan, China, had tested positive for the novel coronavirus that Chinese officials had first reported on New Year's Eve

and were trying desperately and unsuccessfully to play down and contain.

In the weeks and months to come, what most assumed would be a single, compelling story line instead exploded into many stories, each with its own arc, each with stakes that became at turns terrifying and enraging.

On January 21, Chinese officials locked down Wuhan. A week later the World Health Organization (WHO) declared the virus a global health emergency. Three days later, on February 2, global air travel was ordered restricted. The following day the Trump administration called the spreading virus a public-health emergency. On February 6, the United States suffered its first death from COVID-19 in Santa Clara County, California. The second came in the same county eleven days later. Neither victim had traveled, and there was a growing fear that the virus had been spreading in the county for at least two weeks. Two weeks later, on March 11, WHO declared the virus a pandemic, and two days after that the Trump administration banned the entry of non-U.S. citizens from twenty-six European countries.

That announcement came just hours after Breonna Taylor, a twenty-six-year-old medical worker, was shot and killed by police in a raid on her apartment in Louisville. Her death came three weeks after a twenty-five-year-old Black man, Ahmaud Arbery, was chased, shot, and killed as he jogged near his home in Brunswick, Georgia, and shortly before a Minneapolis security guard named George Floyd contracted the coronavirus that was now racing, seemingly out of control, across the country.

Even as hospitals were so inundated with the sick and dying that freezer trucks began appearing because morgues were overwhelmed, Floyd recovered from the virus. He was arrested on Memorial Day when a store owner called police to say that Floyd had tried to buy cigarettes with a fake twenty-dollar bill. The senior officer on the scene, Derek Chauvin, pinned Floyd to the ground and kept his knee pressed on Floyd's neck for eight minutes and forty-six seconds, even as bystanders called out that he could not breathe and recorded the incident on their phones.

The first protest over George Floyd's killing by a police officer came the following day in Minneapolis. Within days, there were protests across the country, most of them spontaneous. On June 6 alone, two weeks after Floyd's death, half a million people in 550 cities and towns across the country took to the streets, protesting his death as well as that of Ahmaud Arbery, Breonna Taylor, and other Black people who had died in police custody. The protests reached 40 percent of the counties across the country. They were overwhelmingly peaceful even as they were criticized by the president and his supporters for occasional acts of violence. The protests were striking in their persistence and the diversity of those who took part, many in masks to protect themselves and those around them from the virus that by June had killed 124,000 Americans, among the 489,000 who had so far died worldwide.

In August, after police shot and paralyzed a twenty-nine-year-old Black man, Jacob Blake, in Kenosha, Wisconsin, protests surged again, with athletes from the National Basketball Association, Women's NBA, Major League Baseball, and Major League Soccer boycotting games in protest. On the second day of protests in Kenosha, Kyle Rittenhouse, a seventeen-year-old white teenager who had made his way there from Illinois with an assault rifle, allegedly shot and killed two protestors and injured a third. President Trump suggested Rittenhouse had acted in self-defense.

By then, the virus had devastated the economy. By May 2020, more than 20 million Americans had lost their jobs. The losses struck everywhere as businesses, office buildings, schools, restaurants, theaters, museums, courthouses, municipal offices, and stores deemed nonessential were forced to close as the virus exacted an ever-greater toll.

Among the hardest hit were newsrooms, which by December 2021 had shed 6,150 jobs even as the need for journalists to cover the rapidly accelerating stories grew more urgent. Those losses were the latest in what had been more than a decade of decimation of American news organizations. With revenue in rapid decline since 2005, around 37,000 journalists lost their jobs as employers cut positions even as they pressed their remaining slender staffs to maintain what coverage they could.

In January, it appeared that if history, tradition, and convention were guides, the story of 2020, which meant the story of the election, was going to be told as campaign stories had always been told, through polling and through reports from the campaign trail and demographically illuminating communities—"they voted for Obama in 2008 and 2012 but pivoted to Trump in 2016"—by reporters from national news outlets who would spend a week or so "taking the country's pulse," often starting with a stop at the local diner. There would be punditry, too, and commentary and a good many off-the-record comments in the mix from political operatives who, as always, went on the record only to offer anodyne quotes about the state of the campaign or their candidate's fortunes.

Although this work was hard and often well done, political reporters would find themselves caught in a competitive cycle in which the hunt for news, especially when it played into a horserace narrative, obscured what was more subtle and arguably more significant.

But was there another way to tell this tale, one that would transport readers to some of those very communities that had been rendered all but invisible because there was no one to find and tell their stories? They would ideally be communities where the drama was high because the outcome would be in doubt, places where the forces shaping life in America—race, poverty, immigration, climate change, social dislocation—were felt acutely.

No one place could claim to tell America's story, but there were communities that, when taken together, could create a mosaic that could capture a great deal of what Americans had on their minds and in their hearts, first as the long countdown to Election Day began and then, very quickly, as the world turned upside-down. That kind of journalism would require time and knowledge, which meant storytellers who knew those communities intimately—reporters who lived and who had or continued to work there.

It would also mean giving those reporters license to tell what they had learned in ways beyond the traditional forms. In truth, many journalistic conventions were a relatively recent phenomenon, one that began after World War II and that had nonetheless became so ingrained in American journalism that it was hard, short of an hour or two on a library's microfilm machine, to recall a time when local journalism could be funny, intimate, chatty, verbose, folksy, weepy, and disarming and, depending on the town, the writer, and editor, could very much have its own distinctive voice.

And that, in turn, posed a question that went to the heart of local journalism's struggle to survive: Was there a different way to do the work? Was there an approach that readers who had abandoned so many local papers might be drawn to and perhaps find essential?

For decades, people had turned to their local papers for news that spoke directly to their lives, their concerns, their neighbors, their towns. And then they began to stop doing so. But why? Was it the ability to learn what they needed to know through their social media feeds? Did national news outlets answer all their questions? Or, as many began to suspect, was the news carried by those papers always secondary to what subscribers really valued, which was what appeared in the classified advertising columns? And, the reasoning went, if the classified ad business was collapsing and newspaper revenues plummeting, was there really a point in having a local paper at all?

As dispiriting as that argument was, it was essential to consider if local journalism was to find a way to recover. What if local journalism as it had become widely practiced was no longer valued by the people it was intended to serve? Across the country, both at start-ups and legacy news organizations, experimentation had become the order of the day. Like most experiments, many failed. Some succeeded. If experimentation could happen online or at the national level, why not locally?

And that is what set this particular experiment in motion. The experiment that became *American Deadline* began with a search for towns that had seen their local journalism collapse and for writers who were still there, ready and eager to report. The search extended across the country and led to four towns: McKeesport, Pennsylvania; Bowling Green, Virginia; McAllen, Texas; and Macon, Georgia. Both McKeesport and Bowling Green lost their newspapers. McAllen's and Macon's newspapers endure but are not what they once were.

These places evidence many of the economic and social challenges that are tearing the United States apart. McAllen, on the border with Mexico, is on one of immigration's front lines; McKeesport has struggled with the impact of the decline in manufacturing jobs; Macon grapples with the legacy of America's troubled reckoning with race; Bowling Green is a largely rural place whose residents have grown increasingly alienated from the increasingly blue cities in Virginia.

The search led as well to four journalists who, as one of them put it, knew their community so well that they understood they still had much to learn about it: Sandra Sanchez, Jason Togyer, Charles Richardson, and Greg Glassner.

Each was well practiced in traditional journalism. But that is not what was being proposed. Instead of the usual fare of news stories and features, these four journalists were asked to try something new: a dispatch, written as if they were writing a letter to a friend. Freed from the constraints of form, could they rediscover their singular voices and, when they did, use those voices to capture each month what they deemed essential about their towns and how they were experiencing the tumultuous events of 2020?

McAllen sits in the Rio Grande Valley, deep in southern Texas on the border with Mexico—a region of 1.6 million people, mostly Hispanic, where there is no local NPR station. Sandra Sanchez had been the opinion editor of the local paper, the *Monitor*. She was now a correspondent for *Border Report*, an online organ that covered life along the southern border. The voting demographic is mostly Democratic, but the ruling and upper classes, as she puts it, "are overtly Republican."

In the 1980s, McKeesport, Pennsylvania, became one of the earliest victims of the contraction of America's manufacturing sector—and it has never really recovered. On an electoral map, McKeesport appeared as a blue dot surrounded by a sea of red. Jason Togyer had been a reporter for the *McKeesport Daily News* and now ran a nonprofit news website, Tube City Online. Located about twelve miles southeast of Pittsburgh, the city's population has gone from a World War II–era high of 55,000 to about 19,000 today. A small pipe mill now employed fewer than 200 people. Before its demise, the *Daily News* saw its circulation drop from around 40,000 to 7,000 before it folded in 2015 after 131 years.

Charles Richardson, the former editorial page editor and columnist at the *Macon Telegraph*, liked to say that Macon is a midsize city that thinks it is a small town, adding that in Macon, as in "many places in the South, issues of race can quickly arise during any point of conflict." Though the city is full of stately historic homes and downtown brims with restaurants and tony lofts, just a few blocks away are blighted areas that, he said, "are difficult to ignore." It is a place where you are considered a true "Maconite" only "if you are a native or if your grandmother was born here" and "where people are distrustful of outsiders and their ideas."

And then there is Bowling Green, Virginia, the seat of Caroline County. It is quiet, mostly rural, with 20 percent of it currently being farmed but with a few new gated communities thrown into the mix. Greg Glassner had been the editor and columnist for the *Caroline Progress* before it went out of business in 2018 after ninety-nine years. "It has been said that the only three topics that draw a crowd here are guns, dogs, and football," he said. In 2008 and again in 2012, Caroline County voted for Barack Obama. Then in 2016, it became one of only five counties in Virginia to pivot and vote for Donald Trump. In 2020, it switched back again and voted for Joseph Biden.

The stories that would become *American Deadline* began in early 2020, before the pandemic, before George Floyd, before it was clear which Democrat would challenge Donald Trump. In the months that followed, dispatches would come from the border town of McAllen, where Trump wanted to build his wall; from Macon, where a mayoral election was growing more fraught over the ever-present issue of race; from McKeesport, where resentment and grievance were rising among Baby Boomers seeing their world collapse; from Bowling Green, where local pastors were leading a campaign to take down the statue of a Confederate soldier. COVID-19 came late to Bowling Green even as it upended life in McKeesport and in Macon, where the funeral for a janitor one hundred miles away became a superspreader event. McAllen became one of the nation's COVID hot spots as the virus raced through the community, finding its way into Sandra Sanchez's home.

There are two ways to read the stories of *American Deadline*: in real time, as it happened, week in and week out, and retrospectively, taking in the year in a single, contained sweep that allows readers to see and remember all at once.

The story each journalist set out to report exploded into new stories, revealing, painful, and frightening.

Change also came to the storytellers in ways that could not be foreseen in the early winter of 2020.

NOTE

1. Penelope Muse Abernathy, *News Deserts and Ghost Newspapers: Will Local News Survive?*, Expanding News Desert (Chapel Hill: Haussman School of Journalism, University of North Carolina, n.d.), https://www.usnewsdeserts.com/reports/news-deserts-and-ghost-newspapers-will-local-news-survive/.

2. Clayton Christiansen, *The Innovator's Dilemma : When New Technologies Cause Great Firms to Fail* (Boston: Harvard Business School Press, 1997).

1

THE MYSTERY OF CAROLINE
COUNTY, VIRGINIA

Bowling Green

Bowling Green, Virginia, the seat of Caroline County, is about seventy-seven miles south of Washington, DC, and forty-two miles north of the governor's mansion in Richmond, where armed gun enthusiasts gathered in 2020 to protest any and all attempts to limit firearm ownership.

Despite Caroline County's geographic proximity to the state and national capital, its residents appear somewhat insulated from political turmoil. It has been said that the only topics that draw a crowd here are guns, dogs, and high school football, although the Caroline Cavaliers have had some lean years, so even that is in doubt. The county's 31,000 residents, most of them employed, underemployed, or retired, live in single-family homes within relatively quiet communities or scattered about the rolling rural landscapes. Twenty-eight percent of the population is Black, nearly 5 percent Hispanic or Latino, and about two-thirds white. A few residents claim ancestry from the Indigenous peoples that greeted John Smith and other English settlers in the early 1600s. Over the past fifty years, several gated lake communities, one golf course community, and a Disney-like subdivision called Ladysmith Village have sprung up, bumping up the population somewhat and changing some of its traditional characteristics.

But at heart Caroline County is one of the last rural areas along the Interstate 95 corridor and has yet to be overrun by apartment complexes and commercial development. In theory, more than 90 percent of the land is available for agriculture and forestry, although only 20 percent of its 549 square miles is actively farmed. Low hills and shallow valleys dot the landscape. If you go to the Visitors Center in Carmel Church, which is more of a destination for hungry travelers than for the community, you can't miss the reproduction of a thirty-three-foot prehistoric whale skeleton found twenty feet down in a local quarry in 1990, a reminder that this area was once under the sea.

Overshadowed by its more populous and prosperous neighbors, Caroline County has been in the national or international news spotlight only on rare occasions. A mention came after the presidential election of 2016, when it was determined that Caroline had been one of five "pivot counties" in Virginia. Its voters gave Barack Obama a twelve-percentage-point win over John McCain in 2008 and an eight-percentage-point win over Mitt Romney in 2012. But then they reversed course in 2016, giving Donald Trump a five-point victory over Hillary Clinton, who won the overall vote in Virginia.

For ninety-nine years, the residents of Caroline County were served by a lively weekly newspaper, the *Caroline Progress*, which was family-owned and operated for most of its existence. Staff size and page count dwindled after the paper was purchased by a Tennessee-based chain in 2007. The March 28, 2018, issue announced that it was the newspaper's last.

How Caroline County voters would feel come the Super Tuesday Democratic primary in Virginia on March 3 and ultimately in the presidential election in November was anybody's guess. How did the residents of this county deal with the loss of their local newspaper, and what impact did it have on their lives and political decisions in 2020? These and other issues are explored in later dispatches.

For the most part, county residents here are resilient and self-sufficient. Many backyard gardens dot the landscape, and hunting and fishing are popular pursuits. The county sheriff's department is a well-trained and equipped force, but many farmers and homeowners are also prepared to defend what is theirs.

The more than seventy churches in the county range from small country chapels to large and opulent edifices. In the old days, the churches were also the social center and, along with rural post offices and general stores, the communication centers of their communities. To some extent, that remains true, especially in the Black community. Other community organizations, such as the Mason and Moose Lodges and the Ruritan and Rotary Clubs, have been augmented by community centers, four libraries, and the relatively new Caroline County Y. Food—be it fried chicken, oysters, fried fish, blue crabs, salt fish, or biscuits and sausage gravy—is a big draw for gatherings and fundraisers.

If you are one of the millions of motorists who pass through the western third of Caroline County each year on I-95 or the parallel U.S. 1, you may be unaware that this county exists. People have traveled through here for centuries, but only a relative handful have decided to put down stakes. Revolutionary War troops marched through on the way to Yorktown and Union, and Confederate troops marched through on their way to battles around their capital, Richmond. Amtrak passenger trains pass through Caroline on their way from Richmond to Washington but no longer stop at the abandoned stations at Ruther Glen, Penola, Milford, Woodford, and Guinea.

Approaching on I-95 from the north, you endure the inevitable traffic snags of rapidly growing northern Virginia before

getting the first clue that you are approaching someplace different in the form of a new and prominent brown directional sign
announcing the way to the "Stonewall Jackson Death Site" in
Caroline County. Thomas "Stonewall" Jackson, the Confederate general, was gravely wounded by friendly fire at the Battle
of the Wilderness and was carried by his men as far as Guinea
Station at the northwestern edge of Caroline County, where he
died on May 10, 1863. A national monument and restored house
still mark the spot. It was known as "Stonewall Jackson Shrine"
for more than nine decades. But "shrines" are perceived as places
of worship and veneration, and the National Park Service
renamed it in the fall of 2020—a decision influenced in part by
controversy and violence in Richmond and Charlottesville over
statues memorializing the leaders of the Confederacy.

Southbound travelers wishing to avoid the logjams around
Washington, DC, and northern Virginia can instead cross the
Potomac River from Maryland, continue through King George
County, and traverse Caroline County diagonally on U.S.
Route 301. That way, you pass through Port Royal, population
205, one of two incorporated towns in the county. This was a
bustling tobacco port back in colonial Virginia, when ocean-
going sailing ships were able to navigate the Rappahannock
River as far north as the rapids in Fredericksburg.

If instead you approach from the south, on I-95, the first clues
that you are coming up on Caroline County would be the signs
for the Kings Dominion amusement park, just south of the
North Anna River, and for Meadow Event Park in Caroline
County. Once known as the Meadows, this former horse farm
was the birthplace of Caroline County's most famous native son,
albeit one with four legs, not two. Secretariat, thoroughbred
horse racing's Triple Crown winner in 1973, was born in Caroline

County, as was his stablemate, Riva Ridge, who won two legs of the Triple Crown in 1972.

In some respects, change comes slowly to Caroline County and its residents, many of whose families have lived here for generations.

Bowling Green, population 1,166, is the sleepy county seat in the approximate center of the county and looks much the same as it did fifty or even one hundred years ago, although a few storefronts that once housed mom-and-pop businesses are vacant. Most county residents drive to Hanover County to the south or suburban Fredericksburg to the north for their shopping, dining, and entertainment. Bowling Green was a bustling community during World War II, when Fort A. P. Hill was quickly created to meet the training needs for a rapidly growing U.S. Army. The 77,000-acre military outpost still occupies a large chunk of the county, and as many as 70,000 soldiers and airmen receive short-term training here each year, though the base's permanent party of military and civilian employees is minuscule. While local residents are patriotic, the fact that the army post removes 22 percent of the landmass from the local tax base while contributing little to the local economy is a source of friction. The fort's old USO club now houses the Bowling Green Town Hall and a community center used for weddings.

In Caroline, several large warehousing operations, an electrical-component manufacturer, and a cluster of truck stops and fast-food eateries provide some jobs, as do agriculture and forestry. But 70 percent of the county's workforce commutes to jobs beyond the county's borders. Many drive as far away as the DC Beltway or to Richmond for lucrative jobs in technology, manufacturing, government, and government contracting. The county maintains an inventory of attractive properties already zoned for business or residential expansion, including a 1,200-acre tract that includes a proposed commuter-rail station, but to date there have been few takers.

Like many living in the southeastern states, Virginians and Caroline County residents struggled with a depleted economy and racial segregation for many years after the Civil War or, as some still insist on calling it, the "War of Northern Aggression." In 1958, in a well-known incident based in the county's Central Point, Richard Loving, a quintessential white southern good old boy, and Mildred Delores Jeter, a young neighbor of Black and Native American ancestry, married in Washington, DC. After returning home, they were arrested by Garnett Brooks, Caroline County's archetypical knuckle-busting southern sheriff, and charged under the state's racist antimiscegenation laws passed in 1924.

The Lovings fought their prison sentences and were thrust, somewhat reluctantly, into the national spotlight when the U.S. attorney general Robert Kennedy and the American Civil Liberties Union championed their cause. The U.S. Supreme Court eventually ruled in their favor nearly ten years later in the landmark 1967 *Loving v. Virginia* decision. After that, the Lovings returned home and lived in peace and relative obscurity for eight years until their car was struck by a drunk driver, and Richard was killed. Mildred survived and lived until 2008. In 2018, a long-overdue historical marker was dedicated to the couple.

2

WHAT'S VEXING MACON, GEORGIA?

Macon

On January 20, 2020, some three hundred residents of the city of Macon in Macon–Bibb County, rose early to attend the annual 7:30 a.m. breakfast to honor Dr. Martin Luther King Jr. This was the breakfast's thirtieth anniversary, and many of those present—thirty years older, wiser, grayer, and balder—were the same who had attended the first breakfast in 1990, four years after the first observance of the national holiday honoring Dr. King.

The breakfast is interdenominational and nonpolitical, although most local politicians regularly attend, and, most important, the breakfast draws a racially mixed crowd, something you don't see often in Macon. However, the march that followed, originating from four points in the city and converging downtown at the Government Center, showed little diversity among the 1,000 or so marchers. They arrived beating drums and singing civil rights–era songs, "Ain't gonna let nobody turn me 'round, turn me 'round. / Ain't gonna let nobody turn me 'round. / I'm gonna keep on walkin', keep on talkin', marchin' into freedom land."

The events of the day celebrating King's life and legacy depict in sharp relief the core of Macon–Bibb County. As for many small southern cities, race and racism have vexed Macon. The races, mostly Black and white, play nice with each other because each plays in their own separate and unequal sandbox.

The city of Macon had humble origins. It began as a small military outpost perched high on a hill overlooking the Ocmulgee River. Though European settlers were new to the area in the 1800s, Native Americans had inhabited the lush, game-filled forests for 13,000 years before their arrival. Macon is now the center of a wider area referred to as "Middle Georgia," an eight-county area with 420,000 people, and Macon–Bibb County's contribution to that number is 154,000.

Location has always been Macon's blessing—eighteen miles northwest of the geographic center of the state of Georgia. A river runs through it, as do Interstates 75, 475, and 16. A 960-acre Norfolk Southern rail yard also calls Macon home, bolstering the city's central location.

Fifteen miles south of Macon, built on land donated by Bibb County, lies the state's largest industrial complex: Warner Robins Air Force Base. The 7,000-acre complex employs 23,000 civilian and military personnel, with an annual payroll of $1.43 billion. The base pumps an additional $492.7 million into the area with local construction, contracts, and procurement. Another $1.2 billion in local jobs are directly attributable to the base.

The city the base calls home, Warner Robins, is the new kid on the block. In 1942, Macon was already 119 years old when the small farm town of Wellston was transformed into the city of Warner Robins. Even with the ballooning of Warner Robins's population to 74,000, Macon remains the cultural center of Middle Georgia.

Having such a large employer in the area is a blessing—until it isn't. Whenever voices in Washington, DC, start discussing military cutbacks, Middle Georgia gets nervous. Although the

Base Realignment and Closure process is nothing new, where other communities caught colds when their bases were shuttered, a fatal case of economic pneumonia would occur in Middle Georgia.

With every turn of the head in Macon, warm breezes of history fill the senses—from historic homes such as Hay House, built in 1855, which featured a natural ventilation system long before the White House got similar relief from summer's heat and humidity—to the Ocmulgee Mounds National Historical Park, where the Mississippians constructed huge burial mounds.

From atop the largest of them, the Great Temple Mound, fifty feet above the already high elevation of the area, you can see several church steeples across the river. Macon believes it has more churches per capita than any other city in the state; more than two hundred are registered in the county.

Those churches are an example of the different sandboxes the communities play in. Up a slight hill from the Government Center, the two steeples of First Baptist Church of Christ (1887) look south down Poplar Street and serve a predominantly white congregation. Facing east sits the majestic Saint Joseph Catholic Church (1841), its two steeples rising two hundred feet toward heaven, its congregation also largely white. Black Catholics attend Saint Peter Claver Catholic Church (1888), located in the Pleasant Hill community, a mile away. Turning down New Street, with its double steeples facing south, is First Baptist Church—yes, another one, but this is a Black congregation that was organized more than a quarter century before the adoption of the Emancipation Proclamation, its brave former pastors' names engraved on the front steps' risers.

In the next block, named Cotton Avenue because it was the route that bales of cotton traveled to the river for transport, sits Steward Chapel African Methodist Episcopal (1865). Across the street, Dr. Martin Luther King Jr. visited another Black church, Tremont Temple Missionary Baptist Church (1897), but it was demolished and replaced with a Dunkin' Donuts. There was an effort to save the structure; there is a very active historical society, sometimes referred to as the "hysterical society," but its efforts were too little, too late. Also torn down in the same block was the unoccupied home of Charles H. Douglass (1870–1940), a wealthy African American who owned several businesses, but his wealth brought a Ku Klux Klan bounty on his head.

Just one block west from these churches is another reason Macon is the center of Middle Georgia: Navicent Health operates its largest facility, the Medical Center, with 637 beds. The sprawling complex is the county's largest employer and is one of only five level-one trauma centers in the state. But news coverage of this large economic engine has all but disappeared. In December 2018, the hospital announced a strategic alliance with North Carolina's Atrium Health, a much larger system. Macon's newspaper, the *Telegraph*, in spite of being given early access to Navicent's CEO, only covered the merger with collaborating news operations and little local flavor—not the extensive coverage the subject deserved. And that's not all the news that's gone lacking—county commission meetings, school board meetings, even sports coverage have dwindled from the printed pages of the *Telegraph* and its digital site. The three-story newspaper building that once housed more than four hundred employees, with a private elevator for the publisher, has been sold. The paper's parent company, McClatchy, filed for bankruptcy protection on February 12, 2020.

History dominates the relationships of Macon's people, and that history created the sandboxes. Public schools didn't integrate until 1970—sixteen years after the *Brown v. Board of Education* Supreme Court decision—and the transition was far from easy. Not only were Blacks and whites sitting in the same class-rooms for the first time but also, at least for the white students, boys and girls, too. The six formerly all-white high schools and the two Black high schools merged.

School integration ushered in white flight. In 2016, there were eighteen private schools in the county with a combined enroll-ment of 4,304 students. As of January 2020, the public-school system had 21,752 students, down from 23,835 last year. The public-school district is 77 percent African American, 13.3 per-cent white, and another 9.5 percent Hispanic, Asian, or multi-racial. The student population in the system has the highest rate of poverty in the nation, according to the district, and 100 per-cent of the students receive free or reduced lunch. The white stu-dent population dropped by almost 1,400 students from 2019 to 2020. Where did they go?

The private schools have been around for decades, but now three charter schools also operate in the county; only one, Hutchings College and Career Academy, is under the direction of the local school board. The other two are state supervised and have a combined student population of 2,203: Cirrus Academy, is 100 percent African American, and Academy for Classical Education, which started out as a public charter before joining the state system in 2019, is 72 percent white.

Macon is also a center for higher education, with Wesleyan College (the first institute of higher learning for women in the world), Mercer University, Middle Georgia State University, and Central Georgia Technical College all located there. Mercer University, formerly a Baptist-affiliated school, pulled itself out of the segregated sandbox in 1963 when it admitted Sam Oni, a Christian convert from Ghana. Oni's experiences at Mercer were indicative of race relations in Macon at the time.

In the fall of 1963, Tattnall Square Baptist Church, founded in 1891 and located on the Mercer campus, refused to allow Oni into its worship service. Church deacons stopped him at the door, but he refused to leave, and police were called. The saga really began that summer when the church's pastor, Thomas J. Holmes, and assistants Doug Johnson and Jack Jones attempted to use the Gospel to show their congregation of 2,000 that not accepting all who wanted to know Christ wasn't Christian. Two students in Upward Bound (a Mercer program designed to prepare local high school students, mainly African American, for college-level work) attended a service. In response, the church voted to bar "Negroes" from attending. The very morning Oni attempted to enter the sanctuary, the church had voted to dismiss all three of its pastors. The incident drew national attention and was depicted in the book *Stem of Jesse: The Costs of Community at a 1960's Southern School* by Will D. Campbell. The church was forced to leave campus and move to the northern suburbs, where it still exists today and remains predominately white.

Though Macon's in-town area is full of stately historic homes, and the adjacent downtown—which in 2012 was barely awake—is now brimming with more than fifty restaurants and almost nine hundred tony lofts, just a few blocks away blighted areas are difficult to ignore. The county has been unable to stem the spread of shabby, boarded-up, or neglected properties. A blight survey in 2017 identified 3,700 unoccupied structures, mainly in the urban core populated by African Americans. The poverty rate of Macon-Bibb citizens stands at 25.7 percent, almost 40,000 of the county's population.

Macon–Bibb County is blue amid a surrounding sea of red. In the 2016 presidential election, Democrat Hillary Clinton carried it with 59 percent of the vote, whereas Republican Donald

Trump carried all the contiguous counties by 59 percent or more. More areas of stress are to come with the 2020 election season, but initially that stress does not come from national politics. Macon-Bibb votes on whether to elect its first new mayor since 2008 in May, and of the announced candidates one of the strongest is Black. Black voters have an advantage of 12,108 registered voters over white voters in mayoral races and a 9,548-vote advantage in other races. However, in the 2018 midterm election, voter turnout for the entire county was a dismal 25.6 percent.

As the saying goes, "follow the money," and this election season is no exception. Each of the three major white candidates for mayor has $377,135 in their campaign accounts; the major Black candidate, $41,859. The sandboxes are set.

3

RED STREETS VERSUS BLUE STREETS IN MCKEESPORT, PENNSYLVANIA

McKeesport

About six years ago, I started doing a weekly talk show for one of the AM radio stations in my hometown, McKeesport, Pennsylvania, about twelve miles south of Pittsburgh.

The show was the station manager's idea, and we both stood to benefit: he got free content, and the community website I run, Tube City Online, could expand its audience. Plus, having a talk show gave me an excuse to sit down, unscripted, and pry into my guests' lives. For someone who's naturally nosy (in western Pennsylvania, we say "nebby"), the gig was almost too good to be true.

I have deliberately steered away from politics. As a newly minted tax-exempt corporation, Tube City needs to stay nonpartisan, but that hasn't stopped us from discussing issues or talking to elected officials. I've also talked to musicians, artists, volunteers, clerics, LGBTQ rights activists, labor union leaders, and pretty much anyone else who can spare a half hour.

The show has featured a lot of entrepreneurs, too. In November 2016, a local independent retail store was celebrating its seventieth anniversary, and I asked one of the managers to come on the air with me.

Celebrating seventy years in retailing is a milestone anywhere these days, but it's especially noteworthy in McKeesport.

In the 1950s, the city's retail district was one of the busiest in Pennsylvania, behind only Philadelphia and Pittsburgh, with department stores, dozens of specialty shops, a half-dozen movie theaters, and several five-and-ten stores—including, not incidentally, "Store Number 1" of the GC Murphy chain, whose five hundred locations in about twenty eastern states were managed from a ramshackle office complex on McKeesport's Fifth Avenue.

Back then, about 55,000 people lived in McKeesport—and that figure is deceptively low. Because of the arcane way that Pennsylvania defines municipal borders, McKeesport was ringed with other municipalities, such as Port Vue, Duquesne, and West Mifflin, that were home to another 150,000 residents who shopped and worked in the city.

At any given time, 7,000 to 10,000 of those people worked at U.S. Steel's National Works—a massive complex stretching nearly two miles along the city's Monongahela riverfront, where iron ore, limestone, and other raw material entered at one end and finished steel pipes left by trains and barges at the other. The pipes and tubes—from which McKeesport took its nickname, "the Tube City"—ranged from a few inches to several feet in diameter and were used in everything from medical and nuclear equipment to the "Big Inch" and Alaskan pipelines.

The development of suburban shopping malls and, especially, the decline of basic steelmaking in the Pittsburgh area gutted McKeesport's downtown. Between 1979 and 1985, according to one estimate, 113,200 manufacturing jobs were eliminated in the Pittsburgh area. Roughly 28,000 of them were at U.S. Steel facilities in McKeesport and the neighboring communities.

Allegheny County—which includes both McKeesport and Pittsburgh—lost roughly 25 percent of its population between 1960 and 2000. McKeesport's population fell to about 19,000 by 2010, many of whom are retirees on pensions or the working poor in service jobs. McKeesport's median household income in 2020 was $28,750—roughly half of the Pennsylvania median of $56,951. Retailers faded away or moved to more prosperous communities.

Still, there are some bright spots, and there's been some new activity downtown recently; none of us who stayed in McKeesport are willing to give up on the city. But it's fair to say that thirty years after the exodus, vacant buildings still dominate the downtown district. Thriving in that environment is an achievement for any business, which is why I was happy to talk to my guest on that gloomy, gray morning in November 2016.

After the interview, I walked him to the parking lot outside. "How are things?" I asked.

"Fine, except I can't believe people were so stupid to vote for Trump," my guest said. Not only did he find Donald Trump's victory to be personally offensive, he said, but it also threatened his business: most of the items in his store were imported, and a prolonged tariff war would have the potential to drive up prices. Many of my guest's customers were public-school districts, which could be expected to face budget cutbacks under a Trump administration.

"How could people be so stupid?" he asked

Our cars were parked in the 800 block of Walnut Street. Opposite us was the Salvation Army, and that was one of the livelier places on a Friday morning.

Next door was a decaying four-story apartment building that had originally housed a car dealership. The most recent first-floor tenant, a used-furniture store, had gone out of business. The two houses behind the apartment building were abandoned and condemned.

One door down, blue plastic tarps flapped from the roof of a defunct Baptist church, its stained-glass windows long gone. Dirty mattresses sat out front on the sidewalk.

At the end of Walnut Street, we could make out the last remaining remnant of U.S. Steel's pipe factory, an electric-resistance weld mill employing about 150 people. Because of a slowdown in the natural-gas industry, the facility was idled, and most of the workforce was laid off.

And in front of that mill, at the corner of Walnut Street at Lysle Boulevard, we could see the one-time home of my former employer, the *McKeesport Daily News*.

In my childhood, the *Daily News* was a prosperous, 45,000-circulation evening newspaper locally owned by the Mansfield family. From 1923 to 1934, the publisher, William D. Mansfield, also served in the Pennsylvania State Senate. A beautiful four-lane bridge leading into McKeesport bears his name, and a wing of the city's hospital was named for the family.

As the city's retail district collapsed, pages of department store display advertising vanished from the *Daily News*. For a while, the paper survived on real estate, automotive, and help-wanted advertising, but by the early 2000s even those sources were shifting to the internet.

In 2007, the *Daily News* was purchased by the conservative philanthropist Richard Mellon Scaife, and its circulation was added to that of the *Pittsburgh Tribune-Review*—part of his strategy to outflank the *Pittsburgh Post-Gazette* by acquiring small newspapers in Pittsburgh's suburbs.

Following Scaife's death in 2014, the *Tribune-Review* retrenched, selling off many of those smaller weeklies and dailies and closing others, such as the *McKeesport Daily News*, which by 2015 had seen its circulation fall to 8,600 and which printed its final edition on December 31, 2015. Now, in 2016, the presses were gone, and the plate-glass windows on the Art Deco building where they had run were covered with plywood.

Tube City Online was trying valiantly to fill some of the gap left by the newspaper's closure. Just before the *Daily News* closed, I worked with local funeral directors to begin publishing their obituaries online. We recruited freelance writers to cover some community meetings and events, and we launched an internet radio station. We were offering a fraction of the *Daily News*'s content—but it was better than nothing.

As the store owner and I stood there in the November gloom, I gestured to the closed church, the abandoned houses, and the boarded-up newspaper office at the end of the street.

"Look around you," I said. "One candidate said she was going to keep everything status quo. She actually said that. The other guy promised he was going to fix manufacturing and put people back to work."

"No one really believes that," my guest said. "What, that the steel mills are going to come back? Trump's going to bring back the steel industry?"

"No, but McKeesport has been suffering for years," I said. "Then you hear Hillary Clinton saying that America is already great, and we need to keep the status quo, and if I'm standing in this parking lot, I'm thinking—we want to keep this? This? And then this celebrity comes along and promises he's going to put people back to work and make everything great again. I'm not saying they made the right choice—I'm saying I can sympathize with anyone who decided to take a chance."

I still sympathize with Trump voters. But I have to admit that the dominant narrative—that Rust Belt places such as

McKeesport voted for Donald Trump because of decades of decline and deep-seated economic anxiety—is seriously flawed.

McKeesport residents, despite all their city's struggles going back to the Reagan years, voted overwhelmingly for Hillary Clinton in 2016. Clinton won twenty-eight of the city's thirty-two voting precincts—many of them by more than fifty points. One small precinct in the city's Seventh Ward went for Clinton by a margin of 164 to 8.

Meanwhile, neighboring White Oak is a relatively well-to-do community (median income $56,316) and now houses much of the retail and professional activity that was once located in McKeesport's downtown. Voters there went for Trump, 2,375 to 1,764.

In nearby Liberty (median income $47,425), voters favored Trump, 780 to 451, and Elizabeth Township (median income $60,068) went for Trump by nearly a two-to-one margin.

Besides their relative prosperity, what sets these three communities apart from McKeesport is their racial makeup.

According to the U.S. Census Bureau's most recent estimates, 60 percent of McKeesport's residents identify as "white alone," roughly 34 percent as "Black or African American alone," and roughly 5 percent as two or more races.

In White Oak, 94 percent of the residents identify as white. In Liberty, it's 97.6 percent. And of Elizabeth Township's 13,271 residents, only 167 (1.3 percent) identify as "Black."

Across Allegheny County, voters in 2016 chose Clinton over Trump, 366,934 to 259,125. But on an electoral map of the county's precincts, it's almost comically easy to see which municipalities are mostly white and which ones have a high percentage of Black residents.

According to the census, Duquesne, directly across the river from McKeesport, is roughly 30 percent white, 57 percent Black, and 12 percent mixed race. Voters there chose Clinton over Trump, 1,780 to 430. Dravosburg, which is part of the McKeesport Area School District, is 94 percent white. Voters there chose Trump 473 to 342.

If it's too simplistic to say that "economic anxiety" motivated voters in 2016 in the Rust Belt communities around McKeesport, it's also too easy and wrong to say they were motivated totally by racial attitudes.

Yet there may not be another part of the United States that is so sharply divided along racial and economic lines as the Pittsburgh metropolitan area—or where those racial and economic characteristics map so closely to political attitudes.

We all know about the gaps between "red states" and "blue states" and the divide between "rural" and "urban" Americans. Around Pittsburgh and McKeesport, it's "red streets versus blue streets" and "red suburbs versus blue suburbs," and although the stakes are smaller, the gaps between the two sides are no less real.

4

FIGHTING THE WALL ALONG
THE RIO GRANDE

McAllen

The Rio Grande is just a trickle in many parts of West Texas, but it grows in force, depth, speed, and character as it rolls through communities in deep South Texas, heading toward the Gulf of Mexico. Along the way, this curving international boundary meanders past towns and county seats, past historic cemeteries and schools, and alongside highways. By the time it empties into the gulf, just east of Brownsville, the ancient river is rolling at fast speeds, wide, a sustaining life force for so many in this border region.

The Rio Grande is the sole drinking-water supply for the 260,000 people in Laredo. It's what farmers rely on to water their crops and cattle. It's a fishing ground for many. And it's where children crack *cascarones* (colored eggshells) on Easter as families celebrate their most sacred holiday by barbecuing and picnicking on its banks. The river serves as the common link for dozens of South Texas communities, all of which have Hispanic-majority populations with unique traditions and share similar economic and familial bonds with their sister communities south of the river border in Mexico.

The river became a source of consternation and controversy for many communities in South Texas once Donald Trump began building a thirty-foot-tall metal border wall—a wall that blocks some communities, such as Laredo, from its water source.

It is with that backdrop that river expert Tricia Cortez, who heads the Rio Grande International Study Center, a nonprofit that studies the river, took to the Rio Grande with some friends to make a statement. Rowing side by side in two kayaks, Cortez and three others paddled just below the Juarez-Lincoln International Bridge (called "Bridge 2" by locals), where city leaders from Laredo and Nuevo Laredo in Mexico were holding their annual International Bridge Ceremony on February 22, 2020. As tradition, leaders from both sides walk to the bridge's midpoint, the international boundary line, to *abrazar* (embrace) and demonstrate goodwill for the next year.

House Speaker Nancy Pelosi attended. So did almost every dignitary in the area from Laredo and Nuevo Laredo, along with costumed mariachi singers and other celebrants. The public's attention, however, was fixed on Cortez and her group as they floated below, holding a banner between the two kayaks that read #NoBorderWall. Spectators on the bridge poked each other and pointed, while Cortez filmed from the water with her cellphone.

Cortez said she protested because, with the presidential election nearing, she realized that she had to speak out against Trump's divisive rhetoric, aimed particularly toward minorities and immigrant-rich Hispanic communities such as Laredo. Cortez, a San Antonio native who moved to Laredo in 2001 to be the city hall reporter for a local newspaper, a position she held until 2008, says she will no longer watch on the sidelines as a border wall is built through her hometown or as Trump overtly links immigrants with "criminals," as he did during the State of the Union Address.

"The way that they characterize the border and the way we live, I just can't stomach that," Cortez said. "I'm filled with grief and sadness and anxiety and depression thinking about the wall and how it will rip through our city and these lands so flippantly, with complete disregard to our history, our culture, our ties to the land, and our ties to the river. And to know that it's being done for political gain for a presidential campaign, I just find so repulsive and dangerous."

Cortez intends to keep her eyes open and her voice loud, organizing events to inform others about the border wall. This is especially necessary because "the local newspaper has sadly atrophied" from its heyday when the newsroom of the *Laredo Morning Times*—one of the oldest newspapers in Texas—was filled with reporters like herself, hitting the streets and covering every aspect of their beat, holding elected officials accountable. Today, the paper reports a circulation of around 6,000. The few remaining reporters do not have the resources or voices necessary to spur the kind of movement that Cortez says is necessary to counter what Trump boasted in his 2020 State of the Union Address would be "a long, tall, and very powerful wall."

Cortez, a soft-spoken, forty-five-year-old Princeton University graduate and mother of two young children, admits she is an unlikely leader and says she has never acted quite like this before. But as the executive director of the Rio Grande International Study Center, she realizes that she has a unique platform that enables her to educate and motivate her community. It's a platform she is now fully utilizing. In the past few months, Cortez has led a protest march, a river sit-in, and the recent kayak stunt. And in the remaining months leading up to November, she plans to hold several more events.

"We're not going to take this lying down. We can't," Cortez said. "Laredo was founded alongside and because of the river, and the city is built right up to the river—neighborhoods, parks, ranches, everything is built right up to the river. It's a very real asset for us, and what infuriates me is that we're not worthy of the same federal protection and federal laws that every other place in the United States is worthy of."

Looking back on how the country and Laredo got to this point, Cortez blames herself.

It was her own gullibility, she said, that prevented her from realizing how Trump's slights toward minorities indicated his desire to enact policies that would deny human rights to some by preventing asylum seekers from entering U.S. soil.

"When Trump first got elected, I really tried to keep an open mind," Cortez said. She even praised his trade dealings with China and credited him with improving the U.S. economy.

But she vividly recalls the exact moment last summer when she realized his "true intentions" and how they could hurt her people, her community, and her region. That was on Sunday, July 14, when Trump singled out four minority Democratic female members of Congress—Representatives Alexandria Ocasio-Cortez of New York, Ilhan Omar of Minnesota, Rashida Tlaib of Michigan, and Ayanna Pressley of Massachusetts—as un-American by tweeting that they should "go back" to the "places from which they came."

Omar was born in Somalia; the others were born in the United States. If Trump felt that way about those elected officials of color, then how did he feel about other women of color, such as herself? Cortez wondered. She found out the next day when in an impromptu news conference Trump said that the women were "free to leave" the country if they were unhappy, and he accused them of hating America.

"I didn't approach his presidency already *cerrada* [closed off]. I tried to stay open," Cortez explained. "Whether you agree with his politics or not, he made it seem like they [the women representatives] weren't part of the American fabric. They weren't white enough. And for me that was *ya* [enough]; I could no longer take it. No more Donald Trump for me."

That moment propelled her into hyperawareness, and she was set on protecting her border town—a town that is older than the United States, founded in 1755 and at one time the capital of the Republic of the Rio Grande, a short-lived independent nation. Laredo is a town that hosts month-long celebrations of George Washington's birthday and massive *quinceañeras* every weekend and has the nation's largest port of entry for importation of goods from Mexico. It's a place where families walk across the various international bridges to Nuevo Laredo to visit relatives and loved ones after Sunday church services, a place where residents might not be wealthy of coin but are rich in love and families and proud of their heritage and culture. It's a place where communities on both sides of the Rio Grande are bound by the river—not separated by it.

Cortez plans to host an event each month leading up to the election in every area of Laredo, from the richest to the poorest neighborhoods. Each event will include giving out river and border wall maps "so they can see how impacted they'll be," she said. "We are trying to connect the dots between us and other active groups along the border to try and apply as much pressure as we can." The center has also joined a lawsuit with Earthjustice, challenging the president's declaration of a national emergency on the southern border. As head of a nonprofit center that receives tax funds for support, Cortez is not allowed to endorse a candidate, but she says she has no trouble pointing out that what Trump is doing is wrong, and she vows to use whatever is necessary, including the mighty Rio Grande, to make her point.

5

ARE DEMOCRATS AN ENDANGERED SPECIES IN CAROLINE COUNTY?

Bowling Green

For decades, quiet and rural Caroline County, Virginia, could be counted on to vote for Democrats in presidential elections, while more conservative and populous neighbors were turning out in droves for Republicans.

In 1988, Caroline gave Mike Dukakis a win over George Herbert Walker Bush, the only county in the region to do so. In 1992, Bill Clinton got 48.6 percent of the county's votes, in contrast to 38 percent for Bush and 12.5 percent for Ross Perot. In 1996, Clinton trounced Bob Dole, 53.5 percent to 38.6 percent, with Perot grabbing 7 percent. Al Gore took 51.7 percent of the county's vote in 2000, over 46.4 percent for George W. Bush.

Only in 2004 did the Republicans eke out a victory—by 121 votes, with G. W. Bush taking 50.2 percent of the vote to John Kerry's 49 percent. Then in 2008, Caroline's voters came back and gave the Democrat Barack Obama a convincing 55.45 percent to John McCain's 43.5 percent. Obama triumphed again in 2012, besting Mitt Romney 53.3 percent to 45 percent.

But then came 2016, with a political neophyte, Donald Trump, taking a narrow 50.2 percent to 45.1 percent victory over his vastly more experienced Democratic opponent, Hillary Clinton, who carried Virginia overall. Caroline County was one of only five "pivot counties" in the state—localities that voted twice for Obama and then reversed course for Trump.

Was this a fluke? Or a sign of shifting political loyalties?

We won't know for quite a while. And before we get to that rather large question—in Caroline County and nationwide—we have to consider whom the Democrats would pick. To begin the inquiry, I attended a February 8 meeting of the Caroline County Democratic Committee.

It was not an easy meeting to find. The Democrats' website and Facebook page still advertised the January meeting. I stumbled across a mention of the February meeting in a video posted on the One Caroline Virginia Facebook page maintained by Tony Ares, who had tried unsuccessfully to start up a local newspaper after the ninety-nine-year-old *Caroline Progress* ceased printing in 2018 and left a void in the civic conversation. In a video on his Facebook page, Ares noted there would be free coffee and donuts at the event.

As it turned out, there were more donuts than people. Most who did attend were older Democrats who knew about the meeting via the grapevine. Committee members briefly discussed their frustration over difficulty in communicating with the electorate, especially with recent newcomers to the county, of which there are a number. In 1988, 6,292 Caroline County residents voted for president. In 2016, 14,863 did so out of 18,229 eligible voters. By March 2020, the number of eligible voters in the county had swelled to 20,508. How many of them would turn out in November and how many would be Democrats were anyone's guess.

The chairman of the County Democratic Committee, Floyd Thomas, was cautious on that question. An erudite sixty-four-year-old Black man who had grown up in White Plains, New York, Thomas had spent every summer of his youth on his uncle's

farm near Bowling Green here in Caroline County. He graduated from Howard University with a degree in architecture and
met his wife, Linda, originally from Baltimore, while they were
students there. They moved here in 1987, and four years later he
was elected to represent Mattaponi District on the county board
of supervisors. Linda Thomas has twice served as president of
the Virginia NAACP.

As local party chairman, Thomas has thus far remained
above the fray, not picking a favorite among the crowded field
campaigning in advance of Virginia's primary vote on Super
Tuesday, March 3. He said that there are as many opinions in
Caroline as there are candidates. The one unifying force, he
said, is to get a Democrat in the White House.

I asked Thomas if, given recent population increases, Democrats are now outnumbered by Republicans in Caroline County.
He said he does not see "a total shifting in philosophy." There
are more independents now than before, he added. "Virginians
are uniquely independent," and independents can vote Democratic. He pointed to local victories for Democrats in 2017, 2018,
and 2019 as evidence.

Up to a week before March 3, the primary did not seem to
create much of a stir in central Virginia. Several candidates
opened campaign offices in Richmond and northern Virginia in
early February, and a relative handful of neighborhood canvass-
ing "events" were listed in counties adjacent to Caroline. TV ads
for the two billionaires then in the race, Mike Bloomberg and
Tom Steyer, began to appear. But yard signs and bumper stickers were virtually nonexistent until just days before the primary.

An exception to this was in the town of Ashland, eight miles
south of Caroline County. There, a former mayor, Jim Foley, was
one of the first in the area to jump on the Pete Buttigieg bandwagon. "It was before the first debate, and he did a Fox News

town hall," Foley said. "I sought out more of his public speaking. Everything I heard resonated with me. It was like he was the adult in the room."

Foley holds a CPA and master's in finance, and he is director of pricing for a major Richmond law firm. He and his wife, Lorie, have lived in Ashland for twenty-four years. "I have family members who voted for Trump, and I think Buttigieg could win them over the most easily," Foley said. Bernie Sanders, he argues, "won the left wing, but I worry that he would not be able to beat Trump."

"Around the holidays I was kind of obnoxious and wore 'Pete' buttons to everything I went to," Foley added. "People said, 'He's too young . . . we like him, but blah, blah, blah.'" This criticism did not deter Foley, who stocked up on bumper stickers and yard signs and offered them to friends and neighbors. "Pete is really focused on a post-Trump world. He is a true uniting candidate who can pull us together as a nation."

Except he didn't.

I contacted Foley after Buttigieg dropped out, and he admitted he was "bummed out."

But Foley said he'd switch to Biden and explained his thinking: "I worry about his gaffes and fading mental facilities. But he really is a safe choice and known commodity. He will surround himself with professionals." And "anyone he picks for VP will be an improvement over Trump."

As for Senator Sanders, stated Foley, his "boldest plans will not get through Congress even if the D's control the senate. But a more practical and appealing version of those plans may emerge will be very good for the USA."

As for Bloomberg, Foley said just a day before Super Tuesday, "he joined because of the disjointed D field, and now that support is coalescing around Biden, Mike's reason for being [in the race] is gone."

Dr. Stephen Farnsworth was not dismayed by the relative quiet in central Virginia prior to Super Tuesday. He is a professor of political science and international affairs and founder of the Center for Leadership and Media Studies at the University of Mary Washington in Fredericksburg, one of two colleges within a thirty-minute commute from Caroline County. He has been observing politics in Virginia for more than two decades.

"I think the Virginia outcome is very uncertain," he said a few days before Super Tuesday. "Candidates are looking at an electorate that is of two schools of mind. One is that they agree with their views. Another perspective is, 'Which candidate has the best chance of beating President Trump?'"

"It is more calculated this year," Farnsworth said. "It is wait and see." He noted, too, that Virginia was seeing high levels of voter interest and participation, including high absentee voting and high interest on college campuses.

Five days before Super Tuesday, Farnsworth served as moderator of a forum on policy, and more than seventy voters—many of them still undecided at the time—gathered on a cold, windy night in the basement of the Fredericksburg Public Library to hear the views of four of the remaining Democratic primary candidates at the time on health care, climate change, and education. Well-prepared surrogates spoke on behalf of Joe Biden, Pete Buttigieg, Bernie Sanders, and Elizabeth Warren.

A former Bowling Green town councilman, Matt Rowe, senior geographic information systems analyst for rapidly growing Stafford County, represented Buttigieg. Rowe said he got on the former Indiana mayor's bandwagon about eight months ago because of Buttigieg's "realistic" approach to solving many of the problems that face the country. Rowe heard Buttigieg speak at the 2019 Blue Commonwealth Gala, an annual fundraiser, and was hooked. "He is an amazing orator and has a great read for where we are as a country."

Other speakers at the Fredericksburg forum were equally well informed and passionate about their candidates. Dr. Jay Brock, a past president of the Fredericksburg Area Medical Society, graduated from McGill University in Montreal and began his medical practice in Canada under a single-payer health system. He spoke on behalf of Senator Sanders, likening the American health-care system to the casinos of Las Vegas. "Like gambling, the system is set up so the house always wins, and the house is the health-care companies. It's wasteful. Who would even want to keep that system?" Brock asked. Moderate plans just perpetuate the waste, he said. "Only Bernie's plan eliminates the health-care industry and is truly affordable."

Senator Warren was represented by Johanna Guzman, a former Fulbright Public Policy Fellow and visiting researcher at Oxford University, who has degrees in biophysics and microbiology. "Fear, uncertainty, and doubt are used to protect the health-care system. Why would anyone want to perpetuate a system that doesn't put us first?" she asked the audience. At the present time, she said, "health care isn't considered a right; it is considered a business. Elizabeth Warren has a plan to change that. She has a *plan!*"

Biden was represented by Henry Thomassen, a resident of nearby Stafford County and a retired Exxon-Mobil executive who called himself "a proud Democrat for over twenty-five years with a strong record of community activism." Thomassen said that Biden's plan for health care, like those of all the contenders, "will increase taxes. But not as much. It is more modest."

Many Virginia Democrats had to revise their thinking on the eve of the primary following announcements that Steyer, Buttigieg, and Amy Klobuchar were abandoning their campaigns. I asked Rowe where that left him, and his answer was, perhaps, telling.

"With Pete dropping out, I have immediately switched to Joe Biden. I think that's what Pete wanted us to do," said Rowe, who added that he would be switching gears and preparing for the Democratic Convention for the First Congressional District of Virginia.

When Super Tuesday finally arrived, voting lifted the fog.

Caroline County gave Joe Biden a resounding victory with 64 percent of the votes. Bernie Sanders trailed with 23.6 percent, followed by Mike Bloomberg at 8.17 percent and Elizabeth Warren at 5.62 percent. Biden's margin in Caroline was much larger than it was statewide, although he was victorious there nonetheless with 53.3 percent of the vote.

Perhaps more significant than the percentages was the voter turnout on a windy, overcast primary-election day. This year, 3,952 Caroline County residents voted, compared to 2,561 in the 2016 Democratic presidential primary. Direct comparisons are problematic because there was no Republican primary; Republicans and independents were eligible to vote in the Democratic primary, and the number of registered voters was higher than in previous years.

Nonetheless, the number was encouraging news for the Caroline County Democratic Party chairman, Floyd Thomas. "That's great," he said. "It will take a while to see how many of those were first time voters and how many didn't vote in 2016," he added.

Matt Rowe, the Democratic chairman for the First Congressional District, was also cheered. Having backed Buttigieg until he dropped out, Rowe spent the final hours of the campaign trying to steer Buttigieg and Klobuchar supporters to Biden. "It certainly helped when Pete endorsed Joe. That sealed it," he said after the polls closed.

How all of this would affect the Virginia congressional primary in June and then the big one, the presidential election in November, remained to be seen.

6

YES, DOROTHY, WE ARE WAY OUTSIDE THE BELTWAY

Macon

Wwhat happens to a rising city with contentious elections, deep racial fault lines, twenty-four candidates for two U.S. Senate seats, a host of local races, and a newspaper too inadequate to help voters navigate it all?

While the rest of the nation is enthralled with the presidential election, Macon–Bibb County and the rest of Georgia don't seem to be paying much attention. They are more focused on local and statewide politics. By the time the state's Democratic primary was held on March 24, Georgia did not have much sway in the Democrats' choice for presidential nominee, and Trump had already been declared the winner in the Republican primary. There was more concern, even trepidation, about the coronavirus threat to the upcoming International Cherry Blossom Festival, March 27 through April 5, which features 350,000 Yoshino Cherry trees and attracts visitors from all over the world.

Georgia, because of the retirement of Senator Johnny Isakson for health reasons, has to choose two senators this year. While Senator David Perdue is the incumbent Republican, winning six years ago by beating Michelle Nunn, daughter of former senator Sam Nunn in a $24 million race, the vacated

Senate seat is drawing the most attention and angst in Georgia's Republican circles.

In January 2020, Governor Brian Kemp of Georgia, a Republican, had appointed Kelly Loeffler, an Atlanta financial services executive and owner of the local Women's National Basketball Association franchise, to fill the Isakson seat. President Trump had implored Kemp to appoint Trump's top ally in the House, Representative Doug Collins, from Georgia's Ninth District, and Collins openly lobbied for the seat. Twenty-three days after Loeffler was sworn in on January 6, Collins announced he would be challenging her, forcing state and national Republicans to choose sides. Now dueling attack ads are being seen back to back to back in all the state's major media markets. Loeffler pledged to spend $20 million of her own money to keep the seat. It was already a nasty race, and each day it has gotten nastier.

Loeffler and Collins face off in a "jungle primary," and they won't be alone—four other Republicans qualified for the race. A jungle primary is a no-holds-barred election featuring candidates of all political parties. Reverend Raphael Warnock, pastor of Ebenezer Baptist Church, the same church where Martin Luther King Sr. and Jr. held the pulpit, is the most notable Democrat, but there are six other Democrats, and seven more candidates qualified as either Libertarian, Green Party, or independent. The jungle primary will be held November 3, the same day voters go to the polls to elect the next president. If none of the twenty candidates reach the 50-percent-plus-one mark, a runoff will be held January 5, 2021. And that is just to fill the unexpired two years of Isakson's term. The winner will have to run again in 2022.

Not to be left out of the fun, three Democrats are seeking to unseat Senator Perdue: former Columbus mayor Teresa

Tomlinson; 2018 lieutenant governor nominee Sarah Riggs Amico; and former congressional candidate Jon Ossoff. In the 2017 special election for Georgia's Sixth District, Ossoff had lost in the most expensive House race in history to former representative Karen Handel, who subsequently lost to Lucy McBath in the 2018 midterms.

For all its importance, this election season finds the local newspaper, the *Telegraph*, unable to invest in much coverage. Though a new regional executive editor responsible for the *Telegraph*, the *Columbus Ledger-Enquirer*, and Mississippi's *Biloxi Sun Herald* as well as a new senior editor have been named, it's hard to say what impact they can have. There are too many local races for the newspaper's meager staff to follow. The new appointments were made on February 5. Eight days later, McClatchy, owner of the *Telegraph* and twenty-nine other newspapers, filed for bankruptcy. It was a stunning turn of events for the 193-year-old newspaper, founded just three years after the establishment of Macon.

On almost everyone's mind are local nonpartisan elections to be held May 19. Not only will a new mayor be selected for the first time in twelve years, but eight of nine seats of the Macon–Bibb County Commission are being contested, plus five of six board of education seats.

Retirement, the search for higher office, and term limits are responsible for the vacancies. The May 19 election is also primary day for the partisan offices for sheriff and district attorney. Interest in the local elections is high drama.

One of the reasons for the high turnover in elected officials is consolidation. Although the mayor had always been limited to two four-year terms, former city council persons and county commissioners are for the first time limited to three 4-year terms. None has reached that threshold, but age and infirmities have

taken their toll. Seven of the commissioners are in their late sixties and seventies. But other factors make this election season
like none other.

The race for mayor has three white candidates and two African Americans—all men. The tension in the contest, once again,
turns to race. The leading African American candidate has run
an effective campaign, although the white candidates have out-
raised him by hundreds of thousands of dollars. African Americans have a distinct registered voter advantage of more than
12,000 votes—if they go to the polls. If no candidate reaches the
50-percent-plus-one threshold, a runoff will be held on July 21.

The race has the potential to get testy, particularly between
the leading African American candidate, Cliffard Whitby, and
Lester Miller, a school board chair. There is bad blood between
the two that has the potential to divide the county along its
already deep racial fault lines.

When Mayor Robert Reichert assumed office in 2008, no one
knew he would be the last mayor of Macon before consolidation of city and county governments. Consolidation was a process that had begun as early as 1923, when a grand jury decided
that having two governments was inefficient. But voters saw it
differently and turned down referendums to merge the governments in 1929, 1933, 1946, 1960, 1972, and 1976. Aside from the
referendums, two government-approved study committees had
studied consolidation in 1983 and 1999. Finally, in early 2012, a
measure to consolidate the governments passed the Georgia
General Assembly and was approved by voters in July of that
year. It helped that both Reichert and Bibb County Commission chairman Sam Hart endorsed the idea and worked for its
passage.

Reichert, elected as a Democrat, inherited a city with budget
issues. The previous mayor on several occasions had to take out

tax-anticipation notes to make ends meet until property taxes flowed in again. Then came consolidation and an edict in the legislation that required the new government to cut its budget by 20 percent within five years. Reichert eventually had to offer early retirements and use other devices to keep the new Macon–Bibb County from taking on more water. The county has made a dramatic turnaround from having a negative fund balance to a $13 million surplus. An almost vacant downtown has morphed into an area that Reichert said "has come to life; a Phoenix has risen from the ashes of decades of disinvestment and businesses moving out."

But there was no "Phoenix rising" at the *Telegraph*. In 2006, the *Telegraph* employed about 320 full- and part-time employees. The signs of distress by 2007 were also being felt in the rest of the newspaper industry. At the *Telegraph*, circulation was approximately 67,500 daily and 89,500 on Sundays, down from more than 100,000 in the early 1990s. In 2009, printing was outsourced—first to the *Telegraph*'s sister paper in Columbus at a cost of almost sixty jobs and later to the printing presses of the *Savannah Morning News*, 165 miles southeast, with papers trucked back to Macon Sunday through Friday. By 2018, the circulation numbers were bleak—19,169 daily and 23,716 Sunday. The *Telegraph* stopped printing its Saturday edition this year. Layoffs, buyouts, and retirements became the order of the day. The Great Recession and the paper's lack of digital prowess hit the *Telegraph* hard.

Advertising and shopping were migrating away from brick-and-mortar locations and into the digital realm. The *Telegraph*, once an advertising juggernaut that could demand high rates for its printed pages, was being assaulted from all sides—television and digital—and it was slow to realize its new place in the world. Digital subscriptions were woefully low, and a push by corporate to accelerate movement to digital in a market that loved its printed product was not well received. A former vice president of news for McClatchy admitted that for some markets, including Macon, the transition was too aggressive.

Now, with pivotal elections on the horizon, the *Telegraph*'s position as a hearty, trusted media voice had never been weaker. Where would the citizens of Macon–Bibb County get the information needed to make informed decisions come May 19? Could other outlets fill the gap? Some were trying.

7

FEAR AND LOATHING IN THE TIME OF CORONAVIRUS

McKeesport

Until the COVID-19 pandemic finally came to western Pennsylvania, I wasn't sure whether the phrase "year of fear" applied to us because it presumes that we all were afraid of something.

My neighbor across the street—the one with the flag that says "TRUMP 2020: NO MORE BULLSHIT"—wasn't feeling anything but excitement over the prospect of another four years of President Trump.

The people who were likely feeling fear were the parents of the Black and immigrant kids who wait for the school bus on the next corner and have to walk past that flag every morning. Or at least they were waiting for the school bus until Pennsylvania's governor Tom Wolf ordered all of the state's schools closed for two weeks, beginning March 16, in response to the COVID-19 pandemic.

As in much of America, in western Pennsylvania COVID-19 went from being an afterthought on the news to dominating everyone's lives in what seemed like an eyeblink. On March 13, the first confirmed case of COVID-19 was reported in the western half of Pennsylvania, and on March 14 Allegheny

County—where Pittsburgh and McKeesport are located—had its first two confirmed cases.

At the web newspaper I edit, *Tube City Almanac*, our usual mix of police-blotter news, school board meetings, and community announcements was suddenly scrapped and replaced with nothing but closures, cancellations, and warnings.

As a small-town community news website, we tried to keep our COVID-19 coverage as local and practical as possible. Based on the feedback from our social media feeds, most readers appreciated that approach. A few even thanked us.

But a handful accused us of spreading "fake news."

Take, for instance, what happened on March 15, when officials in the nearby city of Clairton announced that a resident had tested positive for COVID-19 and was hospitalized.

Clairton is home to a major U.S. Steel coal by-products plant that has been blamed for causing serious air-quality problems in the McKeesport area. After a fire in 2018 damaged the plant's emissions-control equipment, air-quality monitors around McKeesport on numerous occasions recorded the highest levels of sulfur dioxide and other air pollutants in the entire United States. Several environmental activists and public-health advocates called for the plant to be shut down completely.

Whenever *Tube City Almanac* writes about pollution problems at U.S. Steel's Clairton plant, we are inevitably criticized by a handful of readers who accuse us of an "anti-industry" agenda. And when we posted the item about a Clairton resident being diagnosed with COVID-19, one reader from McKeesport accused the website and the Clairton City Council of pushing a "hidden agenda" to "create more unnecessary panic."

The same reader added a few minutes later: "You watch too much TV . . . turn off the TV and pay attention to the real world and apply common sense . . . it's not rocket science."

I checked the reader's Facebook wall and saw that he'd recently shared a post from Milton Wolf, a Kansas Tea Party activist and physician. "The media is creating an all-out panic," Wolf wrote. "They are destroying small businesses, crushing 401(k)s, and worse yet, terrifying people. They are rooting for recession, destruction, and death. The mainstream media is [sic] garbage. They are the enemy of the people."

A few hours later we reported on Governor Wolf's decision to order all restaurants and bars in the state closed. A reader commented, "Hey Mr. Wolf, what's wrong with you? Are you going to reimburse all the businesses you are telling to close down? You're wrong."

A reader from nearby Irwin, Pennsylvania, was blunter: "Fuck Tom Wolf. . . . He just wants you all to be broke."

It goes almost without saying that each of the negative comments were left by older white folks.

A lot has been written—some would probably say too much—about the way that Trump successfully tapped into a sense of grievance in these voters and how he rode it into office with the help of places such as western Pennsylvania.

There was, indeed, a strong sense of grievance here, especially among the Boomer generation. There's also a strong suspicion of authority figures that flares up at times like these when we've been asked to trust faraway experts to know what's best for us.

The grievances have their roots in the industrialization of this valley, and the mistrust of authority figures is a direct result of the big bargain people here made—a deal that turned out to be a lie.

During most of the twentieth century, if you worked for our major industrial employers—companies such as U.S. Steel, Jones & Laughlin, Westinghouse Electric, and Union Switch &

Signal—you knew they were poisoning our air and water, and you knew that you stood a decent chance of being injured or maimed on the job.

But the bargain you made was that in exchange for these sacrifices, with the protection of industrial trade unions you would be paid well, and when you retired, you would have a pension waiting.

In the 1980s, workers kept up their side of the bargain, but U.S. Steel diversified into oil refining and closed down much of its steel production; Westinghouse Electric merged with CBS and exited manufacturing altogether; Union Switch & Signal went overseas; and Jones & Laughlin (by then known as LTV) imploded after two bankruptcies. Pension plans were liquidated for pennies on the dollar or bailed out by the federal government.

Corporate America left western Pennsylvania a toxic mess, both literally and figuratively, and stripped away our livelihoods and identities. Of course we're bitter.

When that crash hit, those who could moved away. Those who couldn't tended to be midcareer Baby Boomers with mortgaged houses that suddenly couldn't be sold at any price. Those folks are now in their sixties, seventies, and eighties, and many of them are still very, very aggrieved.

Some of them found solace in attending their churches or by becoming supernostalgic for the "lost America" that Ronald Reagan told us had been destroyed by "unions" and "minorities" and "welfare queens."

From about 2004 to 2014, I worked Sundays at two AM radio stations just outside McKeesport, where we aired mostly paid programming—polka music and evangelical preachers. (I liked the polkas more than the preachers.)

One of the songs the preachers often played—I would occasionally hear it twice in the same afternoon—was "We Want America Back" by the Steeles, which includes the lyrics

Something is wrong with America . . .
We must return to the values we left,
Before this country we love is totally lost.
We want America back
From those who have no self-control . . .
It's time for the army of God to arise,
And say we want America back.

What do they want back? The familiar past, before they were afraid for their futures. From whom do they want it back? The usual groups. Their secular children and grandchildren, who don't attend church. Feminists. LGBTQ rights activists.

For many of them, the real "years of fear" began on September 11, 2001, and went into hyperdrive when Barack Obama was elected president in 2008. I'm hardly the first one to point out that the Tea Party was (more or less) a white backlash to a Black president.

The rise of the shambolic, lurching authoritarianism of the Trump administration may represent "years of fear" for many Americans, but for aggrieved, older white folks in western Pennsylvania, Trump's election eased their fears of an uncertain future.

On Flag Day last year, I bought red, white, and blue cupcakes to take to work. The cashier, a nice, older white lady, said to me, "I'm so glad people are free to love America again." She wasn't being ironic.

For a long time, I had the sense that Bernie Sanders might have been the only Democratic presidential candidate who could tap that sense of grievance. He's their age, he's white, he supports gun ownership, and, like them, he's mad as hell about the loss of their American dream.

The polls tell a different story. Sanders hasn't connected with that generation at all, at least in the Pittsburgh area. When they hear that he's a socialist, they don't think of modern-day Denmark or Sweden. They remember 1970s Poland and Czechoslovakia.

My wife gets a monthly magazine from the William Penn Association, a fraternal organization in Pittsburgh for Hungarian Americans. A few months ago, one of their columnists wrote of traveling to Hungary to visit relatives and looking through artifacts they had saved from the communist era—ration books, identity cards.

That's what people here remember about socialism: sending blue jeans and toys to relatives behind the Iron Curtain and hearing horror stories from relatives who had escaped to the West.

To them, Sanders was a big unknown, and that makes them more fearful, not less. They don't want to see any more radical changes because all the ones they saw in their young adulthood—deindustrialization, corporate raiding, stock manipulations—worked out badly for western Pennsylvanians.

Trump, besides tapping into their grievances, also promised there are no unknowns because he knows everything, whether he's discussing the economy, the military, or COVID-19.

For a lot of people in western Pennsylvania, President Trump didn't represent three years of fear. He represented a return to a romanticized pre-1965 America—the America of the first few seasons of TV's *Mad Men*, when white men might often be wrong but were never mistaken.

It's no wonder that so many conservative Christians flocked to Trump; evangelicalism, too, promises certainty—that everything, from a stock-market crash to COVID-19, is part of God's plan.

Sure, the voters who most connect with Bernie Sanders today are those age eighteen to forty-five for whom the American economic system isn't working. But the American economic system failed eighteen- to forty-five-year-olds in western Pennsylvania more than thirty years ago. Those people are now forty-eight- to seventy-five-year-old Donald Trump voters—and, it appears, possibly Joe Biden voters as well.

Where Sanders and Elizabeth Warren promised change, and people like Pete Buttigieg and Kamala Harris were types of change (one is young and openly gay, the other is Black and female), Joe Biden is white, cisgender, straight—and old.

In her essay "Bernie Angry. Bernie Smash!" for the *New York Times* on March 4, 2020, Jennifer Finney Boylan touched on another aspect of Biden's appeal—that he represents the "happy warrior" strain of American politics. She suggested that after three-plus years of Trump's endless rage, Americans weren't looking for another angry man in the White House, even if that man (Sanders) was justifiably mad as hell about the same things that have made them mad for the past thirty years.

Could Biden help alleviate those voters' fears through positivity, while still connecting with their sense of nostalgia for a familiar (but imperfect) past? We would likely to know well before Pennsylvania's primary, scheduled for April 28—assuming concerns over COVID-19 didn't lead the state to postpone voting, as Ohio did.

On March 22, the mayor of Clairton confirmed that the resident who had been hospitalized for COVID died the day before, on March 21. This was the first death in Allegheny County attributable to COVID-19.

COVID-19, of course, represented our ultimate existential fears—illness, incapacity, death. On this front, too, Biden tried to reassure anxious voters by promising them that a Biden administration would have handled the early stages of the pandemic far better than the Trump administration.

At that point, I suspected that all but the most hardcore Trump supporters in western Pennsylvania—say, my neighbor with the "NO MORE BULLSHIT" flag and the types of folks who attacked the *Tube City Almanac* for pushing a "hidden agenda" by even reporting on COVID-19 cases—would agree.

8

IN THE RIO GRANDE VALLEY, A BORDER CLOSES, AND SIGNS OF A WALL APPEAR AS THE PANDEMIC SPREADS

McAllen

Standing on the banks of her family's Texas property, Nayda Alvarez shuddered as she stared out across the deep waters of the Rio Grande, her eyes fixed on Mexico. It was March 7, and she couldn't stop thinking that President Trump would likely close the U.S.-Mexico border, citing concerns over the coronavirus spread. Most of all, she feared that he would find a way to blame Mexicans and those trying to migrate from the South for the current crisis despite the fact that Mexico had only a couple of reported cases and the United States had hundreds. If he did this, he would very likely be able to further his political agenda and presidential campaign promise to complete the border wall, she pointed out.

Alvarez, a forty-eight-year-old high school teacher, mother, and grandmother, has lived in rural Starr County in deep South Texas for four decades. For her, the border wall is personal because it is slated to cut through her family's land. When Trump officially announced he was closing the U.S. borders with Mexico and Canada for all "nonessential travel" on March 20 to stop the spread of COVID-19, Alvarez worried for what was to come.

"He's going to use it as an excuse because his main priority was to close the border three years ago, and this is just going to be the excuse he needed," she said mere hours after the closure took effect.

Trump's order was announced at a ninety-minute White House press conference during which he berated *NBC News's* White House correspondent Peter Alexander, who asked the president what he would "say to Americans who are watching you right now who are scared." Trump, who for weeks had downplayed the seriousness of the virus, saying it would "vanish" on its own, turned on Alexander, calling the question "nasty" and accusing him of being a "terrible reporter." The next day, also during a White House coronavirus media briefing, Trump again lashed out at the media, charging the *Washington Post* with being "fake media" and hyping unnecessary hysteria and "lies" about his administration and its handling of the deadly, novel virus.

For Alvarez, Trump's systematic approach to dismissing anyone or any group who disagreed with him was proof that he would stop at nothing to further his political causes, even during such a dire time. Despite the fact that much of the nation was on lockdown because of the coronavirus, including Starr County, Alvarez said that construction on the border wall continued in her small, rural South Texas county, and she feared it would soon begin near her home, located six miles in between the county seat, Rio Grande City, and the town of Roma.

When COVID-19 first gripped the world's attention, Alvarez thought it would perhaps divert Trump from building a border wall. But even during this national crisis—in which several states, including California, New York, Illinois, Connecticut, Oregon, and New Jersey, ordered residents to shelter in place— Alvarez noted that wooden survey markers were planted on her property, pink ribbons affixed on top of them fluttering in the wind, indicating the planned construction path of a border wall.

Alvarez positioned outdoor cameras throughout her property, which includes her grandfather's house and her father's house in a close-knit alcove down an unmarked dirt road. She monitors the cameras twenty-four/seven to try and stop surveyors from entering. But the stakes were put on her family's property in February 2020 without her permission when she went to Washington, DC, to testify before Congress about her opposition to the border wall. Other markers could be seen cutting a path through neighboring fields of this tiny community of about three hundred people fifty miles west of McAllen, Texas.

The juxtaposition of the markers indicated that her home was directly in the path of the wall, or what the U.S. Border Patrol calls the "Border Infrastructure System." This system would include a thirty-foot-tall border wall with steel bollards and a concrete base, tall overhead floodlights, underground sensors, infrared cameras, and an all-weather road laid parallel to the barrier. From the placement of the current stakes, the 150-foot "enforcement zone" system was lined up to go right through Alvarez's four-bedroom, one-story, ranch-style home.

On her roof, Alvarez painted a message to Trump in white block letters: "NO BORDER WALL." She painted it in the summer of 2015 right before Trump, then a presidential candidate, flew into Laredo, about one hundred miles northwest of her home.

"I'm going to lose my access to the river. I'm going to lose our customs, and, mind you, over what? A campaign promise. That's the way I see it," Alvarez said as she eyed the two-hundred-meter-wide divide between the two countries that she loves.

Alvarez is a Democrat. Leading up to the March 3 Texas primary election, she campaigned in Starr County for the little-known immigration lawyer Jessica Cisneros, a twenty-six-year-old who challenged Henry Cuellar, longtime Texas Democratic congressman and vice chairman of the House Appropriations Subcommittee on Homeland Security. Cisneros was backed by U.S. representative Alexandria Ocasio-Cortez, who helped Cisneros raise nearly $1 million in campaign funds from sources outside the state of Texas. Although Cisneros lost, it was by just 2,746 votes—48.2 percent to 51.8 percent for Cuellar—and the race had given Alvarez hope that change would come during the November general election.

As the Democratic presidential candidate field becomes smaller and smaller, Alvarez is still not sure whom she will back, but they have to promise to abolish the border wall, she said. Alvarez had been leaning toward Senator Elizabeth Warren, who, before dropping out, proposed an agenda that would defund the border wall and use billions of dollars to help stop COVID-19.

To many, the river is the Rio Grande, but locals refer to it as the "Rio Bravo" (Mean River) because of its unseen ferocity. Alvarez pointed to the top currents that swirled one way, but underneath, she said, is an undertow that goes the other way. They never swim in the waters, she said. They respect the river and celebrate it. They gather on its banks and barbecue on a grassy spot free from prickly pear cacti and brush. It is a safe place for her three grandchildren to run and frolic without the fear of rattlesnakes.

"I have lived on this land for forty years alongside where my grandfather lives. I worry about my father's health once our land is taken. This land is where my daughters were raised and where I see my grandchildren play," Alvarez told lawmakers during her five-minute speech before a House committee investigating the wall. "This is not only my home, but it is a place of gathering for my family. It is part of my family history and my inheritance passed down to me from my ancestors—a tradition I intend to continue. However, this ancestral home will be destroyed by the construction of the border wall."

U.S. Customs and Border Protection announced that it had awarded a $179 million contract to a New Mexico company to build fifteen miles of border wall through Starr County. The entire fifty-two miles of the county, from end to end, are supposed to be walled off, according to CBP.

Alvarez has "been sued by the government" for eminent domain so that it can gain access to her land to survey it. She had a federal court hearing scheduled for April 14 in McAllen.

"The government has offered me just one hundred dollars for this access, which is what they think is a fair price for giving up so much. And this is the land of prosperity?" she testified in Congress on February 27. "There is already a natural barrier created by a tall bluff from the river. No explanation was ever given to me as to why the government plans to spend billions to construct an artificial one, except for the expensive needless campaign promise. There has been no transparency, and we have been intimidated by the government to sign over our rights to our land. We have been talked down to by government officials who think we're not aware of our rights."

Alvarez, who has been a teacher for twenty-two years, said that at this point in her life she is looking toward retirement, but she has instead become a vocal opponent to Trump's plans.

This was the second time she testified before Congress against the border wall. The first was a year earlier, and she expressed disappointment that her efforts did little good.

Since then, Trump's administration has waived dozens of laws to expedite the construction of the border wall. In October 2019, the Department of Homeland Security announced it was waiving rules for the border wall construction in South Texas, including environmental regulations that protect endangered species, laws pertaining to the Safe Drinking Water Act, and federal procurement regulations.

Alvarez said she became the subject of social media threats. She worried for her family's financial future if a border wall takes over her home and property. And in the time of coronavirus, she worried about her family's health and access to her friends and relatives across the Rio Grande. Her doctor is located across the river in Ciudad Miguel Alemán in the northern Mexican state of Tamaulipas. On the day Trump announced the travel ban, Alvarez hastily crossed the Roma–Ciudad Miguel Alemán International Bridge into northern Mexico and paid $97 for a two-month supply of her father's diabetes medication, which, she said, costs $700 in Texas.

Trump's travel restrictions still allowed crossing for medical purposes as well as commerce and cargo. But Alvarez worried that the entire border would shut down soon and that they might have to spend significantly more money on medication in Texas than in Mexico.

Alvarez didn't know if her upcoming court hearing would be postponed, but as she observed, regardless of the coronavirus outbreak, construction was continuing on border wall sections in Starr County.

"Will I still have a home at the end of this?" she asked. "I will lose my way of life. My privacy. My access to a beautiful river. My plans for the future are now filled with uncertainty," she said.

9

THE GHOST OF A WEEKLY COVERS THE PANDEMIC

Bowling Green

F or ninety-nine years, the residents of Caroline County, Virginia, were served by a lively weekly paper, the *Caroline Progress*, family owned and operated for most of its existence. The newspaper was how this quiet rural county talked to itself. And in the pandemic, I found myself thinking about how it would help its readers if it were still around.

On the pages of the *Caroline Progress* in normal times, people read about births, deaths, and weddings; church notices, coming events, sports victories and defeats, government meetings, political intrigue, highway accidents, and fires. Readers also found thoughtful editorials on local and national issues, op-ed pieces, and a multitude of letters to the editor, particularly in election years.

In the nearby town of Ashland and neighboring Hanover County, the *Herald-Progress* served a similar function until it, too, shut down in 2018 after 131 years of service. By the end, the *Caroline Progress* and the *Herald-Progress* were essentially one newspaper put out by a single editor, one full-time and one part-time reporter, and a few freelancers. The two papers died on the same day.

I was editor of the *Herald-Progress* from September 2004 until I retired in November 2012, and I continued to be part of it in several ways, sitting in as transitional editor several times from 2014 to 2017 as well as providing freelance stories and columns up to the end in 2018.

Historically, employees of both papers were for the most part longtime county residents, emotionally and economically invested in their communities. In 2007, Lakeway Publishers of Morristown, Tennessee, acquired the *Caroline Progress* and three other Virginia newspapers and then added two other local papers, including the *Herald-Progress*, to the chain the next year. All six papers were slowly gutted over the next decade, and in 2016 the office in Bowling Green was closed, with operations consolidated in Hanover County.

On the afternoon of March 26, 2018, the group publisher walked into the *Herald-Progress/Caroline Progress* office and instructed the remaining staff to change the lead story: the March 28 issue would be the last for both papers, a concise notice from Lakeway Publishers above the fold on page 1 read. Employees were told they would be paid for that week and the following week. That was the severance package. The editor did not have time to toss together a proper sendoff in the final editions.

Both newspapers left a huge news vacuum in their wake, one that still exists. I have found it particularly noticeable in 2020.

The global pandemic that has changed the lives of almost everyone in the world has made it even more apparent that the residents of Caroline County need a vibrant local newspaper. To test this idea, I created a scenario in which the *Caroline Progress* is still a functioning newspaper in 2020, much as it had been in 2015. How would it serve its readers? How would its stories and editorials differ from what is being served up by twenty-four-hour TV news, distant newspapers, and social media?

I sought input from two former associates, Dan Sherrier and Sarah Vogelsong. Sherrier was a bright, young college graduate when I hired him in 2007 as a reporter at the *Herald-Progress* in Ashland. He survived my curmudgeonly mentorship until after I retired. He then left the business to teach kickboxing and pursue creative writing in fantasy and science fiction genres, only to return as editor of the *Caroline Progress* in 2014. In 2015, he moved over to become editor of the *Herald-Progress* for another nine months.

Sarah Vogelsong was the part-time reporter at the *Caroline Progress* for two years, spanning my time there as well as Sherrier's. She went on to become a reporter at the daily *Progress-Index* in Petersburg, where she won a number of Virginia Press Association awards. She is now the environment and energy reporter for the *Virginia Mercury*, an online publication.

Vogelsong:

> Church is a huge part of life in Caroline. I think you could easily say it's the glue that binds much of the community together (for better or worse!). I think we'd look at how the churches kept themselves going during this time, both in terms of providing spiritual guidance to their congregations and how they assisted in providing services to community members in need.
>
> Caroline is one of the state's biggest soybean producers, and farmers everywhere have been hit hard by the economic meltdown associated with coronavirus. I think we'd track how the county's farmers and Farm Bureau were handling their planting decisions, getting credit and workers, and generally keeping afloat.
>
> The closest hospitals to Caroline are in Fredericksburg or down in Richmond. We might have looked at how residents were accessing medical services, and maybe how the poorer members

of the community, without access to a car, were handling decision making about whether they should get tested.

Caroline's broadband was beefed up in the past few months, but
that was a huge issue for years, and I think we would have looked at
how students and workers were managing—or not managing—to
get their work done with poor internet connection.

And, of course, money was always tight in Caroline. What
decisions and sacrifices would the Board of Supervisors have to
make when it came to the budget, given certain revenue declines?

Sherrier:

If the *Caroline Progress* was still around, I think we would have
attempted to cut through the noise of the twenty-four/seven news
cycle, where everything is frequently dialed up to eleven, which
can result in understandable skepticism from people.

I would have wanted to talk to any local medical experts, if
available, to help distinguish between the valid warnings and the
fearmongering. We could also have talked with mental health
experts to help people cope with the isolation. On the economic
front, we could have talked with local businesses about how
they're coping with the situation and how they're still serving the
community, if they're still in a position to do so. Certainly, we
could have kept people up to date about what's open, what's
closed, and what's operating in a temporarily different fashion.
We would have been in a position to zero in on these local enti-
ties much more so than other news outlets.

We might also have looked at the ways people in the community are helping each other out—good deeds, neighbors looking
out for neighbors, that sort of thing. The lack of sports and public events would free up considerable space for COVID-19

coverage, and I'm sure we'd have found plenty to cover on that subject.

For more than a quarter century, I put together editorial and op-ed pages in the four weekly newspapers for which I worked, attempting to inform, educate, and entertain readers in a responsible manner.

My theoretical editorial and op-ed pages in March 2020 would have praised Governor Ralph Northam of Virginia for his leadership in addressing the COVID-19 crisis. Northam got off to a shaky start in his first year in office over his awkward handling of a racist photo that had appeared in his medical college yearbook page. After that, he took his licks from the pro-gun lobby. His handling of the COVID-19 crisis, however, has redeemed him in the eyes of many Virginians. A pediatric brain surgeon, Northam quickly realized the magnitude of the problem and the need to act, getting ahead of the federal government in closing schools, bars, restaurants, and many government offices, limiting public gatherings to no more than ten, and promoting social distancing.

In his press conferences, Northam spoke with authority and decisiveness, deftly avoiding the mixed signals that came from the federal government. Also praiseworthy were the efforts of the Caroline County Board of Supervisors and School Board in closing the public schools, libraries, county buildings, and other public areas days ahead of neighboring counties. As of April 1, Caroline County had just one case of COVID-19, a forty-three-year-old nurse who works at a Richmond-area hospital and was quarantined at home.

I would have used the editorial pages to bring the readers' attention to people like her: those who were on the front lines risking their own health. Also deserving of praise were the many volunteers who distributed meals to children who would have normally been receiving lunches and breakfasts at school. Our local restaurant workers and store employees would have also found themselves on the editorial pages.

Finally, I would have pointed out how the pandemic encouraged many people in Caroline County to put aside their petty social and political differences and work together to help their neighbors get through the crisis—by getting them groceries, prescriptions, and other necessities or simply cheering them up during difficult times.

In 2015, the *Caroline Progress* was published by a barebones five-person staff: editor, part-time reporter, advertising representative, graphic artist, and receptionist. The paper was job-printed by a daily newspaper in Hopewell (which also has since then gone out of business), and it was distributed by one contract employee who filled the vending boxes and store racks and delivered subscribers' papers to the post office for mail delivery. If the paper had continued into 2020, all of these employees would have been able to practice basic social distancing on the job. This staff could have functioned well during the pandemic.

Each week our theoretical newspaper would have provided a place to post closing and modified hours for businesses and government offices. Readers who benefited from the many acts of random kindness would have a place to express their gratitude. Others could have made suggestions or appeal for help through letters to the editor. The many official government notices and legitimate health tips generated during this crisis would have been printed on the news pages or posted to our website, accessible without forcing people to wade through countless government websites and Facebook posts of cute animals or what people ate for breakfast.

In short, a functioning local weekly newspaper would have been of real value to the people of Caroline County in a time like this. The *Caroline Progress* is missed.

10

STANDING ON SINKING SAND, LIVING IN LIMBO

Macon

On March 20, 2020, Pastor Ronald Eugene Terry Sr., the shepherd of New Fellowship Missionary Baptist Church, one of largest congregations in Macon, died. Reverend Terry had led the church since its founding in 1978 and was one of the most respected and beloved ministers in the area, honored for his work as a chaplain as well as with the Cherry Blossom Festival and the National Baptist Convention, USA, where he was president of the music auxiliary.

Under normal conditions, even Terry's large sanctuary in East Macon would not be able to hold his funeral. Services would probably have been moved to the Macon City Auditorium, site of Otis Redding's funeral on December 18, 1967, after a plane carrying Redding and members of the Bar-Kays band plunged into Lake Monona outside Madison, Wisconsin. Redding's homegoing was attended by music industry legends James Brown, Wilson Pickett, Sam and Dave, the WLAC disc jockey John R., and 4,500 others, and Terry's services would have attracted an equally stellar cast from the gospel music realm, fellow clergy members, and local, state, and national political figures. But the conditions were anything but normal.

In an executive order on the same day as Reverend Terry's death, however, Mayor Robert Reichert of Macon "strongly encouraged" all funeral directors to "avoid conducting any indoor funeral service, whether in the mortuary chapel or any place of worship unless no more than ten people" were in attendance.

His edict went further. Funeral directors were told not to provide limousine services; rather, "guests should ride in personal vehicles." And finally, Reichert's order advised "any customers wishing to have a large memorial service to do so after the current public health emergency has resolved."

While Reverend Terry's family was faced with this dilemma, it was no different for families all over Macon–Bibb County—or, for that matter, all over the country. The edict regarding memorial services was personal for Mayor Reichert; not only had the community lost a leader and friend, but two days earlier Macon–Bibb County deputy Kenterrous De'Wayne Taylor was killed responding to a burglary call when his cruiser overturned. Normally, when a law enforcement officer dies in the line of duty, hundreds of his colleagues from around the state gather in full-dress uniforms, bagpipes sound, and the processional can be miles long. Not this time. The graveside services were restricted to family only.

Ultimately, Reverend Terry's services included a viewing at his church the day before his burial, but only two people at a time could enter the sanctuary. His burial was limited to family, but only two at a time could approach his casket.

Earthquakes are a tricky phenomenon. Most depictions feature large cracks in the earth's surface, but most quakes don't cause buildings to fall into crevices or roads to buckle; rather, an unsettling sudden motion creates instability in body and mind as the ground—thought solid—shifts. The rapid spread of COVID-19 has been just such an earthquake, and the aftershocks—day by day by day—put every aspect of normal life in the United States in doubt.

Now in addition to deaths without funerals, there are elections without campaigns, schools without students, religions without services, and newspapers with few reporters.

In Middle Georgia, the ripple from the first shockwave started innocently enough; in fact, it was thought the COVID-19 earthquake wasn't all that bad. On Thursday, March 12, all University System of Georgia (USG) college presidents received an encouraging message about COVID-19 from the board of regents advising all twenty-six USG institutions to remain open because the risk was low.

Only hours later, though, the board reversed course and ordered its institutions to halt face-to-face classes. The system's 163,754 employees and 328,712 students were tossed into limbo. "Students who are currently on spring break are strongly encouraged not to return to campus," said Teresa MacCartney, executive vice chancellor for the USG. By March 16, the USG closed all residence halls, canceled all face-to-face classes, and canceled or postponed graduation ceremonies.

There are two USG institutions in Middle Georgia: Middle Georgia State University, with its five campuses in Macon, Warner Robins, Cochran, Eastman, and Dublin, and Fort Valley State University in Fort Valley. The state also closed the Technical College System of Georgia, with eight campuses in the area, and private Mercer University and Wesleyan College also closed down and moved to online instruction.

On Friday, March 13, the 2020 Masters Golf Tournament was postponed. Fred Ridley, chairman of Augusta National Golf Club, which hosts the legendary tournament, explained,

"Unfortunately, the ever-increasing risks associated with the widespread coronavirus COVID-19 have led us to a decision that undoubtedly will be disappointing to many." The tournament has a $120 million economic impact on the Augusta, Georgia, area. Although a golf tournament can be rescheduled, other events have not been as fortunate.

Earlier that same day, Macon's Cherry Blossom Festival, which draws thousands of visitors from around the world, was canceled. "This is a rapidly changing situation," said Cherry Blossom Board chair Alex Habersham. "After meeting with public health officials . . . we recognize that even with the plans being made for additional hand-washing stations, table and ride cleaning, and regular reminders, there would still be a risk by having a large number of people in close proximity." This would have been the ten-day festival's thirty-ninth year. The festival's economic impact, according to a University of Georgia study, has usually been between $10 and $12 million—money now gone.

Later that day, the Bibb County School System decided the entire system would shut down and transition to digital platforms for teaching.

On March 19, Atlanta-based Delta Airlines, the world's largest airline by revenue, cut 70 percent of its flights, and 10,000 employees took voluntary unpaid leave. Delta accounts for 79 percent of Hartsfield-Jackson International Airport's traffic, and the busiest airport in the nation has an $82 billion economic impact on the region. Many would-be travelers' canceled plans, affecting the hospitality and tourism industries. Atlanta was to host the Final Four before the NCAA ditched March Madness because of the virus, costing the city an estimated $106 million.

The same day as Delta's announcement, Mayor Kiesha Lance Bottoms of Atlanta by executive order closed all restaurants (limiting them to delivery or takeout), bars, nightclubs, private social clubs, fitness centers, gyms, movie theaters, bowling alleys, and arcades in the city's limits. Atlanta averages 56 million tourists annually, and according to William Pate, president and CEO of the Atlanta Convention and Visitors Bureau, tourism supports 223,000 jobs and brings the city $16 billion. "Tourism," Pate said, "is the gasoline that drives the city's economic engine." In 2019, tourism had brought the Peach State $66.2 billion.

The palatable fear brought by national, state, and local politics has been surpassed by the alarm wrought by COVID-19, and that's saying something. Forty-six candidates are fighting over eighteen local elected offices in Macon–Bibb County, including for mayor, county commissioner, school board positions, sheriff, district attorney, state Senate seats, Water Authority officials, plus two U.S. Senate seats, but the public focus has shifted away from politics. Elbow bumps have replaced handshakes, and houses of worship are streaming services online and told parishioners to stay home even before a statewide ban began.

The building enthusiasm for the Democratic ticket—whether Bernie or Joe—vanished from seismographs before Biden took decisive victories in Arizona, Florida, and Illinois on March 17. President Donald Trump is the only name on the Republican ballot, but everyone in Georgia would have to wait because the state's presidential primary was moved from March 24 to May 19, even though 279,000 Georgians have already cast early-voting ballots. And then there is serious talk of delaying the primary until mid-June. Not that it really matters—the state's influence on the national tickets won't register a blip on the Richter scale whenever its primary is held.

Governor Brian Kemp, who has thus far handled the crisis well, came under fire when he ordered a stay-at-home decree on April 2—but only partially and much later than other governors. His order superseded ones given in communities that had taken a tougher stance, notably the beach communities of Tybee Island and St. Simons Island. Those communities closed their beaches, but Kemp's order opened them up again, and the mayors of those communities have publicly expressed their dismay. When asked why he waited so long, Kemp replied, "Finding out that this virus is now transmitting before people see signs." However, Dr. Anthony Fauci, the lead member of the White House coronavirus task force, had been talking about asymptomatic transmission as far back as January 31.

The virus has exposed usually hidden strategies to suppress voter turnout in the state. Fearing increased participation, Republicans were seething at Secretary of State Brad Raffensperger, a fellow Republican, for deciding to send every active voter, 6.9 million of them, absentee-ballot request forms. State Speaker of the House David Ralston (R–Blue Ridge) said, "This will be extremely devastating to Republicans and conservatives in Georgia. . . . Could it jeopardize Republican control [of] the House and Senate in the state? Could it jeopardize, you know, other races up and down the ballot in 2020?" Ralston said his concern was over voter fraud.

With the ban of gatherings of no more than ten people, municipal candidates are basically treading water. The normal glad-handing, Sunday morning church visits, and campaign rallies are now relegated to virtual spaces and to those with war chests who can afford television ads. Two mayoral forums, one sponsored by the Greater Macon Chamber of Commerce and the other by the League of Women Voters, have been postponed indefinitely.

On April 5, the *Telegraph* posted its first stories featuring local races since March 6. Craig Forman, president and chief executive officer of McClatchy, owner of the local newspaper, said in an op-ed printed in the March 22 edition, "Our 30 newsrooms are uniquely equipped to go deep into the communities they cover with boots-on-the-ground journalists. This is what we do. This is what we've always done." Really? McClatchy had filed for bankruptcy protection. Staff positions at its papers—those "boots-on-the-ground journalists"—had been decimated by layoffs and buyouts.

But the *Telegraph* was far from the only newspaper in the state having financial hardships related to COVID-19. The *Marietta Daily Journal*, a newspaper staple for a county just north of Atlanta, announced the reduction of its seven-day-a-week print schedule to Tuesday through Saturday. The *Rome News-Tribune*, distributed an hour northwest of Atlanta, would do the same. The *Gainesville Times* and the *Forsyth News*, both in towns about an hour northeast of Atlanta and twenty miles apart, went to a Wednesday- and Saturday-only schedule. All of these newspapers have an online presence, but would that help readers wedded to their print editions in the heat of this political season in the midst of a frightening pandemic?

By April 1, Governor Brian Kemp closed all public schools and issued a shelter-in-place order for the entire state.

The Georgia Municipal Association asked the leaders of all 538 cities in the state to declare public-health emergencies and shut down nonessential businesses within their boundaries. The Georgia Department of Public Health updates the number of COVID-19 cases daily at noon. The statistics of the number of cases, of those hospitalized and deaths, are accelerating at an alarming rate. As of April 1, there were 82 confirmed cases of the virus originating in Macon-Bibb and surrounding counties as of April 1. By April 6, that number was 154, with eleven deaths.

Such is the new normal. The COVID-19 earthquake has shaken our very core, and, as for any earthquake, recovery will take time because the aftershocks—possibly the strongest—are yet to come.

11

TRANSPARENCY IN A TIME OF PANDEMIC

McKeesport

As I got ready to head out the door on April 1 to cover a McKeesport City Council meeting, I could tell my wife was worried. Over eight years of marriage to a part-time community journalist, she had put up with a lot, including endless late-night meetings and noisy interviews conducted over speaker phones. Last summer, we were on vacation when my cell phone rang. It was an elected official who wanted to pitch an idea.

"He just calls you on your cell phone while we're on vacation, and you answer?" she said. What could I do but shrug? I'm used to a lot of reactions from her when I'm heading out to cover a story—including encouragement and sometimes bemusement—but fear was a new one.

"Do you really have to go?" she asked.

A week earlier, Allegheny County had been among the first in Pennsylvania to be placed under a stay-at-home order by Governor Tom Wolf. The order—closing all nonessential businesses—was later extended to each of the state's sixty-seven counties as health officials worked to slow the spread of the novel coronavirus.

By mid-April, there was some evidence that Wolf's order was "flattening the curve." More than 1,000 cases of COVID-19 were reported in Allegheny County, including 55 deaths and 180 hospitalizations, but health officials said Pittsburgh-area intensive-care units hadn't yet been overloaded like those in Detroit and New York City.

That's not to say we were out of the woods. Fire departments and ambulance crews were asking for donations of personal protective equipment of any kind, including face masks. At a nursing home in Beaver County, north of Pittsburgh, officials presumed that all eight hundred residents and staff had been infected with coronavirus after more than one hundred tested positive. A local ice-skating rink was being prepared for possible use as a morgue.

Unemployment was rampant. When the Greater Pittsburgh Community Food Bank, located across the river from McKeesport in Duquesne, began directly distributing boxes of food to needy families on March 30, cars lined up for miles. From the window of my home office, I could hear helicopters from Pittsburgh's TV news stations circling overhead, filming the traffic.

I was lucky. My day job allowed me to work from home, while employees of accredited media outlets were exempt from the governor's stay-at-home order. At the nonprofit community journalism website I run, Tube City Online, I laid down guidelines for our freelance writers and radio-show hosts. At the radio studio, no guests were permitted until further notice, and all hosts were required to disinfect anything they touched on the way in and out, using hydrogen peroxide spray and wipes we provided.

I also asked our freelancers to keep doing their best to cover our communities. "If you regularly attend a community meeting, and you feel safe continuing to do so, those meetings are still important—maybe more than ever," I told them on March 18.

"If you attend, practice good social distancing—avoid handshakes and stay at least six feet away from people," I said but

added, "Remember, in Pennsylvania, public meetings by government officials mean *public* meetings—you have a *legal right to
attend* except in certain limited circumstances."

Some of the communities we cover canceled their meetings.
But a few, such as McKeesport, had business that needed to be
done. After promising my wife that I'd put my clothes in the
washer as soon as I got home and that I'd shower in the basement before I went upstairs, I went to McKeesport's public-
safety building, wearing a windbreaker, nitrile gloves, and a
face mask.

"Here comes the Orkin man," joked one councilman when I
entered council chambers, but they were taking social distancing rules seriously. Just four council members—the minimum
needed for a quorum—attended in person, and each sat six feet
apart. Three others participated over the phone. Mayor Michael
Cherepko submitted his remarks in writing. Only I and Jeff Stitt,
a reporter for the *Mon Valley Independent*, were in the audience.
The meeting began at 6:45, the voting was at 7:00, and I was
showering in our basement by 7:30.

In any community, there's a delicate relationship between
local officials and members of the media, but it's especially ten-
uous in a small town. A reporter in a large city can afford to be
confrontational with officials because if they won't talk, there are
plenty of other people who will leak information. But in a small
town, there are fewer alternative sources to call on. There are
social complications as well. Reporters who live in the community they cover, as I do, are likely to bump into the mayor shopping at Giant Eagle or see a council member at church on
Sunday.

To be sure, I'm always concerned about becoming too chummy
with the people I cover. But being completely aloof simply won't
work. Besides, even if I wanted to become more adversarial,

Pennsylvania has some of the weakest open-records laws in the country.

Take police reports. As a rookie reporter in the late 1990s, I had to follow up on the deaths of residents killed in car accidents in Florida and Tennessee. I was amazed when sheriff's deputies and highway patrol officers there would say, "Do you just want me to fax you the report?"

Such access simply isn't granted to reporters by police in Pennsylvania. By law, the only document police are obligated to show us is what's called "the blotter"—the daily log of people who are charged with crimes. Police aren't required to show us any reports or statements from witnesses. Many police departments in the state, including McKeesport's, do cooperate with the media, but some won't even offer a "no comment."

The state's so-called Sunshine Act requires municipal councils and authorities to hold all votes and deliberations "at a meeting open to the public." But there are broad exemptions to which topics must be discussed in public—among them the hiring or firing of employees, union contracts, and even the planning of emergency preparedness. No wonder the Center for Public Integrity gave Pennsylvania an "F" grade and ranked it forty-fifth out of fifty states for government accountability and transparency.

As a reporter for the former *Pittsburgh Tribune-Review*, I once arrived at a borough council meeting in a well-to-do suburb only to be kept waiting in the hall. "We're meeting in executive session," the council president said. "For what?" I asked. "To discuss sewage," she said. I was soon on the phone to the city desk, where an editor called the newspaper's attorneys. The meeting was opened.

That was twenty years ago. These days, many local newspapers are barely covering municipal meetings, let alone keeping attorneys on retainer to file emergency motions on behalf of reporters. Tube City Online has needed the help of attorneys on a few matters, and most of them donated their time, but with a yearly editorial budget of less than $20,000, we certainly don't have someone on retainer.

The situation in Pennsylvania is further complicated by our fractious system of local government. Allegheny County, with 1.2 million residents, has 130 separate incorporated municipalities, ranging in size from the city of Pittsburgh (population 301,000) to Haysville Borough (population 70). Each has its own mayor or board of commissioners, and most maintain their own police and fire departments.

Until the coronavirus pandemic, almost none of the local communities had ever attempted to stream a council meeting over the internet—meaning if you wanted to know what was being discussed, you had to attend, even during a national emergency.

And now because of coronavirus precautions, going to court to challenge efforts at secrecy is all but impossible. Many court offices are currently closed to the public, except for life-and-death filings. So too are municipal offices, which means I can't even see the minutes of past meetings we may have missed.

The natural instinct of many government officials even during normal times is to withhold information from reporters—sometimes for nefarious reasons but often for innocent ones. In smaller communities, part-time officials may simply not know what information is allowed to be made public or think routine business isn't newsworthy.

But these are nothing like normal times. Officials withholding information is especially problematic during a crisis, when rumors and misinformation can spread quickly.

I participated in a private online forum for local journalists across the United States. An editor in another state said that its local health department refused to answer any questions about the spread of COVID-19 in its community, citing "HIPAA regulations." When the editor asked how releasing the requested statistics would violate patient privacy, the department simply ignored her question.

At the same time, we have a federal government run by an erratic and authoritarian president with a known habit of lying, repeatedly. Is it any wonder that some local and state officials choose to follow his lead?

There is going to be massive fallout from this pandemic beyond the human health impact (which is almost unimaginable in our lifetimes) and beyond the economic impact (which is going to make recent recessions seem mild).

But I also am afraid of another, less obvious outcome: that many government agencies are going to use this pandemic as an excuse to do even more of the public's business in secret. And I think a substantial percentage of Americans—many of whom have internalized President Trump's message that reporters are "the enemy of the people" who concoct "fake news"—is going to let them.

I see people on social media complaining that they are bored being cooped up at home. Personally, between doing my regular nine-to-five job and then trying to hold Tube City Online together at night and on weekends, I have been busier than ever. And when my work is done, in the wee hours of the morning I sometimes lie awake in the dark, cycling from anger to panic to resolve to regret and back again.

Bored? Really?

I think anyone who is bored isn't paying enough attention.

12

COVID-19 HAS CHANGED
HOW WE REPORT STORIES
ON THE BORDER

McAllen

Before the Southwest border was shut down to all unnecessary travel on March 20 due to the coronavirus, I journeyed regularly to Matamoros, Mexico, to report on a tent encampment of 3,000 migrants who—under the Trump administration's Migrant Protection Protocols program—were forced to remain in Mexico as they awaited their U.S. immigration proceedings.

I remember the migrants' giggles as Dr. Jill Biden, the wife of the former vice president, visited their camp this past December, passing out tamales while trying to speak Spanish. They did not laugh at her attempts and gratefully accepted the plates, many of which fell afterward into the puddles of muddy rainwater that had deluged the city just hours before her visit. At the time, Joe Biden was low in the polls. Now Biden was the presumptive Democratic nominee after Senator Bernie Sanders dropped out of the race and on April 13 heartily endorsed him.

I have not been able to cross the border since its closure, and I now rely on phone calls and social media updates on the asylum-seeking migrants whom I used to visit regularly. They rely on donations and volunteers coming in from Brownsville,

Texas, to keep them alive while they wait for their immigration hearings, all of which have been postponed.

I have been told that buses are being sent to the camp daily to transport migrants to the southern Mexican border town of Tapachula, near Guatemala. Families living in Matamoros have long told me stories about the mistreatment and conditions in Tapachula. Now, with the Executive Office of Immigration Review postponing hearings, the earliest reset for mid-May, I wonder how many of the families I built a rapport with will remain there in limbo.

Seeing the abject poverty they live in always shocked me, and yet they always appeared approachable, optimistic, and friendly. I would often return to my cozy home after visiting, feeling guilty knowing that they were sleeping on the dirt ground in forty-degree weather or enduring one-hundred-degree-plus days with just one bottle of water each, if that. There is one image of three little boys clad only in underwear diving from a rock in the Rio Grande—laughing and playing as the carcass of a cow floats past them—that will never leave me.

I wonder if the garden plot at the tent encampment, set off by a rope made from clothing scraps, has borne any vegetables. I wonder if the ovens that the many industrious families carved from the mud on the banks of the Rio Grande are still being used to boil chicken and rice soup. Mostly, I wonder every day how many of these families living in such unhygienic conditions are sick with COVID-19.

The changes happened so quickly.

One month ago, I traveled to San Antonio, the outskirts of Houston, and rural Starr County in the span of a week to work on stories. I was at the Alamo, where protesters were picketing a Border Security Expo conference VIP dinner they felt should not be held on such sacred grounds. I interviewed a released migrant, and I went to the little colonia of La Rosita to meet Nayda Alvarez for this very series, the bold woman who has painted "NO BORDER WALL" on her roof in the hopes that U.S. Customs and Border Protection will stop trying to access her land to put up part of the border wall there.

Despite cultural norms in South Texas, I stopped cheek kissing in early March. The last hand I shook was at the Border Expo in San Antonio on March 11, the day the World Health Organization declared COVID-19 a pandemic. However, press conferences were still being held at the time, and I found myself standing uncomfortably with my tripod, hip to hip beside other reporters, trying to hold my breath.

As President Trump shut down the Southwest and Canadian borders to unnecessary travel, I applied lipstick with my fingers while waiting for a live shot with a San Francisco station. Instantly I worried that I had just infected myself as I crouched on a sidewalk outside the McAllen City Hall. When I filmed inside a Walmart, looking for families shopping together en masse without protective facial coverings or gloves, I nearly dropped my camera as I neared a group that included children and a grandma.

After nearly thirty years in newspapering, during which I worked as a reporter for *USA Today* and the *Fort Myers News-Press* and as an editor at the *Waco Tribune-Herald*, the *Austin American-Statesman*, and the *Monitor* in McAllen, Texas, I am finding multimedia reporting to be a challenging, exhausting, and exhilarating new experience. I am currently a multimedia journalist at *Border Report*, an online publication from Nexstar Media Group, America's largest local television and media company, with 196 TV stations nationwide. Every story I produce is expected to have a video component to be shared with the company's TV stations, but with the coronavirus pandemic that has become harder and harder to do, and every story potentially puts me at risk of exposure.

The South Texas region that I cover is massive. I report on an area that is five hours by car from east to west and four hours from north to south, stretching from the southwestern town of Laredo—across the Rio Grande from Nuevo Laredo, Mexico—to the gulf coast city of Brownsville and north to San Antonio. All of my stories are original content, and 99 percent are ideas that I pitch to my producers. I'm grateful to be fed story ideas through an elaborate web of sources from many different states. I'm able to set my own schedule, work weekends as needed, and rely on my producers to help me with the technical and visual aspects of multimedia reporting that do not come naturally to me.

I absolutely love what I do. I believe my role fills the void made evident by the shrinking number of journalists at press conferences, even when national figures such as the head of the Department of Homeland Security come to town to view the progress on the border wall. I feel blessed to be able to give a voice to this border region, which is mostly Hispanic, low income, and so often overlooked by the national media.

But the COVID-19 pandemic has changed the way I report my stories, as it has done for many journalists today. As I prepare to go out on assignments by stuffing disposable vinyl gloves into my fanny pack, putting on a face mask, and grabbing a fifteen-foot coil of cable so that I can use my seven-foot-long boom microphone to maintain proper social distancing from my subjects, there is a real fear in my gut. I believe that my stories are important and necessary. I have chosen to do them of my own volition, but I'm also aware that by doing so I could get COVID-19. Or worse: I could bring the virus back to my eighty-five-year-old father, who lives with me, or to my adult children or my husband.

To minimize my exposure to the novel coronavirus, I, like millions of Americans, have learned to embrace Zoom conference calls and Webex meetings. But they're not the same as attending live press conferences, and typing questions off to the side in a group chat does not ensure that they are answered. Public-relations directors can now pick and choose with impunity the questions they answer or even acknowledge. I have also learned that sometimes when I press officials for comment, some of the slicker ones have learned to answer in Spanish, making my job all the more difficult.

When I do go outside, it is as briefly as possible. And, honestly, I find that I am so preoccupied with worry over the "invisible enemy," as President Trump referred to the virus, that sometimes I don't always ask the questions I intended to or film in the way I wanted to. Usually, I end up doing one take and one quick interview. Then I throw out the gloves, lather hand sanitizer on my exposed skin and steering wheel, and try not to touch anything else until I return to my home office, where I promptly shower down and change before writing my piece. I shouldn't complain. Physicians are the real front-line heroes in this pandemic. Some are living in backyard tents to minimize exposure to their families. Others have caught the virus, and some have died.

Maybe it's my age. I'm in my fifties now and not the carefree journalist I once was. In 1992, I covered the Los Angeles uprising for *USA Today*. On the second night of chaos, I was with my husband, then a reporter for the *Washington Post*, when a police officer yelled at us. We had come into an area through which, the officer said, bullets had just rained. He pointed at bricks on a building pockmarked from shell shocks. He told us which way to drive and not to stop for anything—anyone or any lights. He then radioed his colleagues to tell them a couple of bone-headed journalists were coming that way and to let us pass. In 1989, I covered the decimated island of Puerto Rico following Hurricane Hugo with just a backpack, a single bottle of water, and a couple cans of tuna. And twenty-five years ago this month, I flew to chilly Oklahoma City on April 19, 1995—the day the Alfred P. Murrah Federal Building was bombed, killing 168 people—without a coat.

But during the pandemic I appear prepared for a nuclear winter every time I step outside my home. And when I return, everything gets Cloroxed and disinfected to the point that I think I am losing my fingerprints. After every assignment, I mentally reset my fourteen-day quarantine clock in my head to track any symptoms.

In my little corner of the world, it has truly become a year of fear unlike anything I have ever experienced while covering stories. I keep thinking about the migrants I am no longer able to see. The camp in Matamoros identified seventeen cases of clinically suspicious COVID-19. Some have recovered, but the camp holds 3,000 migrants. Are the migrants as afraid of this virus as the rest of us? Or have they already suffered enough to get this far north that they live more in fear of the lawmakers in Washington, DC, who malign them and ensure they stay south of the Rio Grande, a stone's throw from their destination?

13

HOW THE PANDEMIC IS PLAYING IN RURAL VIRGINIA

Bowling Green

In comparing rural Virginia and big cities, I am reminded of a man I once interviewed who had grown up in rural Virginia during the Great Depression. I anticipated tales of woe. Instead, he said he had noticed little difference: "We were poor before the stock market crash and poor afterwards." His family raised and canned fruits and vegetables from their garden, slaughtered a few hogs in the fall, and kept chickens and a single milk cow.

I am aware of at least three acquaintances around here who have built backyard chicken houses in the past month.

The threat of COVID-19 exists in rural communities such as Caroline County, Virginia, of course, as well as in large metropolitan areas, and our lives have changed in many ways since mid-March 2020. Despite this, when I saw photos and videos of empty streets in New York, Chicago, Rome, or Paris, it was somewhat difficult for me to relate. In Caroline, with about 30,000 residents spread out over 549 square miles, the changes are not as striking as they are in the big cities.

My rural-delivery mailbox sits on U.S. 1, once the major north–south route from Maine to Florida. From a lawn chair, I can hear almost every car, truck, or motorcycle that passes by.

While there are lulls in traffic flow now, that was also true before COVID-19.

People are still out and about in Caroline County, albeit in fewer numbers than before Governor Ralph Northam closed all public and private schools on March 13 and limited social gatherings to ten people. Executive Order Number 53, which Northam issued on March 24, closed to the public "nonessential businesses" such as hair salons, barbershops, spas, and tattoo parlors and limited restaurants to take-out and delivery. That order was to end on April 23 but then was extended to May 8.

The difference between rural Caroline, with thirty-two COVID-19 cases and one death as of May 1, and New York City, with more than 167,000 cases and 13,000 deaths, is more about lifestyle, geography, and population density than numbers. Caroline had no reported COVID-19 cases until April. That number has increased at an average of slightly more than a case per day since then. Up to then, there had been one death, although neighboring King George County, which is less populous and even more rural than Caroline, had four, the most in the Rappahannock Area Health District, which includes four counties and the city of Fredericksburg. As of May 1, the district had seen 506 cases and 11 deaths.

Most Caroline residents abide by the COVID-19 laws and guidelines, and most of them wear face masks in public. On visits to my local supermarket during the early-morning seniors-only hour, I observe many masked shoppers. On a rare midafternoon trip last week, however, I was appalled at how many people, many of them young, roamed the aisles and conversed in the parking lot without coverings. Perhaps it is provincialism or bravado, but a lot of folks around here appear to be playing the odds on what could prove a deadly game—if not for them, then for others. All too often someone says to me as they downplay the pandemic, "I don't know anyone who has even been infected, do you?" It is almost like declaring that the earth must be flat because you don't know anyone who ventured beyond the horizon and returned to tell about it.

As the weeks of self-distancing continued and balmier spring weather arrive in 2020, people realized that drastic lifestyle changes are not going away quickly. Many activities were canceled or at least postponed. The May 2 Caroline Spring Festival bit the dust, as did the annual Caroline County Agricultural Fair, scheduled for June 17–20. Ashland's popular Strawberry Faire, usually held in early June to coincide with berry season, was also canceled, as were a number of smaller events.

Meanwhile, many Caroline residents are out of work, and a few have shuttered their small businesses or have faced severely reduced revenues. In February, Caroline County had a workforce of 15,687, according to the Virginia Employment Commission. Only 513 residents, or 3.3 percent, were classified as unemployed. But during the five-week period as COVID-19 restrictions took effect, 1,452 people from the county applied for unemployment benefits.

Still, generally speaking, Caroline County has weathered the storm better than many other communities. Although county officials have long sought more manufacturing and retail employers, the very fact that we have so few of them may make it easier to survive the next year or two.

The local school system is the county's largest employer, and teachers and administrators are still being paid. Some money is being saved because the school bus fleet is idle, and buildings are dark. Still, many parents have had to balance homeschooling while trying to work at home. Everyone has had to endure some life changes.

The largest private employer is the McKesson Corporation's warehouse, which distributes pharmaceuticals and health-care products to hospitals and pharmacies. If any industry is pandemic proof, that one should be, according to Gary R. Wilson, Caroline County's director of economic development. Wilson also oversees tourism, though, and the outlook there is bleak. "Tourism? Right now, it's a shambles. The state fairgrounds [are closed], and Kings Dominion is just not happening," Wilson said, referring to Caroline's Meadow Event Park and the nearby amusement park in Hanover County. "Right now, we are marketing restaurant take-out to our own citizens and local ag businesses."

There are only three small shopping centers in Caroline County, plus a small downtown shopping district in Bowling Green. Most of the stores and restaurants there are still open, although restaurants struggle through lean times by offering curbside pickup and delivery. The county's two supermarkets are busier than before the COVID-19 pandemic, and employees struggle to keep the shelves stocked. Caroline County has few businesses that were deemed "nonessential" by the governor's order.

One relatively new employer that was less fortunate was Coastal Sunbelt Produce, which just a little more than a year ago had taken over the warehouse once operated by Russell Stover candies. Coastal Sunbelt's client base consists of restaurants and resorts, and the parent company has already announced layoffs.

"Unlike several neighbors, our county is not very dependent on sales and meals taxes," Wilson noted, although he added that Caroline will take a hit from tourism-generated gasoline taxes if things don't pick up soon. The county has several major truck stops that are still clogged with tractor-trailer rigs—but bereft of cars driven by the usual tourists headed to and from Colonial

Williamsburg, Virginia Beach, and the Outer Banks of North Carolina at this time of year.

County administrator Charles Culley and his staff have scrambled to come up with a workable budget that will go into effect July 1. "The budget challenge is something everybody is facing," Culley said. About lost sales tax revenue, he said, "A million dollars at least, and that's just a guestimate. They are much behind getting reports to the treasurer's office. You can look at what we normally do and cut back 75 percent and have some idea." One blessing: the county has a deep reserve fund, Culley pointed out. "People have been wanting to use it over the years, and we have resisted. It gives us some buffer. We can pay bills. We will be alright for a while."

Culley expected little or no help from the state or federal government.

"Historically, when the state runs out of money, they cut out things," he said. Virginia is expected to take a big hit from lost taxes on gasoline and lost retail sales tax and state income tax. State lottery ticket sales decreased dramatically in March, and April's figures are expected to be even lower.

"Managing through a pandemic is nothing anybody in the management field has ever done," Culley said.

In the first weeks of the pandemic, there appeared to be a relaxation of the political sniping that often is so prevalent on social media. As the days wore on, however, people became more restive.

As media criticism of President Trump's handling of COVID-19 increased, his defenders became more vocal, and criticism of Governor Ralph Northam of Virginia, a Democrat, ramped up accordingly. Stray volleys at Northam started showing up on local Facebook pages. One referred to "King Ralph's reign of tyranny." Another post questioned how Northam could appear so well groomed if barbershops were on the list of nonessential businesses. A story circulated for several days that Northam was sneaking off for holidays at a vacation house on the North Carolina Outer Banks in defiance of a temporary ban there on nonresident property owners. That charge was put to rest by a Republican member of the state legislature.

Still, the story reappeared in a professionally produced video put out by a conservative organization called LifeSite about the "Liberate Virginia" protestors who walked and drove around Capital Square on April 15, honking their horns while the House of Delegates met. This is the second such protest against the governor's order to keep some businesses closed. It appeared to be attended by a loose mixture of gun enthusiasts, antiabortion groups, Trump boosters, and a few people whose line of work was deemed nonessential under the governor's edict.

Generally speaking, Virginians seem to approve still of the governor's handling of the COVID-19 crisis. The *Free Lance-Star* of Fredericksburg, a paper often stinting in its praise of Democrats, published an editorial that called Northam the right man for the job. After detailing Northam's bungling of some issues early in his term, the editorial continued: "Suddenly, the best possible person to have at the state's helm seems to be an unassuming, well-informed doctor who calmly tells us hard truths, who doesn't use the pandemic to self-aggrandize, who doesn't try to lay the blame on others."

Still, the Facebook wars continue. Clearly exasperated by the mean-spirited tone of many posts, Steven B. Tucker, who started a Caroline County, Virginia, residents Facebook page back in 2015 that now had more than 5,000 users, posted the following message on April 20:

If the Coronavirus has proven anything, it's that Republicans and Democrats are so partisan, so hateful and suspicious of each other, that they've made a virus into a purely political ordeal.

Frankly, this virus pales in comparison to our real problems in this country and what's sad is that nothing, not one damn thing will change. Nothing positive will come out of this. No light at the end of this tunnel. No silver linings. But I bet left-wing and right-wing people will hate each other even more now. We haven't even begun to get what we deserve.

14

A GOOD IDEA AT THE TIME

Macon

There was a slow-moving, surreal, multipolitician train wreck in Georgia, and the carnage is strewn across the Peach State's landscape. Aside from the COVID-19 virus that has infected 33,833 and killed 1,405 as of May 11, this train wreck started, oddly enough, as though Georgia had escaped the fate of so many southern states led by Republican governors. Governor Brian Kemp, leader of the largest state east of the Mississippi, appeared to be rational in his approach to COVID-19.

On March 12, Governor Kemp held a press conference in the state capitol building. At his side were the lieutenant governor, the state Speaker of the House, the mayor of Atlanta, the state public-health commissioner, the governor's Coronavirus Task Force members, and others. He cut nonessential travel and told state workers to telework. Although he didn't close schools, leaving that decision to local districts, he did cut visitation to the state's prisons. He also announced four new coronavirus committees for emergency preparedness, economic impact, physicians, and homelessness. Kemp was widely hailed for his efforts.

In the days following, Kemp came before the media to give detailed reports of how many confirmed cases of the virus and deaths there were in the state and whether victims had underlying health issues. On March 14, he declared a public-health emergency and called upon the Georgia National Guard. On March 16, he ordered all public schools and colleges to close; on April 1, he extended that order for the rest of the school year. But he faced criticism for not issuing a shelter-in-place order. That order would come on April 2—fifteen days after Keisha Lance Bottoms, Atlanta's mayor, proposed a "stay-at-home" order for the city but delayed it on Kemp's request.

On April 2, Kemp finally shut down every bar, restaurant, nightclub, gym, barbershop, beauty salon, massage parlor, live-performance venue, and amusement park. Governor Kay Ivey of Alabama and Governor Tate Reeves of Mississippi would follow Kemp's lead and issue statewide shelter-in-place orders the next day. Kemp continued to be at the top of his game. On April 5, he appointed Bernice King, Reverend Dr. Martin Luther King Jr.'s daughter, as cochair of the new Coronavirus Community Outreach Committee.

During a press conference on April 8, Kemp was asked why he finally declared a shelter-in-place order. Kemp said, "What we've been telling people from directives from the CDC [U.S. Centers for Disease Control and Prevention] for weeks now is that if you start feeling bad, stay home. Those individuals could have been infecting people before they ever felt bad. *But we didn't know that until the last twenty-four hours.*"

The press corps was flabbergasted. Dr. Robert Redfield, director of the CDC, had said in mid-February that asymptomatic transmission of coronavirus was possible. That was just the beginning of Kemp's derailing.

Then on April 20, Kemp announced, "Given the favorable data, enhanced testing, and approval of our health-care professionals, we will allow gyms, fitness centers, bowling alleys, body

art studios, barbers, cosmetologists, hair designers, nail care artists, estheticians, their respective schools, and massage thera-
pists to reopen their doors this Friday, April 24." Kemp also
stated, "This measure will apply statewide and will be the oper-
ational standard in all jurisdictions. This means local action cannot be taken that is more or less restrictive." He delayed opening restaurants and other facilities until April 27.

All over the state, elected officials were flummoxed.

Members of Kemp's coronavirus committees were caught flat-
footed because he had not consulted them. Bernice King took
to Facebook to say, "I'm not sure that we are understanding the
importance of balancing the economy with a commitment to
humanity." Mayor Bottoms told CNN, "We really are at a loss,
and I am concerned as a mother and as the mayor of our capital
city." Hardie Davis Jr., the mayor of Augusta, the state's second-
largest city, told CNN, "If we move as swiftly as the governor's
proposing right now, we could find ourselves mashing the gas
on the economy when in fact we need to be putting the brake
on where we are right now."

Bo Dorough, the mayor of Albany—an area the virus hit so
hard that for a time it was second in transmission rates to New
York—said, "We're simply not ready to reopen. I mean, we have
sixty-two people on ventilators. I think it's rather imprudent to
set dates as opposed to goals. I mean, even the White House says
we're going to do this in phases. And if you look at the four criteria for phase one, we haven't met but one of those criteria."
Mayor Van Johnson of Savannah said when learning of Kemp's
announcement, "To be absolutely clear, I was just as surprised
as the rest of the world."

Mayor Robert Reichert of Macon said, "He didn't allow any
flexibility for local government to add to or take away from his
order, so we are without the authority to pass any order or

legislation that would be in conflict with the governor's order."
Macon–Bibb County sheriff David Davis said, "I hate to think
that Georgia is part of a grand experiment to see how reopening things will affect the virus. You might say we're the guinea
pigs. It's sad that we're getting so many conflicting notices and
conflicting statements from the so-called experts." Dr. Keren
Landman, a specialist in infectious diseases, wrote an opinion
piece in the *New York Times* titled "Georgia Went First. And It
Screwed Up." She wrote, "For better or worse, the governor has
made our state the nation's canary in this particularly terrifying
coal mine."

On April 22, the Macon–Bibb County Board of Health
passed a resolution asking Kemp to rescind his order. The board
had just heard on April 20 from Navicent Health's chief medical officer Dr. Patrice Walker, "We expect our surge to be some
time now in mid-May." Board member Chris Tsavatewa said,
"We are behind in this state. Our per capita testing is abysmal."
As of May 11, only 12.37 percent of the state's population had
been tested, and the infrastructure for contact tracing was
nonexistent.

Liz Fabian, one of the most well-known and respected journalists in Middle Georgia, was the only reporter at that board
meeting. Fabian's journalism career began in high school when
she wrote for the Georgia Military College newspaper. When
she entered Georgia College and State University intending "to
study theater and become a big star," she did a morning news
program on the campus radio station. She said the journalism
bug hit the morning of November 5, 1980. When Georgians went
to sleep the previous night, Senator Herman Talmadge, a Georgia legend, was thought to be the winner over Republican Matt
Mattingly, but they awoke to find Mattingly had won. Fabian,
for the first time, heard the AP wire machine's bell, a bell that

rings only when there is a big story. "It was such an interesting feeling about having news you could share with someone right away, things they didn't know." The rest was history. The journalism bug had sunk its teeth into her and didn't let go.

Fabian started her career in television and has done stints at all three local network affiliates. Her first, in 1982 at WCWB, paid her $150 a week, but it was an important training ground where she learned to do weather. Those skills took her to the newly established Weather Channel, based in Atlanta. At each stop, budget cutbacks left her holding the short end of the stick. In 2003, she went to work at Macon's daily newspaper the *Telegraph*.

An excellent journalist and versatile writer, not common for someone making the transition from television to print, Fabian did everything from covering early weather podcasts for the paper to anchoring the news desk for a newspaper-sponsored morning talk show from 2007 to 2012 that aired on ABC and Fox affiliates and on the most powerful AM radio station in the market.

But in February 2019, Fabian was once again caught in the budget vice. McClatchy, the *Telegraph's* corporate owner, found itself squeezed after acquiring Knight Ridder newspapers in 2006. The Macon paper had already jettisoned its sports reporters and editor, editorial page editor, senior news editor, and executive editor in 2017 and 2018. Now Fabian, along with 450 McClatchy employees fifty-five years of age or older with ten years of service, were given the choice to voluntarily retire or stay. "They really weren't interested in holding on to anybody with experience," Fabian said. "And that was one of the things that stuck with me. 'Do I really want to stay?'"

Craig Forman, the CEO of McClatchy who a year earlier had received a $35,000 a month stipend for housing—up from $5,000 on top of his \$1 million salary and \$1 million bonus—said of this early retirement offer, "This will be a one-time opportunity. We do not anticipate another." Famous last words. McClatchy filed for bankruptcy protection the following year.

"I worried about the things we reported about and cared about," Fabian said about her decision, but she got some good advice: "They are paying you to leave, not paying you to try to stay." After putting out a few feelers, she was interviewed by one of her former television employers to take the place of an anchor out on maternity leave. Everything sounded good, so she signed her retirement papers. The budget gods would strike again. The station didn't replace the anchor, laid off its sports staff, and reassigned other personnel.

The *Telegraph* shared a building on Mercer University's campus with the Center for Collaborative Journalism (CCJ), established as an incubator for Mercer's journalism program. The *Telegraph* newsroom of forty people moved to campus in 2012 (the business office remained at another location downtown), but McClatchy started chasing clickbait, emphasizing stories with shock appeal—crime, auto accidents, and mayhem—while county commission, school board, and other important meetings went uncovered. After the purge of 2019, only five journalists remained, unable to help much in the preparation of journalism students.

After Fabian "retired," she was brought in by the university as the civic reporting senior fellow for the CCJ. "It was nice to dig in and cover some of the civic journalism that had been ignored," Fabian said. And that's why she was at the Macon–Bibb County Board of Health meeting on March 22, 2020, when it heard news that Macon–Bibb County had not yet reached its peak for COVID-19 infections. No other media outlet covered the meeting.

So why the sudden burst of speed by Kemp in the midst of the COVID-19 storm? President Donald Trump had already talked about opening the economy by April 12, Easter Sunday, before walking back his statements. Conservative-sponsored protests had occurred around various state capitols, snarling traffic and creating more fear as protesters didn't worry about social distancing or masks. Protesters scheduled a similar demonstration in Atlanta.

Two days before Kemp's reopening announcement on Wednesday, Trump promoted an insurrection in Minnesota, Michigan, and Virginia—all of which had Democratic governors—telling people they should "liberate" themselves from state-ordered restrictions. But then suddenly Trump flipped the script. On April 22, two days after Kemp's announcement to reopen, Trump said he "disagreed strongly" with Kemp's move. "It's just too soon. I think it's too soon; they can wait just a little bit longer. Safety has to predominate." Trump would name Kemp and repeat his criticism the next day.

Kemp was left looking for the number of that Norfolk Southern locomotive that had run him over. Jim Galloway of the *Atlanta Journal-Constitution*, one of the few remaining "dead tree" journalists living in a digital word, wrote in the newspaper's daily digital political newsletter, the *Jolt*: "One of the more remarkable aspects of President Trump's remarks late Wednesday was that he and the governor had had a one-on-one conversation only the day before: the two men spoke late Tuesday in what aides to Kemp described as a productive conversation about Kemp's approach, and top Georgia Republicans said they had no indication that Trump would undercut his strategy."

Galloway went on to explain that Senator Kelly Loeffler—whom Kemp had appointed in January over Trump's objections and who is now facing a primary challenge from Trump ally

Representative Doug Collins—got the worse end of the deal. "In a quirk of timing," Galloway wrote, "she joined the governor on a tele-town hall shortly before Trump's press briefing where she spoke of Kemp's approach as a needed step to help revive Georgia's flagging economy." Collins's spokesman, Dan McLagan, responded, "Poor Kelly did this to herself. She asked Brian to help her across the political street, and they both got hit by a bus, which then got backed over them. And caught fire."

Tim Bryant of WGAU in Athens tweeted, "I'm not a conspiracy theorist, but if I were, I'd look at the developments of last evening and see President Trump putting his thumb on the scale for Doug Collins."

And in late April, citing COVID-19 transmission concerns, a lawsuit was filed asking the U.S. District Court for the Northern District of Georgia to scrap the state's new touchscreen election machines in favor of all-paper ballots. The suit asked the court to delay the June 9 primary for a second time, leaving nonpartisan elections that are supposed to take place May 19 in limbo—again. In the meantime, more than one million voters have requested absentee ballots. Only 483,000 absentee ballots were cast in 2018.

15

IN TOWNS LIKE MCKEESPORT, THE FUTURE WAS ALREADY PRECARIOUS. THEN CAME CORONAVIRUS.

McKeesport

I brace myself when I get an alert that the Allegheny County Police homicide unit is on its way to a crime scene.

The communities we cover at Tube City Online may be small, but they pull their weight in the county's homicide numbers. In 2019, eleven of the county's ninety-five homicides were in three of the five communities we serve. Those municipalities have a combined population of about 34,600 people.

So each time I'm alerted to a possible homicide, I silently pray: *Please don't be us.*

Pittsburgh's TV news viewers are used to seeing the names of communities such as McKeesport, Duquesne, Clairton, and Wilkinsburg mostly in the context of crime reports. Rarely do those TV stations cover any good—or even *neutral*—news from those areas. Naturally, when Pittsburghers find out I live near McKeesport, they ask me if I feel unsafe. "If I did, I wouldn't live there," I reply.

Yet the negative perception is a constant obstacle to efforts to bring back the Monongahela Valley from the economic damage it suffered during the collapse of the steel industry in the 1980s.

It defines every aspect of life here, from attracting commercial development to encouraging potential residents to buy homes. A few years ago, the internet radio station Tube City Online operates had a lively big-band music program hosted by an eighty-something gentleman from Pittsburgh. He gave it up in part because his wife was afraid of him traveling to McKeesport on Sunday mornings. "She sees it on the news all the time," he said, "and she worries about me."

The reality is that he wasn't likely to be a victim of a homicide in McKeesport or anywhere else in Allegheny County, and as a middle-aged white person, I am not, either.

Of the homicides in 2019 across Allegheny County, almost half (forty-four) of the victims were younger than age thirty. While 83 percent of the county's population identify as white, 82 percent of the homicide victims were Black. It's young Black men, not middle-aged and older white people, who are dying at an appalling rate. Too many parents in the Mon Valley have buried their children. Too many teachers at local schools have become accustomed to counseling their grieving pupils, and too many of our pastors have conducted funerals for teenagers they baptized years earlier.

It's not a new trend. Twenty-plus years ago, when I worked at the now-defunct *McKeesport Daily News*, our crime reporter, Bill Kaempffer, was hired away by Connecticut's *New Haven Register*. "They almost didn't call me," he told us as he cleaned out his desk. They had looked at his résumé and thought Kaempffer must be exaggerating the number of murders he had covered for a paper the size of the *Daily News*, which then had a circulation of about 30,000.

The number of homicides has mercifully dropped since those bad old days through a combination of aggressive police work and community-based after-school antiviolence programs.

Technology is helping, too, including cameras at major intersections that can track license-plate numbers of suspects' vehicles. This month McKeesport City Council voted to apply for a federal grant to purchase "ShotSpotter," a computer-controlled network of sensors that can pinpoint the location of a gunshot in less than sixty seconds.

But policing and antiviolence programs don't address the root causes of crime in the Mon Valley or elsewhere, which remain serious poverty and a lack of upward mobility for young people. Children born poor here are likely to stay poor here unless they have a lot of lucky breaks. The very racially segregated nature of Pennsylvania communities means that Black and Latino children are about three times as likely as white children to live in impoverished neighborhoods.

Covering any of these things is a challenge, especially for a tiny, part-time digital news operation such as ours. When I worked for the *Daily News* in the late 1990s, we sent a reporter and often a photographer to every homicide scene to interview family members and witnesses. (During a few particularly bad years, some residents sarcastically called the paper "the *Daily Shooting*.")

These days I'm lucky if I can make one or two phone calls to follow up on a murder, and most of my information comes from official sources such as police or the medical examiner's office. It feels awful to write about a young person only in the context of the incident that ended their life prematurely, but it seems worse not to report it—in my opinion, murder should never become unremarkable.

Ditto for covering our schools. Our freelance writers do their best, but how many good news stories in these school districts go unreported simply because we don't have the time or resources to dig for them? How much of what residents know of their local schools is only in the context of official sources telling us about lower test scores and higher property-tax rates?

In 2016, Donald Trump ran for president on the platform "Making America Great Again." In 2020, he seeks reelection on the slogan "Keeping America Great." In our region, I'm not sure how to quantify "greatness" in the context of serious, widespread poverty that has now spanned two generations and part of a third.

It escapes me, too, how any of the solutions being proposed on the national level—things such as tax credits and college-loan forgiveness—will make a difference in the lives of low-income families who aren't paying much in federal taxes, anyway, and can't afford to send their kids to college.

Everyone who is on Twitter or Facebook passionately arguing about the policies of Biden versus Bernie or Trump versus a third-party candidate or about unfettered free markets versus democratic socialism would do well to remember that those debates are a luxury that many young people in places such as McKeesport, Duquesne, and Clairton aren't able to indulge.

They are too busy focusing on their day-to-day survival.

16

SAVING SANTA ANA WILDLIFE REFUGE EXTENDS BEYOND POLITICAL BOUNDARIES

McAllen

The Santa Ana National Wildlife Refuge is known as the "jewel of the national wildlife refuge system." This 2,088-acre parcel of land hugs the looping Rio Grande on the border with Mexico, south of the small South Texas town of Alamo and across the river from the bustling Mexican city of Reynosa. It is a favorite place for bird-watchers and nature lovers and anyone else in search of a moment of solitude and a peaceful place to reflect while gazing at coyotes and rare species of birds and turtles amid draping Spanish moss trees. The refuge is located at a crossroads of biological diversity. It is positioned along the east–west and north–south juncture of two major migratory bird routes. It is also at the northern tip for many species whose range extends south into Central and South America. The refuge is also a crossroad for politically diverse supporters.

"Winter Texans," as they are called, are retirees who live in South Texas during the winter months. This is a coveted go-to spot for them because it is easily accessible, located in the middle of the "upper" or "lower" Rio Grande Valley (RGV), where the towns of McAllen and Brownsville are. Most Winter Texans live in the two hundred recreational vehicle parks located throughout the RGV. Most are Anglo, and a great many of them are Republicans. They come to the RGV, a Democratic-majority region full of young Hispanics, for several months every year to escape wintry cold states such as Minnesota, Iowa, and Wisconsin.

Besides frequenting local restaurants for early-dinner specials, most Winter Texans stay within their park circuit, where the nightly entertainment ranges from Bingo to square-dancing to bocce ball to park buffets and live music that never seems to end.

But it's places like Santa Ana where very different people—politically, economically, and culturally—meet. Here, on the fourteen miles of winding trails, one can find Hispanic families pushing strollers, with young children trying to catch butterflies, near seniors dressed in camouflage vests with binoculars hanging around their necks as they point quietly to rare birds.

When the Trump administration announced that a border wall would be built through this nature preserve, there was public outcry from nature lovers on both sides of the political spectrum unlike anything heard before in the Rio Grande Valley.

While campaigning against Senator Ted Cruz in the summer of 2017, the former congressman Beto O'Rourke, a Democrat from El Paso, visited the park and walked the dirt trails with a pack of media following him. O'Rourke spoke about the need to save Santa Ana and documented the experience on Facebook Live. He even climbed a metal winding stairwell and filmed from atop a picturesque rope bridge and scenic overlook, where one can spy rural Mexican farmlands in the distance. By using social media, O'Rourke was able to reach a nationwide audience, many of whom had never before seen the splendors of this area.

O'Rourke went on to lose his Senate challenge in a surprisingly close race. But in many respects, Santa Ana was the big winner that day because it thrust the nature preserve into the national spotlight. When Congress during the heated 2019 fiscal budget process voted to approve $1.375 billion in funding for a border wall on the southwestern boundary with Mexico, Santa Ana was listed as one of the handful of places exempt from construction. The others included La Lomita Chapel, Bentsen–Rio Grande Valley State Park, and the National Butterfly Center, all located in the RGV. Lawmakers again exempted Santa Ana when they approved nearly the same amount in the 2020 fiscal budget for the southwest border wall plans.

At the time, environmentalists felt they had scored a victory in their fight against the "militarization" of the South Texas border, and they believed Santa Ana was safe.

But in 2020 Santa Ana is once again threatened because the Trump administration appears to have found a loophole for building the wall on the border of Santa Ana, which many say will decimate the quietness of the isolated reserve. A federal judge ruled that border wall surveyors may enter a disputed swath of land that abuts a corner of the refuge and that they may even trim back and cut vegetation within the park where it is necessary to survey the area for a future border wall. Many South Texas communities along the Rio Grande have become especially concerned since construction on the border wall began to be ramped up during the pandemic by workers, many from other states, who locals fear will bring the deadly virus.

"They're doing this all right in the middle of this pandemic," Ricky Garza, a lawyer with the nonprofit group Texas Civil Rights Project, said during a video call with news media. "We are extremely concerned with this construction never really stopping during this pandemic and a lack of PPE [personal protective equipment] by construction workers who are out there."

Judge Randy Crane of the U.S. Southern District of Texas in McAllen ruled on April 30, 2020, that surveyors may access that section of land, writing that he grants "the right of the United States, its agents, contractors, and assigns to enter in, on, over and across the land" for up to twelve months.

Crane ruled that a one-third-mile-long section of land that abuts the northeastern corner of the refuge is not owned by the refuge and therefore not exempt from border wall construction. When the refuge purchased additional lands from a local farmer in 1978, the land underneath an earthen levee that lines the park boundary was not part of the deal. So although Congress legislated that no border wall may be placed on Santa Ana property, putting one atop the flood levee apparently does not violate any rules.

The dirt levees, which run parallel to the Rio Grande, were built in the 1930s throughout Hidalgo County to control flooding in the delta region. The levees are maintained by the U.S. International Boundary and Water Commission to ensure that water deflection does not violate a 1970 international water treaty between the United States and Mexico. They have become the Trump administration's favorite path for constructing new border wall for miles in South Texas. Survey crews hired by the U.S. Army Corps of Engineers and U.S. Customs and Border Protection were slated to begin work Memorial Day weekend 2020 but were delayed.

Representative Henry Cuellar of South Texas—the only Democrat from the Southwest border on the U.S. House Appropriations Committee and vice chairman of the Homeland Security Appropriations Subcommittee—has vehemently opposed surveyors on the land and the constructing of the border wall so close to the treasured preserve. He says that the building of a border wall on this section of land violates the legislative intent that Congress mandated when it approved funds for the wall.

"The legislative intent was very clear that anything within Santa Ana will be protected, and they should not come in and go into Santa Ana to clear brush," Cuellar told *Border Report* in an interview. Environmentalists complain that the recent turn of events has left them desperate and uncertain of what will happen to their beloved park and other protected areas in the vicinity of the Trump administration's border wall path ahead of the November election. As of May 15, 2020, Customs and Border Protection had completed 187 miles of new border wall, with the goal of completing 450 miles by the year's end, according to the U.S. Department of Homeland Security.

Jim Chapman, the seventy-two-year-old president of Friends of the Wildlife Corridor, a nonprofit support group for Santa Ana National Wildlife Refuge and the Lower Rio Grande Valley National Wildlife Refuge, scrambled to get help. Chapman walked the dirt levee, spotting wooden stakes already placed adjacent to park lands, their pink ribbons marking where the 150-foot-wide enforcement zone would likely extend. A once-lush path of brush was already trimmed back and thin, and Chapman shook his head in sadness.

Customs and Border Protection's border-wall-enforcement zone is set to include an all-weather road, underground sensors, infrared cameras, thirty-foot-tall floodlights, and an eighteen-foot-tall metal bollard wall that will sit atop the levee, mounted on a six-foot concrete base.

Chapman said the floodlights will disturb nocturnal species such as the Mexican free-tailed bat and will threaten already endangered species of tortoise that call this area home and that will not be able to get through the four-inch-wide gaps in between the six-inch-wide metal slats in the wall or under the concrete base.

He was also angry at what he said is the Trump administration's "full-throttle" drive to complete the border wall during the coronavirus pandemic. As a retired physician's assistant who has spent his life working in medicine, Chapman said money is urgently needed to find a cure for COVID-19, not to build a wall to divide the United States from Mexico. "Money for the wall should be given to anything else. There shouldn't be any wall," Chapman said.

Garza, the Texas Civil Rights Project lawyer, said, "The government has filed more lawsuits under the pandemic" to gain land access for wall building, as it has done at Santa Ana. Garza said there are currently more than forty federal lawsuits involving the wall, most at the McAllen federal courthouse. The Texas Civil Rights Project represents several landowners and is keeping an eye out on Santa Ana, which is located just a few miles from its offices in Alamo, Texas.

"What was pretty shocking to see was in Santa Ana the government basically went up to the letter of the law where the prohibitions had been in place, and they had decided to sue the piece of land directly adjacent," Garza said during a call with news media. "It was not violating the letter of the law put in place by Congress, but it was violating the intent."

The question now becomes, What will it take to save this jewel? Will park supporters from both sides of the political spectrum come together to oppose border wall construction? Many of Santa Ana's Winter Texan supporters have uncharacteristically stayed in the Rio Grande Valley this spring because they feel it is safer to ride out the pandemic here. Will they speak out against Donald Trump? Or will they remain silent and allow the cutting down of centuries-old Mexican cypress trees?

17

AT THE EDGE OF A PANDEMIC, ITS DIRECTION UNKNOWN

Bowling Green

On March 13, the same day President Trump announced a national emergency over the COVID-19 pandemic, I was released from Mary Washington Hospital in Fredericksburg, Virginia, after a coronary ablation to get my heart back in rhythm. After four decades of deadlines, bad newsroom coffee, and fast-food meals over my office computer, I was no longer the workhorse I used to be. A triple bypass, a pacemaker installation, and the ablation—all in a span of six months—made me realize that life is fragile. And because I check off so many of the boxes that make a person more vulnerable to COVID-19 than younger, healthier Americans, I vowed to take this pandemic seriously, while still reasoning that the rural community in which I live is less of a target than urban areas.

The young woman who pushed my wheelchair to the hospital entrance told me she was a senior pre-med student at the nearby University of Mary Washington campus, where classes had just been suspended. It was her last day at the hospital because all volunteers were being sent home in preparation for the anticipated wave of COVID-19 patients. As a precaution, a temporary pandemic triage unit had been constructed in the hospital's parking garage. As it turns out, it has not been needed.

Still, we have not been untouched. COVID-19 took a while to creep into northern Virginia and the Richmond area and even longer to find its way to rural Caroline County, which is just far enough south of the nation's capital and north enough of Virginia's capital to stay partially out of the way. The pandemic did eventually find its way here, but not to the extent that many feared. It almost feels as if we are at the edge of a plague—not in it and not out of it either, with the direction uncertain.

The first COVID-19 case in Caroline County was reported April 1. By May 27, the number of cases had climbed to a modest 55, an average of fewer than one case per day. Two deaths were attributed to the disease in Caroline County. The numbers in more densely populated counties around us were far steeper, however. The Rappahannock Area Health District, which encompasses Caroline and three counties to the north plus the City of Fredericksburg, had reported 1,500-plus cases with 18 deaths by the end of May. (Neighboring Spotsylvania County had 571 cases by that time; Stafford, 722; Fredericksburg, 166; King George, 69.) The Commonwealth of Virginia topped 45,000 total cases, with 1,392 deaths. The counties and cities of northern Virginia account for more than half of the state's cases. Richmond and surrounding counties have had the next largest concentration. In the scheme of things, northern Virginia is to the rest of Virginia what New York City is to the Empire State.

Some of the same factors that have hindered commercial and residential growth in Caroline County over the years have turned out to be a blessing during the pandemic. We have only one nursing home of any size, no hospitals, no meatpacking plants, only one significant assembly line, few office buildings, no movie theaters, and only a handful of apartment-building clusters. A couple of restaurants have bars in them, but none draws crowds or stays open until the wee hours. Places where Caroline County residents typically rub shoulders—churches, schools, libraries, restaurants, and the family Y—have been closed or sharply restricted since mid-March.

The number of cases and deaths have continued to rise, however, and those numbers include Caroline's first COVID-19 outbreak, in which five office workers at the M.C. Dean Inc. Modular MEP plant in Ruther Glen, where I live, tested positive. Although no workers on the assembly floor tested positive, the plant shut down for five days and was thoroughly cleaned. This is one of Caroline County's few manufacturing companies, employing about two hundred people.

Another and more alarming COVID-19 outbreak started with one nurse and in five short days involved ten employees testing positive and another nineteen quarantined at the offices of the Rappahannock Area Health District, the very agency in charge of pandemic testing for the area. This news came as the Commonwealth of Virginia relaxed a number of restrictions on business closures and self-distancing.

Although the shelter-in-place mandate is not slated to lift until June 10, it has largely been ignored by many in the state, as have recommendations to wear face masks in public. Alarmed by this, on May 26 Governor Ralph Northam made face masks mandatory in restaurants, stores, and other public places, although enforcement has been left up to the owners and operators of these businesses. A pediatric neurosurgeon, Northam is the only governor in the United States with a medical background. By law, he is not allowed to run again, and it is apparent from his thrice-weekly TV press conferences that he was more concerned with the physical well-being of Virginians than with the ballot box. Still, many Virginians who prefer Donald

Trump's "somebody told me this, so it must be so" approach, find Northam's science-based method of reopening Virginia for business to be too clumsy and slow. This red state/blue state divide is readily apparent on social media and in conversations I have had with friends and neighbors. How this divide will play out politically in 2020 is anybody's guess.

Rob Wittman, our longtime incumbent Republican congressman, also has a background that has been helpful in the COVID-19 pandemic. Prior to being elected to represent Virginia's First District in Congress in 2007, Wittman worked for twenty years with the Virginia Department of Health. He served as an environmental health specialist and was later field director for the Division of Shellfish Sanitation. He has a PhD in public health. Long regarded as a moderate who is strong on constituent services, Wittman has sent out daily briefings explaining the nuances of COVID-19 legislation and how individuals, businesses, and localities can apply for assistance. He has also led a bipartisan effort to protect Virginia fisheries from the harsh effects of the pandemic.

Because Northam and Wittman represent opposing parties, it might be difficult for some Caroline County residents to appreciate how fortunate they are to have two elected representatives with an understanding of pandemics that transcends partisan politics.

The threat of a new wave of infections remains in the back of my mind, but I also look forward to the return of some sort of normalcy—although what shape the new normal will take is anybody's guess at this point. It may be that many cherished traditions will be streamlined or sanitized in our future.

For example, on May 26 the Caroline County Board of Supervisors held a County Budget Hearing that was part in-person and part virtual. Before the budget discussion, though, the supervisors heard from Dr. Donald Stern, the interim director of the Rappahannock Area Health District. Stern said many individuals were walking around with COVID-19 but not being counted in the daily statistics—because they were asymptomatic and did not realize they had the virus. He suggested multiplying the known cases by five to understand the problem. Eliminating COVID-19 is unrealistic until a vaccine is approved, he said. The goal is to "box it in" and slow it down through testing more people, staying at home, wearing a mask when in contact with others, washing hands, and cleaning surfaces. For the budget hearing part of the meeting, staff and members of the public were allowed to send in comments or come in person, register to speak, and then, when called, approach a remote podium.

Caroline High School, meanwhile, held a four-day, graduation-by-appointment ceremony that allowed each senior to arrive with family, get a diploma, and pose for photos that were incorporated into a video. The Health District already has a task force working on ways that area schools can safely reopen in September 2020.

The way we cast our votes in 2020 will be different from how we did it in the past, as will the methods used by candidates to win those votes. Local elections were held May 19 in the Town of Ashland, twenty miles to the south, and in the City of Fredericksburg, twenty-five miles to the north. For the most part, incumbents won easily. A combination of absentee, curbside, and in-person voting was used and functioned well, albeit for a small sample size.

The electoral process will face a larger test on June 23 when primaries are held for the Democrat nominee to run against Wittman in District 1 and for the Republicans' candidate for the U.S. Senate seat occupied by Mark Warner, a Democrat. Local election officials encourage absentee voting for these primaries, using COVID-19 as the reason. Just a few candidates ran—only two made the Democratic ballot for the First District congressional race, and three for the statewide Republican primary. Three hopefuls withdrew or were disqualified for the Democratic primary and seven for the Republican primary. The inability to gather a sufficient number of signatures before the March filing deadlines—a task made far more difficult by the pandemic—undoubtedly helped thin these fields.

The First District Democratic Committee, meanwhile, claimed a precedent of sorts by holding the state's first virtual convention on May 2. The 175 delegates, representing all the counties in the district, normally meet in caucuses that turn into lengthy affairs, complete with speeches, pomp, and posturing. "This one took about thirty minutes," according to the District Democratic chairman, Matt Rowe, a former Bowling Green Town Council member. Similar virtual conventions were held by the Democrats in the other ten districts on three successive weekends, Rowe said. A June 20 Democratic state convention will also be virtual.

Meanwhile, Republicans stuck with in-person conventions, at least to some degree. The First District Republican Party held its convention on June 13 at Caroline County High School. "Due to the COVID health emergency, we will be using a modified convention format authorized by the Republican Party of Virginia that will allow delegates to the convention to vote using 'curbside' voting procedures," noted the district chairman, Bob Watson. The GOP state convention, which had been scheduled for May, was postponed due to the pandemic. A new date has not been made official. "We will not let this setback define our 2020 efforts," said the party chairman, Jack Wilson, in a statement. "Republicans are more energized than ever to flip Virginia for President Trump and send our do-nothing senator, Mark Warner, packing," Wilson added.

Virginia has been slower than other states to reopen many businesses, churches, and attractions. Governor Northam announced a three-phase system, portions of which went into effect on May 15, 2020, excluding the hot spots of northern Virginia and Richmond. Under phase one, Virginia moved to a "safer at home" strategy, which continued the ban on social gatherings of more than ten people and maintained recommendations for social distancing, teleworking, and face coverings in stores and businesses. Businesses were required to make modifications to maintain six feet of physical distancing and increase sanitization of high-contact surfaces. Retail establishments were allowed to operate at 50 percent occupancy, as were restaurants and bars that could offer outdoor dining.

Also under phase one, churches could hold indoor services at 50 percent capacity and could continue to hold drive-in services in parking lots. Many churches in Caroline County took a "wait-and see" stance while continuing to live stream Sunday services. Ashland, which depends heavily on tourism and restaurant revenues, embraced the challenge. Restaurant owners were offered $2,000 grants to purchase outdoor tables, chairs, and canopies, while sections of streets were temporarily closed and turned into expanded sidewalk cafés, which were much used over Memorial Day weekend.

Although many Memorial Day activities were canceled in Virginia, a traditional ceremony went on as scheduled in front of the old courthouse in Bowling Green. Many local veterans participated, along with County Supervisors Jeff Sili and Nancy Long, Sheriff Tony Lippa, and other officials.

"I cannot recall a more emotional moment for me as the Bowling Green District Supervisor, or a time when I was prouder of the partnership between VFW Post 10295 and the county," Sili said in a Facebook post. "We did it, and were able to observe social distancing and quarantine rules still in place. We did not fail those who gave their lives so we can wake up free people each and every day."

18

DIRTY POLITICS IN THE DIGITAL AGE

Macon

COVID-19 has turned the political scene in Macon–Bibb County on its head: no live events, no Sunday church visits, no in-person campaign rallies or forums. However, the campaign season is finally heating up. Candidates are getting their digital legs underneath them: putting their campaign commercial spiels online and employing robocalls. Lots of robocalls.

A bipartisan group of community organizations has tried to help. An online forum for the five mayoral candidates using Zoom was sponsored by the League of Women's Voters, Georgia Women, and LINKS. Eleven days later, the Greater Macon Chamber of Commerce sponsored another one. Forums over two nights for sheriff, county commission, and Macon–Bibb County Water Authority candidates initially drew 4,500 views on Facebook. Although municipal elections are nonpartisan, these forums were sponsored by the Macon–Bibb County Democratic Party.

But things have gotten nasty. Several candidates for mayor, county commission, and district attorney have used push polls that single out one or more of their competitors and propose a question such as "If you knew Candidate A was an ax murderer, would that change your opinion of him or her? Press 1." Although the example question used here is facetious, the technique is meant to alter a potential voter's view of a candidate and is really no poll at all—it just masquerades as one. The real sponsor of the push poll is never revealed.

The race for mayor has been dragged into the deep muck.

On May 14, readers of the *Telegraph* were met with this headline: "Companies Tied to Macon Mayoral Candidate Cliffard Whitby Under Georgia Bureau of Investigation (GBI) Investigation." Whitby is the leading African American candidate for mayor in a consolidated county where African Americans hold more than a 12,000-registered-voter advantage. Whitby had already been acquitted on all charges from a federal case about the same issues.

The new "investigation" stems from Whitby's time as chairman and executive director of the Macon–Bibb County Industrial Authority and calls for an examination of a three-year-old case file. Blair McGowan, the deputy attorney general of Georgia, sent a letter to GBI director Vic Reynolds, saying in part: "I am writing to request that the Georgia Bureau of Investigation open an investigation into possible theft, forgery and false statements involving former chairman/executive director of the Macon–Bibb County Industrial Authority, Cliffard Whitby, and three companies owned by Whitby's family members." This situation is puzzling, though, because the deputy attorney general requested the GBI investigation in March, but the probe didn't become public until mid-May, less than a month before the June 9 election. Who pushed for this investigation at this time is unknown. Although the mayor's office is nonpartisan, partisan politics can't be ruled out. McGowan is a Republican, and at least one of the mayoral candidates has positioned himself as aligned with President Donald Trump.

Three years ago, the Industrial Authority did an investigation of its own in an effort to distance itself from Whitby after he was served with the federal indictment. But that investigation took a nasty turn that reeked of politics. It charged that work on an Allied Industrial Park project wasn't completed, but the authority's own internal documents—with before-and-after pictures—proved the work was in fact completed according to contract, and several authority board members had visited the site according to board records. In addition, board minutes proved Whitby was open about his connection with the three companies before the authority approved the contracts, which had also been subject to competitive bidding. Now enter the GBI to conduct a duplicate investigation on the state level, where all concerned parties already know the outcome—but that outcome won't be revealed to the general public until after Election Day, if then.

Whitby, as head of the Industrial Authority, had a very successful tenure, bringing Kumho Tire, Tyson Foods, Irving Tissue, and other employers to town. Whitby, for the first time in the authority's history, reached out to minority contractors and vendors. Then there was pushback. And there is more to the back story that preceded Whitby's tenure as chairman. The Greater Macon Chamber of Commerce acted as the area's industrial recruiter, but that relationship had been brought to a halt—ruffling feathers in the process—by former Industrial Authority chairman Frank Amerson, with Whitby at his side.

Whitby says the attack is "politically motivated." The *Telegraph* quotes Whitby saying, "Anyone who ever attempts to do anything of substance will always have enemies. In this current political environment, it does not surprise me that after three years, some would choose to bring up these old allegations at the Industrial Authority that were fully reviewed previously."

The Black community has little doubt about the origin and timing of the investigation. Whitby is seen as a hero who has faced down federal charges and supports Black businesses. He has been a thorn in the side of the Macon–Bibb County Board of Education, which has a sorry record of not employing minority contractors in the spending of more than $1 billion in construction contracts in the past dozen years. One of Whitby's opponents in the mayoral race served on the school board and has racked up contributions from the contractors who have benefited from the board's largesse; at the same time, this opponent has openly attacked contracts targeted at minority contractors.

Although the *Telegraph*, the 194-year-old daily paper, announced the investigation, it left the follow-up response, two days later, only to television reporters, choosing not to cover local Black clergy, current and former local politicians, and others gathered to support Whitby. "This is what you call a political lynching," said state senator David Lucas in front of the Macon–Bibb County Government Center. "When you don't want somebody that's talking about serving the community, but you got another part of the community that has another agenda, then they come up with all kinds of tricks." Pastor Bryant Raines said during the same press conference, "What we are experiencing is an intentional assault on the collective consciousness of our community, all in the name of politics."

This election for Macon–Bibb County is pivotal. The mayor's office will be transitioning for the first time in twelve years. Eight of nine county commission seats might have new occupants because only one commissioner doesn't have opposition. Twenty-one candidates are running for those eight seats. No matter who is elected, the commission will have four new members because of the retirement of three members and the decision by one to run for mayor. Four of the eight board of education members will also be new, and the Macon–Bibb County Water Authority is guaranteed a new member because the District 2 representative, Javors Lucas, who served on the authority for thirty-seven years, died at age ninety-six.

This election is also weird. Aside from the municipal nonpartisan races, the June 9 election is a partisan primary for district attorney, sheriff, state Senate, and one of the state's U.S. Senate seats, with seven Democrats seeking the nomination to face Republican senator David Perdue. The other U.S. Senate seat is a "jungle" primary in November that includes twenty candidates of all political stripes, Republican, Democrat, independent, and everything in-between.

Another factor raising its ugly head that will impact all municipal races: the Macon–Bibb County budget. What started as an example of fiscal responsibility has become something else. Before COVID-19, the county was projected to have a rainy-day fund of $28 million, up $9 million from fiscal year 2019, but that changed. One day after early voting began on May 18 this year, Mayor Robert Reichert revealed his 2021 budget, which begins July 1. He seeks to cut $16.6 million because sales tax, hotel-motel taxes, and fines and fees revenue are down because of the COVID-19 shutdown, and so the rainy-day fund has become an undefined figure.

Personnel costs are 80 percent of the county's budget, and Reichert has proposed furloughs for all personnel except those in public safety. That means a furlough of as much as four days a week for Recreation Department employees over the summer. And that means swimming pools will close during the height of what is always a hot summer. Reichert said, "It's hard to imagine a way to balance our budget without adversely impacting our employees." Reichert is also proposing that other county employees lose a half-day's pay each week for the entire fiscal year. "I recognize and understand, however, that this is not what you deserve," the mayor said. "I ask only for your understanding of the circumstances that compel the proposals of this budget."

This proposal has forced all five mayoral candidates, one a sitting commissioner, to chime in and has put four sitting commissioners with opposition in the unenviable position of having to debate and finally vote on the mayor's proposal—up or down—and that final vote will come on Election Day on June 9. "We have to do more with less, and there's going to be difficult decisions moving forward," Larry Schlesinger, a candidate for mayor, said. Commissioner Virgil Watkins, who has two contenders for his seat, said, "We know we need to put paying our employees and adjusting the pay at the forefront."

Will this consequential commission meeting be covered by the *Telegraph*, a newspaper that touts its watchdog responsibility? No. Fortunately, though, the meeting will be livestreamed and reported by television reporters, who have picked up the mantle dropped by the newspaper.

The county isn't the only government looking to cut expenses. Governor Brian Kemp is looking to cut $3.5 billion in the state's budget and has ordered each state agency—from the GBI to the University System of Georgia—to cut budgets by 14 percent, no exceptions. Furloughs were announced for the university system's twenty-six schools at a time when face-to-face classes have had to transition to online classes. Summer classes are being held online only, and it is not known whether students will return to campuses in the fall.

State government has other issues, and COVID-19 is at the heart of them all. Unemployment claims increased by 1,041,401 in April to reach a total of 1,353,921. The unemployment rate hit an all-time high in April: 11.9 percent.

Kemp started opening up the state before any of his fellow governors, and he got hurt in the polls: Kemp was at the bottom of a *Washington Post*–Ipsos poll from May 2020 that ranked all fifty governors for their handling of the virus. But, more importantly, Kemp has paid the price in the health of the people in his state. Several data snafus came from the Georgia Department of Public Health—for instance, one made the trend line in COVID-19 cases appear to decline when in actuality it was flat, and then another inflated the number of tests by adding together the nasal swab (viral) and antibody tests, which artificially increased the number of tests performed and lowered the percentage of positive cases in the state.

At the same time, Dr. Carlos del Rio, chairman of the Global Health Department at Emory University and the dean overseeing physicians at Grady Memorial Hospital, stated that Georgia experienced a 26 percent rise in COVID-19 cases between May 11 and May 18, and those numbers were not all attributable to an increase in testing but to the partial end of stay-at-home orders. Businesses here rushed to open, but was it too soon?

One of the most successful restauranteurs in Macon, the Moonhanger Group, led by Wes Griffith with three downtown eateries, released this statement:

On Tuesday, May 26th The Moonhanger Group made the decision to open our dining rooms at H&H, Rookery, Dovetail and Natalia's. As we prepared to open, we not only implemented the state reopening guidelines and CDC [Centers for Disease Control] recommendations, but we also arranged testing for all of our employees last Tuesday and Wednesday. We were not required to do this but thought it prudent to go the extra mile. Though we didn't have all the results yet, we re-opened anyway. We were confident, based on the low number of positive results reported in Bibb County, that none of our employees would test positive and we hoped to share that news with the public. Unfortunately, and surprisingly, we have employees who have tested positive. All of them were asymptomatic. We feel that the only appropriate thing to do at this point is to close dining rooms at Rookery, Dovetail and H&H. Natalia's (located in the north end of the county) will remain open due to no positive results among the staff. We will spend the coming days retesting, examining the data, and identifying team members who are COVID free. We hope to resume to-go business soon.

No one knows what the future will look like—but it will be far from "normal."

19

HOW FACEBOOK HAS UNDERMINED COMMUNAL CONVERSATION IN MCKEESPORT

McKeesport

A lot has been written about the corrosive effect of Facebook on our national discourse. It's also eroding what people know and what they talk about in small towns like McKeesport. We lost our newspaper, the *McKeesport Daily News*, at the end of 2015. When I was working in print, the rule of thumb was that a healthy newspaper carried 50 percent news content and 50 percent advertising. By that metric, the *Daily News* before its demise was a very unhealthy newspaper—some issues carried less than 10 percent advertising.

How much of Facebook's advertising growth has come at the expense of small daily and weekly newspapers? Facebook allows anyone with a business or organization page to buy advertising. You can market to individual zip codes, behaviors, ages, and interests—almost every demographic category short of directly targeting individuals by name. While your ad is running, Facebook will even show you how many people are interacting with it in case you want to adjust your targeting or your message.

Compare that to print advertising. The Pittsburgh area still has a number of small weekly newspapers, such as the 10,000-circulation *South Pittsburgh Reporter*, which serves three zip codes. A single column inch of black-and-white advertising in the paper costs $9.

For the same $9, Facebook promises to show my ad to 3,300 people in Pittsburgh's south suburbs. It will even tell me who saw my ad and when. No newspaper can match that. If you own a neighborhood coffee shop or car-detailing business and have $50 or less to spend every week on advertising, would you buy four column inches in the weekly, or would you use Facebook? That's what small print papers are up against.

Facebook also sucked away many of the little news items that once populated newspaper columns. When I worked at the *Daily News* and the *Observer-Reporter* of Washington, Pennsylvania, back in the 1990s, we reporters were always filing short, one- and two-paragraph briefs on rummage sales, pancake suppers, volunteer fire department recruiting drives, and pet adoptions. On Saturday, each paper devoted most of a page to church news, and each paid clerks to take wedding and birth announcements.

At Tube City Online, we seldom get those kinds of items. People don't need to filter those announcements through a reporter or news clerk—they post them directly to Facebook.

When the crisis in local journalism began more than a decade ago, there were promises by technology pundits that social media would lead to the rise of "citizen journalism" and that crowd-sourcing of information would replace the work done by professional reporters.

There *has* been a proliferation of community and neighborhood "news" groups on Facebook. In McKeesport alone, at least a dozen competing Facebook groups claim they're devoted to community news. White Oak, a neighboring borough, has at least seven, and Glassport, another adjoining municipality, has five.

But, in reality, few of them post what would be traditionally considered news. Some posts consist mainly of lost-dog reports, reviews of local diners, funny photos, and church announcements. That's pretty harmless and even uplifting, if not particularly informative.

Yet, increasingly, the content put out by some "community news" groups reflects the same dangerous tensions and divisions for which Facebook is being blamed for stoking nationally. A few of them traffic in blatant racism. Black teenagers wandering through a mostly white neighborhood will immediately set off posts about "strange people" being seen walking the streets and reminding residents to "watch your car and lock up your valuables!"

Misleading information dominates other "news" groups. Throughout the COVID-19 pandemic, posts about local businesses requiring customers to wear face masks, for instance, have inevitably led to the same familiar arguments: *Yes, face masks do slow the spread of airborne virus particles. No, you cannot get carbon monoxide poisoning from wearing a face mask.* Yet both theories have passionate defenders in Facebook's "community news" groups.

And we're seeing how misinformation and racism are making their way off Facebook and back into the mainstream conversation in our community and in towns around the country. For instance, on May 26 a Black transgender woman was found dead outside of her apartment building in McKeesport's downtown. Allegheny County police were called to the scene. They concluded she had jumped or fallen from her ninth-story window and that she likely died by suicide.

Normally, Tube City Online wouldn't cover a possible suicide. But it happened on a weekday morning, within sight of McKeesport City Hall, and the victim, Aaliyah Johnson, was a popular performer on the Pittsburgh drag scene with an active social media presence. Her fans and friends wanted to know what had happened—Was there foul play? (As an out Black trans woman, she had received threats to her life.) Also, no Pittsburgh TV stations or newspapers were reporting her death—her friends began speculating whether police were involved in a cover-up.

I called a county homicide detective and was told police reviewed surveillance video from outside of Johnson's apartment. No one other than the victim had been seen entering or leaving before or after the incident. We ran our story the next day.

But in the wake of the George Floyd murder in Minnesota—which set off protests in and around Pittsburgh, as elsewhere—many people were understandably not willing to take police reports about a Black woman's unexpected death at face value.

They wanted the investigation reopened to confirm that no one had harmed her. If Johnson did die by suicide, they asked, did she kill herself because of targeted harassment? And, finally, if she was suicidal, why are there no resources in the McKeesport area for Black people who are LGBTQ?

Rumors continued to swirl. On June 10, police in neighboring Port Vue announced that a "Justice for Aaliyah" protest march was being planned for McKeesport in two days. I made a few calls. I was sitting in the McKeesport police station, reviewing the week's blotter, when one of the march organizers called me back.

He told me a peaceful march was being planned by several groups, including community activists and members of Pittsburgh's LGBTQ community. I called the mayor: McKeesport police would provide traffic control and an escort, he said. Port Vue police said they had been in touch with the Pittsburgh office of the Department of Homeland Security and concluded, "This will be a peaceful gathering from this group[, which] has no history of any aggression or violence."

I walked across the street to our newsroom and posted the story on our website. That might have been the end of it—had not one of those "community news" Facebook groups posted a report that "someone from the city" was calling McKeesport business owners and advising them to close their stores and offices at 2:00 p.m. and evacuate the downtown area because "someone" (supposedly "Black Lives Matter" or "Antifa"—it wasn't exactly clear) was threatening violence.

Within minutes, the post had gone viral.

No one from the Facebook group called police or city hall to verify such calls were being made. McKeesport police issued their own statement via Facebook, denying the report, which set off waves of recriminations—some users defended the police, while others alleged that city officials were engaged in a conspiracy to silence their critics on Facebook. The march in McKeesport, by the way, was peaceful.

Another small town—Bethel, Ohio, near Cincinnati—wasn't so lucky. On June 14, a Black Lives Matter rally of about one hundred peaceful demonstrators was met by six to seven hundred counterprotesters, some carrying weapons, who harassed and threatened participants, according to Cincinnati's WCPO-TV. The counterdemonstration, according to published reports, was organized on Facebook, spurred by rumors that "Antifa" was invading the town.

If McKeesport police hadn't strongly and quickly rebutted the rumors about the Justice for Aaliyah march, and if Tube City Online hadn't published its report about the marchers' peaceful intentions, could something just as bad have happened here?

In 2020, Facebook pledged $100 million to support local newsrooms in the United States and Canada, but only $25 million of that would provide direct grants to news gathering. Assuming a reporter is making only $50,000, with no benefits, that pledge would support 500 reporters for one year. Meanwhile, Pew reports that more than 27,000 reporters have lost their jobs in the United States since 2008, including the ten or so writers and editors who worked at the *McKeesport Daily News*.

Any investment in local news gathering is welcome. But as long as Facebook continues to give an unchecked platform to racists and gossipmongers, allow otherwise well-meaning people to spread false information unchecked, and drain money from local news organizations, the grants are little more than a balm for whatever guilt the company may feel about the problems it's creating for democracy and community life in America.

Facebook reaps the profits. Small towns like McKeesport pay the price.

20

SOUTH TEXAS WAS
REOPENING. NOW COVID-19
IS ROARING BACK.

McAllen

I n mid-March 2020, the United States went on lockdown because of the emergence of thousands of coronavirus cases in major cities on the East and West Coasts, while thousands of miles away in South Texas border residents anxiously waited and prayed that the virus would not make an appearance in their communities.

On March 21, the first case was reported in Hidalgo County, Texas, followed by a second a day later. Since then, cases have slowly trickled in for this border county, where McAllen, its largest city, sits across the Rio Grande from Reynosa, Mexico. However, the situation there did not compare to what was happening in New York City, San Francisco, and Seattle, where health-care workers and hospitals were quickly overwhelmed by the novel and deadly virus.

But a few mandates and directives came from the governor's mansion in Austin. Fearing for his constituents, Judge Richard Cortez of Hidalgo County issued a disaster declaration on March 17 and ordered no gatherings of more than fifty people. Two days later he said no groups more than ten. On March 26, Cortez ordered all "nonessential" workers in the county of 860,000 residents to shelter at home. He also ordered the closure of dine-in restaurants, bars, gyms, hair and nail salons, movie theaters, bowling alleys, and other entertainment venues, saying: "I make this extraordinary move convinced that it is the right path for the safety of the residents of Hidalgo County. I know this will cause hardship, but I am convinced this will save lives."

Elsewhere throughout the state, the onus also appeared to be on local leaders to implement the orders that would safeguard their communities, absent any statewide directives from Texas's Republican governor, Greg Abbott. Similar orders were issued by other South Texas county judges along the border, from Webb County to Cameron County on the Gulf Coast.

As Abbott remained mum, local leaders took the heat, getting blamed for the economic losses that small businesses and communities would suffer during the shutdown. This criticism was especially magnified in South Texas, where hospitals remained on the ready but had few cases to treat.

On April 2, Abbott issued stay-at-home orders for nonessential workers and urged social distancing, but he did not limit the number of people who could gather. He told the state's 29 million residents to "minimize social gatherings and minimize in-person contact with people who are not in the same household . . . and work from home, if possible." He also said that "people shall [sic] avoid" restaurants, bars, hair salons, tattoo parlors, but he did not actually close any businesses or order facial masks to be worn in public.

After a flurry of hoarding that left grocery store shelves bare, residents hunkered down in their homes, resisted the urge to gather with extended Hispanic families, as is traditional in South Texas Hispanic culture, and spent the better part of their days communicating on social media and scouring websites for home-delivered groceries, cleaning supplies, and toilet paper.

On April 7, the first death in Hidalgo County occurred—that of a seventy-six–year-old man from Alamo, Texas, who had "underlying health conditions" and had been hospitalized for "several weeks," the county reported. But even then, the total number of patients being treated for COVID-19 in all of Hidalgo County was just 123.

Across the Rio Grande in Reynosa, Mexico, similar preparations and precautions were not being taken; testing kits were not being procured by Mexican health authorities, and social distancing and masks were not discussed or commonplace.

The Trump administration shut down the southwestern border with Mexico to travel on March 20 but still allowed the back-and-forth crossing of essential workers from Mexico, including those employed at factories known as maquiladoras, which we would later discover were hotbeds for infections and helped spread the virus.

Days passed, and South Texans watched and read harrowing tales of uncontrolled hot spots and families decimated by the loss of loved ones elsewhere in the country. And yet the virus appeared to stay relatively contained here on the border. On some days, no new COVID-19 cases were reported.

But in the northern Mexican state of Tamaulipas, which has two hundred miles of shared border with South Texas, the number of cases was rapidly increasing. By mid-April, South Texas leaders were openly warning that Mexico was expected to hit its peak during the first or second week of May. Although the borders were closed to travel, hundreds were still crossing the international bridges daily, and leaders knew the potential for viral spread was imminent. Warnings were given daily through the media, and South Texans showed a resolve to fight the virus.

But on April 17, Governor Abbott suddenly announced that his administration would begin a phased-in reopening of Texas over the next few weeks, and he made it clear that his orders superseded any issued by local leaders. Heeding Abbott's guidance, Cortez and other county judges began easing restrictions. Over the next few weeks, the South Texas region fell into step with Abbott's orders, allowing businesses to reopen, restaurants to welcome back diners, and even movie theaters to start showing films. South Texans emerged from their homes in dangerous numbers. They went grocery shopping, hung out at malls, flooded beaches on Memorial Day weekend. Fewer and fewer wore masks in public.

However, just a few miles south of the border, maquiladoras were shut down due to infections; pregnant women were forbidden from leaving their homes; and vehicles were limited to no more than two passengers. The Tamaulipas Ministry of Health went from single-digit daily cases to more than 100 and sometimes 150 per day, with many daily deaths reported in the border cities of Matamoros, Reynosa, and Nuevo Laredo. Since it had been reported that Mexico lacked testing capabilities, border leaders routinely warned they thought the infection rate was actually much higher in Mexico. Senator Juan "Chuy" Hinojosa of the Texas State Legislature, a Democrat from South Texas who sits on a committee appointed by Abbott to oversee Coronavirus Aid, Relief, and Economic Security Act funds, told me in an interview that the number of cases in Mexico is believed to be "five times higher" than what the government has said, based on information he has received from sources in Mexico.

This month, the number of coronavirus cases began to skyrocket in Hidalgo County. On June 4, there were 45 new cases—a one-day record. On June 11, there were 70 new cases. On Monday, there were 193 new cases, bringing the total to 1,882, with 23 deaths.

Out of desperation, Cortez reached out to Abbott last week, taking a cue from Judge Nelson Wolff in San Antonio, Bexar County. Both pleaded with the governor to be allowed to implement mandatory face mask rules in their counties. To everyone's surprise, Abbott responded by saying that he had never forbidden them from ordering face masks be worn in businesses. He even told a Waco TV station this had been his "plan in place all along." "Local governments can require stores and businesses to require masks. That's what was authorized in the plan," Abbott said.

That statement prompted *Texas Monthly* to run a story on June 18 headlined "Greg Abbott Invites You to Figure Out What His Coronavirus Executive Orders Allow." The article's subhead read, "A month and a half after telling local officials they couldn't mandate masks, the Texas governor congratulated a local official on realizing that, actually, they could."

Cortez issued a mandatory-mask order for all businesses that took effect on Friday, June 19. But the fear is that it's too little, too late. The virus is now widespread in the community. On June 12, the *New York Times* named McAllen as a coronavirus hot spot.

So, will a thin homemade cotton mask or bandana—most commonly worn here—do anything to stop the deadly virus? It is hard to know, especially with so many mixed messages from Austin that appear to give no consideration to this border region three hundred miles from the state capital but just a thin river away from another country where the pandemic is overtaking entire communities.

21

RACISM, CONFEDERATE STATUES, AND THE VIEW FROM FROG LEVEL, VIRGINIA

Bowling Green

I was surprised by the intensity and ferocity of the demonstrations in the wake of the death of George Floyd, in particular those in nearby Richmond and Fredericksburg, Virginia, and I found myself wondering how we had come to this point.

I realized, though, that I needed help with that question and sought it out. I am the product of a white, middle-class family from the Midwest. I attended schools that were integrated in theory but had only a few or no Black students in attendance. I'm a seventy-five-year-old former newspaper editor who considers himself reasonably enlightened, but I admit that I have no idea what it is like to grow up as a Black man or woman in America—especially in rural areas, where I have spent much of my time since moving to Virginia in 1972.

Still, seeing images of angry protestors clashing with police lines, watching statues being defaced or toppled, and hearing so many voices raised against systemic racism, I get flashbacks of times when I was on the edges of the history of race relations in this country.

1965

On January 21, 1965, in my junior year at Penn State I was among 8,000 students who heard the Reverend Dr. Martin Luther King Jr. speak. This was six months after the Civil Rights Act of 1964 passed and just weeks after Dr. King was awarded the Nobel Peace Prize for his nonviolent campaign against racial inequality. I recall that as we walked over to hear the speech at Rec Hall, there was a lot of jocularity among my mostly white classmates. Walking back to the dorm, we were a quieter group, locked in our own thoughts about Dr. King's words.

1968

When I graduated in 1966, I was called up by the Vietnam War draft, so I went down to the recruiting office and volunteered. Commissioned a second lieutenant in 1967, I was assigned to a training battalion at Fort Eustis, Virginia. When our new battalion commander, Lieutenant Colonel William Smith, arrived, he spotted my journalism degree and invited me to be his chief personnel and administrative officer. For the next year, my office was next to that of this truly inspirational Black man who already had two combat tours in Vietnam as a helicopter pilot.

In truth, this was my first prolonged encounter with a Black man, and Colonel Smith impressed me with his firm belief that anyone regardless of race could succeed through hard work and dedication—in the military, at least. I suppose this experience gave me a somewhat one-sided outlook on race relations because I had little input from Blacks who had tried and failed to break through America's racial barriers or from those who had given up in the face of systemic racism.

APRIL 5, 1968

On Friday, April 5, 1968, I sat at a window table in a restaurant in Washington, DC, with a fellow lieutenant. Having dispatched the official portion of our task that day, we were having a late lunch and discussing sights we wanted to see during our antici-pated weekend in the nation's capital. We asked the proprietor why traffic was so heavy in midafternoon. He replied that Mar-tin Luther King Jr. had been shot the night before and that busi-nesses and government offices were shutting down early in anticipation of riots. When daylight faded, we cautiously picked our way through eerily empty streets to the safety of Andrews Air Force Base. The restaurant owner's predictions were correct— there was widespread violence, looting, and burning of build-ings that night and the next. On the way out of town Sunday morning, we drove through some of the devastated neighbor-hoods. At that time, as an army officer during the Vietnam War and a believer in law and order, I had difficulty understand-ing the rage that triggered the widespread destruction.

1984

Another memory concerns my covering of a voter registration drive in a predominantly Black church in Chesapeake, Virginia, in 1984. The mayor of Chesapeake, my fiancée, and I were the only white people in attendance to hear the Reverend Jesse

Jackson tell the audience about David and Goliath and how votes were like stones lying on the ground, just waiting for someone to pick them up and sling them.

These and other images flashed through my mind as I watched the demonstrations in the wake of the killing of George Floyd and the vandalizing of statues of Confederate soldiers that have dotted the Virginia landscape for 120 years or more.

I could not help but wonder: After the civil rights movement, affirmative action, and the election of so many Black mayors, the first Black governor of Virginia, and the first Black president of the United States, how have we come to this point in 2020? To address the question, I needed to get outside of myself because I have no way of knowing firsthand what it is like growing up Black in Caroline County or America.

But others do.

Dr. Alphine W. Jefferson is one of them. I met him in his office at Randolph-Macon College in nearby Ashland on a campus deserted because of COVID-19. The middle child of five, Jefferson was born in 1950 on his family's small farm near Frog Level, a tiny crossroads community that straddles the Caroline and Hanover County line.

He said he did not know what racism was as a boy, a comment echoed by many who grew up in rural mixed-race communities around here. His father could not read or write, and his mother had a seventh-grade education. The family moved to Baltimore in search of economic and educational opportunities, came back to Frog Level for a few years, then returned to Baltimore again. Jefferson spent nine years of his youth in each place and attended segregated schools in both.

Jefferson is medically color-blind and fought a persistent stutter for the first fourteen years of his life. One teacher tried to tell his mother that her son was "retarded" because he could not color correctly. Yet he graduated from Baltimore's all-Black Frederick Douglas High School and went on to obtain an AB degree from the University of Chicago and both an MA and a PhD from Duke. He has dedicated his life to studying racism in America and to teaching: African and American history at Northern Illinois; Black and urban history at Southern Methodist University; Black studies and history at the College of Wooster; as well as multicultural education at a prison, among other places. Unlike many rural Black families that moved to the city, his family never sold their farm. Jefferson returned to Virginia and lives in the restored family farmhouse in Frog Level. For the past fifteen years, he has been a professor at Randolph-Macon College and is the director of Black studies there. He has organized Juneteenth celebrations on campus and in the community for the past decade.

Jefferson admitted he was as surprised as I was over the intensity and ferocity of the widespread demonstrations in reaction to George Floyd's killing in Minnesota on May 25.

But, in retrospect, he sees a number of factors that help to explain the upheaval:

1. "Very few humans alive could watch that eight minutes of video of a policeman kneeling on George Floyd's neck and not react to it," Jefferson said. "Many whites had not encountered something that obvious, that suggests that level of pathology."

2. "We have been confined in our homes due to COVID-19. Lots of people were glad to have an excuse, any excuse to go outside and to react," Jefferson said.

3. A third factor is economics, with real wages declining since 1973, while wealth at the top grows exponentially. Jefferson cited

"an egregious example" of a CEO who made $52 million last year, "which comes out to $20,000 a minute. We live in a society that is absolutely hypocritical to argue that $15 an hour is too much when corporate America is making thousands of dollars a minute. This is one of the major areas of anger that is simmering beneath the surface today."

4. Another factor, in Jefferson's view, is that "Madison Avenue constantly feeds an appetite for consumption; it urges us to make unwise decisions with our money. Debt is the new slavery."

5. Technology, in particular social media, plays its part: "People have multiple overlapping connections and then find themselves in the street because of instant communication. . . . People can plan an event and determine which people can show up. [Issues] are hijacked by other people. Many of those who demonstrated did not come out to tear down statues," Jefferson said.

Jefferson is one Black man who does not condone the removal or desecration of the many statues in Virginia that commemorate Confederate soldiers at sometimes violent clashes in nearby Richmond and Fredericksburg and even at more peaceful Black Lives Matter demonstrations in Ashland and Bowling Green, with law enforcement officers participating.

"We need somebody who is Black and has studied this for years to say it," Jefferson said: "tearing down the monuments is a dumb idea." Jefferson sees such efforts as ahistorical and self-righteous. "I oppose the destruction and taking down of Confederate statues because we are destroying important primary sources in our national history. These monuments exist in a particular and specific historical context and time frame. Thus, when we remove them, we are altering history. I say leave them and let those who care study their creation and use that information for positive change."

Jefferson says instead we should seek to understand why "these emblems of honor from a long-lost past exist and why have they produced so much anger and hatred today." The efforts to destroy Confederate monuments, he argues, "focus attention away from the real problems of discrimination, inequality, and systematic preferential treatment for America's ruling elite," Jefferson added.

Jefferson said he tells his beginning students that there are three types of racism in America. The first, he said, is individual: "I hate you because you are Black, or I do not like you because you are Black." The second is institutional. Jefferson gave as an example "what Jews experienced trying to get into Harvard decades earlier," regardless of their qualifications. The third is systemic racism: "If you are excluded from those spaces where all the business decisions are made, where money exchange happens, the spaces where corporate elites meet and the inner workings of the government occurs, then you can never be equal," he said.

A considerable amount of Jefferson's research and published writings have to do with housing patterns and how that is also at the core of systemic racism. In one article, "Rhetoric vs. Reality" (1984), he wrote: "Blacks are the inheritors of ghettos, not their creators. Until it is widely known and clearly understood that ghettos are the product of the financial institutions, law firms, and real estate agencies, which benefit from the dual housing market, then whites and blacks will continue to live separately." At the conclusion of that article, Dr. Jefferson wrote: "America does not grant to its black minority the guarantees of its Constitution. The rhetoric does not translate into reality for the majority of the population."

It still doesn't. Thus, perhaps, the rage.

As Dr. King said in that speech I attended fifty-five years ago, "We have come a long, long way in the struggle for racial justice, but we have a long, long way to go before the problem is solved."

22

MACON–BIBB COUNTY VOTES WHILE A NATION PROTESTS

Macon

I n a long-term project such as this, you need a premise to keep everyone on track. Our premise of looking at the 2020 political landscape from four different areas of the country unserved or underserved by newspapers has been blown to hell first by COVID-19 and now by the police killings of George Floyd, which sparked weeks of major protests across the entire country.

A similar murder happened in Macon–Bibb County about seven years ago. Sammie "Junebug" Davis Jr., a forty-nine-year-old Black man with a history of mental illness regularly hung around the Kroger grocery store. Most everyone who frequented the store knew "Junebug." He was a panhandler—and he was big but slow as molasses in winter and no threat to anyone. On a sunny day with a high of fifty-two, four days before Christmas in 2012, eighty-four-year-old Vivian Marable called 911 and told the dispatcher, "There's a guy sitting out front, walking, following me to my car, and asking me for money. It's a big, uh, big Black guy." Aside from Ms. Marable, the one other person who didn't know that Junebug was harmless turned out to be the Macon police officer who responded to her call.

Clayton Sutton, a twenty-nine-year-old officer who had served in Iraq and Afghanistan, arrived at the parking lot with several complaints of excessive force already on his record. Sutton later said that when he approached Junebug, Junebug attacked. Sutton fired his service weapon at him four times, killing him. The Macon Police Department initially said Sutton was there to serve Junebug a warrant and that Junebug had a weapon. There were no warrant and no weapon, but it took the department a week to clarify.

In the end, Sutton wasn't charged in Junebug's killing, and there were three months of marches decrying Junebug's death. A few weeks into it, the Macon Police Department merged with the Bibb County Sheriff's Office as part of the city–county government consolidation, and Sutton had a new boss—Sheriff David Davis. The sheriff has a distinct approach to policing, and that's probably why the county didn't explode into violence over Junebug's murder. Davis wants his deputies to be viewed by the community as protectors, not warriors. The marches over Junebug's death never crossed the line from peaceful to violent. Certainly, the Bibb County Sheriff's Office has all the riot gear and SWATery, but you didn't see deputies in riot gear holding protestors at bay, and you don't see them doing so now.

Two years later, Sutton was involved in another shooting downtown, after which he was placed on administrative duty and ordered not to engage in any law enforcement duties. However, he drew his gun and confronted two men he suspected of theft and was fired for insubordination. He twice appealed his firing, but to no avail. In the summer of 2018, Sutton was indicted for aggravated stalking in Dodge County, south of Macon-Bibb.

Six years after Junebug died, that same midtown Kroger located in the middle of three affluent neighborhoods, closed. The store had been built only after a three-year zoning fight that went all the way to the Georgia Supreme Court. Now the local neighborhoods are left with a twenty-three-acre empty hole, and the closest grocery store is more than three miles away.

Macon-Bibb voters remembered this story this month as they learned of four similar tragedies, two of which occurred in their own state. Breonna Taylor, sleeping in her bed after midnight in Louisville, Kentucky, was killed by plainclothes officers exercising a "no knock" warrant, even though the man they were looking for lived miles away and was already in custody. Ahmaud Arbery was shot and killed for the offense of "jogging while Black" in Brunswick, Georgia, but the vigilantes who killed him were not arrested until a video was leaked three months later. The last straw was Floyd's murder, in all its gruesome detail, and the nation's citizens, Black and white, erupted. Three weeks after Floyd's death and subsequent protests began, twenty-seven-year-old Rayshard Brooks was shot and killed while running from police in what should have been, at most, a simple DUI arrest in Atlanta, Georgia. Officer Garrett Rolfe was fired immediately and later indicted, and the city's police chief, Erika Shields, resigned.

When the citizens of Macon-Bibb peacefully gathered in Rosa Parks Square on May 31, an Ecumenical Day of Solidarity, to listen to faith leaders and pray for the families of Arbery, Taylor, and Floyd, not a rock was thrown as demonstrators sang gospel songs. The Reverend Marvin Colbert, the pastor of Bethel African Methodist Episcopal, said we needed to "come together to have a day of solidarity, not protest. We are moved to come together today to pray."

Sheriff Davis, who attended the gathering, told the *Telegraph*, "The things we're seeing across the country are heartbreaking, and people have to have an outlet for that. They have to have an outlet for that outrage. Very fortunately, we have a good relationship with our community. We're here to support; we're here to show our dismay and disappointment in our law enforcement brethren for treating individuals the way they have."

Two demonstrations were held in Warner Robins; the most recent one on June 13 was titled "Unity in the Community." Marchers, numbering more than five hundred, carried signs and chanted as they marched about two and a half miles to city hall along Watson Boulevard, the city's major thoroughfare. Speakers included Police Chief John Wagner of Warner Robins, Police Chief Steve Lynn of Perry, and Sheriff Alan Everidge of Houston County. At all of the marches in both cities, the demonstrators were ethnically diverse.

"All this is about is having a conversation about things," said Chief Wagner. "That's the strong action of talking and should be what's done. They [the marchers] were very grateful for this, and we'll continue that open relationship and communication."

MAY 31, 1921–MAY 31, 2020

Those attending the Ecumenical Day of Solidarity were aware that ninety-nine years earlier to the day, on May 31, 1921, white residents of Tulsa, Oklahoma, attacked the Greenwood District, known as the Black Wall Street. Three hundred Black residents were estimated to have been killed and buried in mass graves. Hundreds more were injured, and thousands fled. The rampaging white mobs burned everything—churches, schools, and hospitals. Greenwood was the first place in the United States to be bombed from the air. In the end, thirty-five city blocks were torched.

Did members of the white mob get arrested? No, but police and National Guardsmen rounded up every Black resident who was still around, according to the Tulsa Historical Society and Museum. "Over 6,000 people were held at the Convention Hall and the Fairgrounds, some for as long as eight days."

The two white papers in town—the *Tulsa World* and the now defunct *Tulsa Tribune*—mostly ignored the rampage, according to Scott Ellsworth, a professor of African American history at the University of Michigan who has written extensively about the massacre, and as reported by the *Los Angeles Times*.

The *Tribune*, Ellsworth noted, didn't publish a single article about the massacre until 1971. The bottom line is that for half a century the white newspapers of Tulsa intentionally kept the massacre buried. The only outlet to print accounts of the massacre before 1971was the Black-owned paper the *Daily Tulsa Star*, founded in 1913, which was torched during the massacre (it is still in publication as the *Oklahoma Eagle*).

It was in this atmosphere of tragedy and conflict both historical and current—with COVID-19 still having its way and demonstrations all over the nation—that Georgia held its primary elections on June 9.

The biggest upset was in the Democratic primary for district attorney. Anita Reynolds-Howard, an African American, trounced the incumbent, David Cooke, by 9,374 votes. Cooke was hit by a perfect storm because many of his supporters voted in the Republican primary, where he wasn't on the ballot and no Republican candidate ran for the position.

The race for mayor headed to an August 11 runoff between Lester Miller, the top vote getter, and Cliffard Whitby, an African American candidate.

Georgia's two U.S. Senate seats will be decided—in two very different ways—in November. In the primaries, Democrat John Ossoff beat back six competitors to win the nomination outright to face Republican U.S. senator David Perdue. The other U.S.

Senate seat is the subject of a "jungle primary," where twenty-one candidates will seek to fill the unexpired term of Senator Johnny Isakson. If there's a runoff, the race won't be decided until January 5, 2021, and whoever wins will have to run again in 2022.

Locally, eight of the nine Macon–Bibb County Commission seats, the mayor's office, school board seats, and Water Authority positions—all nonpartisan—are in play. In the primaries, voters who selected the Democratic ballot saw the contested races for district attorney and U.S. Senate. Republican primary ballots were mostly perfunctory.

It would seem voters in Macon–Bibb County should have had reasons to vote in the delayed primary, but that was not the case. Only 38,514 ballots were cast in the mayor's race, the only seat besides district attorney that was county wide. That's a paltry 36.3 percent of registered voters. Was COVID-19 or long lines or altered campaigns to blame?

While Macon–Bibb County had its problems on the primaries' election day, and some precincts had equipment malfunctions, the reporting of the voting results was particularly galling. Precinct information on election night was unavailable; in fact, no information was available. Some results dribbled out Wednesday, June 10, but a final tally wasn't released for ten days—not until June 19. The Board of Elections, which normally receives about 3,000 absentee ballots, received 15,000, and the chair of the board said 10,000 of them were marked incorrectly. Voters, instead of filling in the bubble next to their choice, circled or marked an X. Workers had to go through each ballot to make sure votes counted. On top of that, many of the absentee ballots mailed by the state were printed on thinner paper than those locally produced, so the scanners couldn't read them, and they had to be manually tabulated.

Additional problems included 289 people who had been mailed incorrect absentee ballots. Voters who requested a Republican ballot in the Second Congressional District received a ballot for the Eighth Congressional District, and a new database had to be created to count those voters. The Elections Board had to wait for the manufacturer of the $107 million new voting system to merge the new database with the old, and the board's chairman, Mike Kaplan, said on June 16, "They're having an extremely difficult time with that. We would've been done if we had the old system." The Board of Elections has asked for a budget increase before November to handle the anticipated increase in absentee ballots.

Those issues were nothing compared to those in the Atlanta metro area, where hours-long waits to vote were the norm. It was a noxious combination of human error (not enough trained poll workers, many of them new) and equipment issues (some precincts didn't have voting equipment until the morning of the election, and some equipment was delivered to the wrong locations). Polls that were supposed to close at 7:00 p.m. had to stay open past 10:00 p.m. One precinct, where the lines stretched for three blocks, was a nursing home, putting voters and residents at risk of COVID-19. Local officials pointed fingers at the Secretary of State's Office, the agency that oversees elections in Georgia, and state officials blamed locals. Georgia has 159 counties, and each county is responsible for selecting precincts to count votes.

"Georgia, We Must Do Better" screamed the June 10 front-page, above-the-fold headline tagged to the *Atlanta Journal-Constitution* editorial board's opinion. "Georgia blew it—big time," the editorial began. "An election meltdown that had been simmering here for a long time finally boiled over for all the world to see. The election process—what should be a near-sacred ritual of this Republic—quickly developed into what national and local commentators called, with ample justification, a hot mess."

The Georgia State Legislature's Speaker of the House has called for an investigation into primary-election issues, particularly in Fulton County, where there were long wait times at polls, poor poll worker training, and missing absentee ballots. Brad Raffensperger, the secretary of state, has asked the legislature for the power to step in if a county can't perform its election functions. His office's website, where all the statewide returns are supposed to be posted, was useless on election night.

The *Atlanta Journal-Constitution*'s editorial said it best: "The back-and-forth we saw Tuesday was simply childish and unbecoming of the leadership for a state that proclaims itself as world-class. Our elections apparatus certainly and spectacularly failed this week to live up to those claims. And it's fair to ask just what that says about the caliber of leaders we've chosen here."

23

"McALLEN AND SOUTH TEXAS NEED HELP NOW"

McAllen

O n June 29, I attended a press conference at the Hidalgo County commissioners' facility to get an update on the rapidly escalating cases of COVID-19 in deep South Texas. The administrators for seven regional hospitals, the county judge, the county health director, and the county's Health Authority physician urged the community to tread cautiously because deaths were increasing daily. Dr. Ivan Melendez, the Hidalgo County Health Authority physician, was twenty feet in front of me speaking about the need to maintain social distancing, wear facial coverings in public, and limit outings unless absolutely necessary. Then midway through the hour-long press conference, he disappeared.

I later learned that he had received an urgent message telling him to leave the room and get on a call, in which he was informed that he had tested positive for coronavirus. On June 30, I wrote a story for *Border Report* explaining that he had been masked for the duration of the news conference, as had everyone else. I never interviewed him one-on-one because he had left the briefing early, and I counted my blessings that the press corps had been positioned many feet apart in the back of the room, far away enough, I hoped, to avoid contracting the virus.

My husband, Carlos Sanchez, was also at the news conference. A former *Washington Post* reporter and editor for the *Waco Tribune-Herald*, the *McAllen Monitor*, and the *Texas Monthly*, he left journalism this past February to take over as Hidalgo County's director of public information. He had organized the news conference, in fact. He talked to several reporters and dignitaries and made sure everyone had secured the interviews they needed. I watched him have many close interactions with others that day.

Shortly after midnight on July 1, my husband's sixtieth birthday, he shook me awake and told me to get out of the room because he had a fever and body aches. In my sleepiness, I didn't quite comprehend what was happening. I grabbed my pillow and ran out of the room. As I lay on the family-room couch without a blanket, I realized what had just happened, and I began to pray for my family. My eighty-six-year-old father was asleep down the hall. My three young-adult children staying with us during the pandemic were upstairs.

My husband isolated himself in our bedroom suite for the next eleven days, but his fever never broke. We were lucky that this room has a door to the backyard, and I was able to stock the garage refrigerator with drinks and food for him and leave hot meals at his door. He continued to work, however, answering media calls, writing press releases, and soldiering on. He tested negative twice, but we still suspected it was COVID-19.

He almost passed out after facilitating a Zoom press conference on July 9 with a 102-degree fever. My eldest son sent him hot soup, but his appetite continued to decrease, his breathing got more and more labored, and three days later, as the rest of us were about to eat dinner, he suddenly appeared in the dining room and headed for the front door. He was going to the hospital, he announced groggily.

My eldest son threw on two masks and drove him there with the car windows rolled down. Hours later, we learned that my husband had COVID-19. A day later, he was transferred to another hospital, where he was placed on oxygen and given a cocktail of IV drugs and painful blood-thinner injections through his stomach. He was just two miles away from us, but we had no access to him. He would call me on a landline phone when he felt well. In the hours and sometimes days in between calls, I feared the worst. But I knew he was lucky to have gotten into a hospital. Hundreds in the Rio Grande Valley were suffering with this disease at home, unable to get medical care.

Judge Richard Cortez of Hidalgo County announced this past Sunday night that the county had 1,320 new cases and seventeen deaths. Thirty-five died on Wednesday, July 15—a one-day record—and twenty-seven people died on the Friday after that. Altogether so far, 12,263 people have COVID-19 or have recovered from it in this county of just 860,000. The numbers grow astronomically every day as this border region faces what community leaders had so desperately warned could happen when the governor reopened Texas months ago.

With Mexico just six miles to our south and San Antonio four hours away, South Texas was slower to see cases rise and was holding its own until the state was reopened in phases on May 1. By the time the virus was peaking in mid-May in the northern Mexican state of Tamaulipas just across the Rio Grande, bars and restaurants here were allowed to reopen; gyms were accepting patrons once again; and a feeling of complacency began to spread after weeks of tense waiting and worrying over when (or if) the novel coronavirus would strike the region.

It feels as if the rest of the state and the nation do not realize what is happening here. I have spoken to friends in the Northeast and Northwest who are completely unaware that we are the nation's hot spot right now. They are unaware that leaders from the nonprofit Samaritan's Purse came to tour the area on Monday, July 13, to see where they could build a field hospital and/or a step-down convalescent unit for recovering survivors, as the organization did in New York City and Italy. People in the Northeast and Northwest are unaware that suddenly, late on Wednesday, the nonprofit announced it wasn't going to help aid efforts here. The *Wall Street Journal* reported that Governor Greg Abbott dissuaded the group from setting up operations in South Texas.

That deterrence garnered stiff criticism from Representative Vicente Gonzalez, a Democrat in the U.S. House whose hometown is McAllen. "The governor needs to let those who want to help our overextended and exhausted medical personnel in South Texas do so. We have people who are suffering and dying. How can any governor see fit to deny a field hospital and critical medical services to overrun COVID-19 hospitals?" Gonzalez said in a statement. "I urge Governor Abbott to reconsider this decision and expedite the deployment of a field hospital by Samaritan's Purse to the Rio Grande Valley. McAllen and South Texas need help now." The *Wall Street Journal* story also quoted Dr. Melendez, the county's health physician who had tested positive for COVID-19 and had recently been cleared to resume seeing patients. The story said Samaritan's Purse was informed that the governor had sent adequate resources to the region.

Abbott had sent a surge team of health-care workers a few weeks earlier, and an ambulance strike force was also sent to augment transport vehicles for the sick. But as the numbers rose, and hospitals were overwhelmed, it became clear that these efforts were not enough. This region needs help, and it needs it now. Every major media organization was here in town reporting on this story, including the *New York Times* and the *Los*

Angeles Times. On Thursday, Melendez was interviewed on *CBS News* and CNN mere hours apart.

On Monday, July 20, Judge Cortez issued new shelter-at-home orders, which he acknowledged have no legal backing, but in a statement he said, "I strongly hope everyone will voluntarily follow [the orders] so that we can slow the spread of COVID-19."

I wish my husband could shelter at home with us, but he is hooked to tanks of oxygen in a bright, zero-pressure room. They are already discussing discharging him because others need the bed, and he is not on a ventilator. But where would he go? I have been told that if he comes home, the rest of us (five people and three dogs) would have to go elsewhere because of his viral load. A field hospital and convalescent station sure sound like the answer to many of our prayers right now.

24

WHEN A NEWSPAPER DIES,
WHAT FILLS THE VOID?

Bowling Green

For nearly a century, the residents of Caroline County, Virginia, were served by an energetic weekly, the *Caroline Progress*. As I mentioned earlier, on its pages they read about births, deaths, wedding announcements, church notices, coming events, school sports victories and defeats, government meetings, political intrigue, highway accidents, house fires, a variety of other local news and features, as well as editorials, op-ed pieces, columns, and a multitude of letters to the editor, particularly in election years, like now.

In the nearby town of Ashland and neighboring Hanover County, the *Herald-Progress* similarly served generations of local residents until it, too, was shut down after 131 years of service. At the end, they were essentially one newspaper put out by one full-time reporter, one part-time reporter, a few freelancers, and one editor. For a while, that editor was me, from 2004 until I retired in 2012. After that, I continued to contribute a column to the *Herald-Progress* until its demise and to the *Caroline Progress* until its final issue. Both papers died—or, rather, were killed—on March 28, 2018.

The newspapers were the heart of the civic conversation here. Lately, I have been thinking about who and what have tried to fill that void.

The first attempt came from the daily of nearby Fredericksburg, a town that has long regarded Caroline County as part of
its circulation area and for years had cherry-picked the big news
stories and features as well as some advertising revenue. This
policy continues for the most part today. But immediately after
the *Caroline Progress* folded, the owners of the *Fredericksburg Free
Lance-Star* made a bigger move. Residents of Caroline County
began receiving in their mailboxes a free publication called the
Caroline Star Weekly, which featured advertising and store inserts
aimed at Caroline County and stories of local interest culled
from the pages of the *Free Lance-Star*, which produced the
weekly. This endeavor proved unprofitable, and after about a year
the *Star Weekly*, too, ceased to exist.

The Fredericksburg paper itself had struggled for years and
went bankrupt in 2014. It appeared to get a new lease on life
when it was purchased in 2015 by multibillionaire Warren Buffett's conglomerate Berkshire Hathaway. It joined sixty-two
former Media General newspapers, including the state's flagship paper, the *Richmond Times-Dispatch*, which Buffett purchased in 2012. In 2020, however, Buffett gave up on the newspaper business, selling Berkshire Hathaway's newspapers to
Lee Enterprises of Davenport, Iowa, while retaining ownership
in the physical properties. As was widely reported, Buffett was
quoted in 2019 as saying that newspapers are "toast." The sale
was completed on March 16, 2020, just before the pandemic
caused retail advertisers to pull in their horns. Staff cutbacks
resulted, and so today the *Free-Lance Star* as well as the *Times-
Dispatch* limp along with reduced staffs, their pages nearly
bereft of display advertising and stuffed with lengthy Associated Press copy.

Meanwhile, there was another attempt to fill the void. A
longtime Caroline County couple, Tony and Kim Ares, thought

they saw an opportunity when the *Caroline Progress* closed its doors. "We heard a lot of complaints from people when the *Caroline Progress* shut down, and sensed a need," Tony, who is forty-seven, said. "We had some experience in writing and in websites. We listened to a gentleman from New York on how to create a new model of a newspaper with a skeleton crew."

In December 2018, the Areses began printing the *Virginia Connection*, a tabloid that was distributed for free on restaurant countertops and at public gathering places. Paid subscriptions by mail or online were also offered. The content was chiefly press releases from the public schools, county government, and law enforcement; public-school schedules; and other items—all of which could be found online with enough searching. Tony generated photo features on local events, such as the second-grade swim program at the YMCA and the charity Polar Bear Plunge. He also posted videos on the publication's website.

Contributions from the public were encouraged, and the site ran a weekly inspirational column from a local pastor that had also been carried in the *Caroline Progress* for many years before it closed. The new publication's somewhat broad name was intentional: "My thought was, if things took off, we would expand to other news deserts," Tony said.

That didn't happen. Full of enthusiasm, Tony made the rounds, meeting county residents and talking to various organizations. He sold advertising, and he and his daughters, now four and six, drove around the county distributing the paper for the next six months, during which he invested a chunk of the family's life savings in the venture.

Although the *Virginia Connection* was well received as a free publication, it was apparent from stories floating in a sea of white space in the page layouts that the paper was not generating many contributions from the public.

Nor were readers becoming paid subscribers. "Subscriptions were so low, it breaks my soul," said Tony, who also moonlights as the pastor of a church in Dumfries, Virginia.

He readily admits his lack of journalism experience contributed to his downfall. Press releases from politicians were run without being labeled as such, for example, making it appear to at least some readers that the newspaper was endorsing the politicians. "We planned to run a story each week on candidates for public office, but after the first one ran, people assumed we were taking sides," he explained.

Tony had been active in the local Democratic Committee prior to his newspaper venture (and is now part of the local dump-Trump movement), but he stepped down from the role during his newspaper days. He was shocked when some of his editorial decisions were assailed from both sides of the political spectrum. When he commented in print that the incumbent county supervisor for Bowling Green, a Republican, "was 'a hard worker focused on budgetary issues, and a political powerhouse,'" Tony said, "all of my Democratic friends were mad at me." He said he also came under fire from Republicans when he covered Caroline County teachers who demonstrated with other National Education Association members for better pay at the state capital, Richmond. At least one reader accused him of espousing a "socialist agenda."

The only real bright spot was ad revenue, Tony reports. He claims that in a year or two his publication would have been paying its way. But the frustrations and disappointments did not encourage the Ares family to bet their house and remaining life savings on the risky venture. The *Virginia Connection* ceased publication in July 2019.

Would he try again? "If I ever had an influx of money? Yes," Tony answered. He said he still believes that if he could concentrate on the business end of things and hire some professionals for newsgathering, it might work.

Meanwhile, the Areses kept a Facebook presence called "One Caroline Virginia" and kept a space-holding but inactive *Virginia Connection* website, just in case.

Some Caroline news is found in the two regional dailies. The *Richmond Times-Dispatch* considers Hanover County, Caroline County's neighbor to the south, to be solidly in its circulation area and covers some news in Caroline as well. The Richmond paper also operates a free-circulation weekly in Hanover, the *Mechanicsville Local*, which competed against Ashland's *Herald-Progress* for decades. As the *Herald-Progress's* fortunes waned, the *Mechanicsville Local* stepped up coverage of the entire county and started another free-circulation weekly, the *Ashland-Hanover Local*. The two papers successfully wrested the county's lucrative legal advertising away from the *Herald-Progress*, thus hastening the paid-circulation weekly's demise. Though smaller in size, the *Ashland-Hanover Local* fills some of the news vacuum left behind when the *Herald-Progress* failed.

Caroline's residents are lucky that they can still get occasional local stories in the Fredericksburg newspaper, and the person they can thank for that is Dawn Haun, a freelance reporter and photographer for the *Fredericksburg Free-Lance Star*. Now in her late fifties, Haun moved to Caroline County when she was five, and as a teenager she was already working in the news business part-time for the *Caroline Progress*. "When I was thirteen or fourteen, I worked down in the basement in the pressroom, wrapping newspapers to be mailed out and throwing them in the mailbags," Haun said. "I guess I have black ink in my veins."

Haun stayed with the *Caroline Progress* until 1997, when it changed hands. She took a job with the Fredericksburg daily as a graphic designer but returned to the *Progress* after Lakeway

Publishers bought it in 2008. "I came back as a photographer and graphic artist—a little bit of everything," she said. In 2015, she again left the paper and now runs her own business, Wagon Wheel Creations, which offers many of the services she learned in the newspaper industry, including photography, graphic design, marketing, and website design. For the past two years as an active freelancer for the Fredericksburg daily, she has covered Caroline County government meetings and public hearings and contributed photo features and other stories.

Still, the *Free Lance-Star* can devote only so much space to Caroline County, which represents only a small slice of the regional daily's circulation and ad revenue. For the most part, in 2020 news-thirsty residents of Bowling Green and Caroline County must depend on all-too-rare reports on crime or social hot topics from the Richmond TV news, the *Richmond Times-Dispatch*, and somewhat scattershot social media.

For a portion of the sort of local news, social events, and opinions that Caroline County readers once found tucked away and organized in the pages of their home county weekly, residents can comb through a variety of Facebook groups, websites, and other social media. That process can be exhausting, though, and it is easy to miss something unless the searcher is dedicated.

One of the most popular Facebook groups in the county is Caroline County, Virginia, Residents, which was started in 2015 by Steven Brodie Tucker, a Caroline middle-school teacher. Tucker and the site's co-administrator, Susan Sili (the wife of Jeff Sili, chairman of the Caroline County Board of Supervisors), strive to maintain a pleasing yet responsible balance of local news and opinion. "It's meant to be a positive mechanism for spreading news while trying to build up the community," Tucker said.

Because of the co-administrators' interests and connections, these pages carry a great deal of county government news and school news as well as notices about farmers' markets, fairs, and other community events, such as COVID-19 testing. They also offer pet and wildlife photos, scenic views, inquiries about where to get a good plumber or electrician, jokes, comments on local restaurants, and other ephemera, plus the unavoidable political crossfire in this year of COVID-19, Black Lives Matter demonstrations, and the presidential election.

Although useful, such Facebook groups do not offer the same experience as a traditional weekly newspaper—with its familiar organization of news, feature, editorial, sports, and church pages as well as, more important, its staff of dedicated news professionals who are paid to surface stories and report them. Still, they help Caroline County residents stay in touch and maintain some sense of identity—for the time being, anyway.

25

TO SCHOOL OR NOT TO
SCHOOL—A BURNING QUESTION

Macon

S tudents in the Bibb County School System have among the highest levels of poverty in the nation. That makes the decision on how to reopen in the fall of 2020 very difficult for the school board.

Many families don't have internet access, computers, or tablets. Although the system would provide computers or tablets, the student's home must have internet access to be eligible for digital instruction. Many teachers are not comfortable or skilled in digital instruction. And though digital learning is an option, registration for it closed in mid-July. The system is still devising the protocols for distanced learning. And the top-of-mind worry continues to be COVID.

After the pandemic hit and schools were closed in mid-March, through the Central Georgia COVID-19 Response & Recovery Fund, the Community Foundation of Central Georgia (CFCG) provided, among 103 grants totaling $1.26 million, a $15,000 grant to Houston County schools to fund internet access to 935 families. The Bibb County School System matched the foundation's grant. The CFCG also granted $28,500 to Baldwin County schools, northeast of Macon–Bibb County, to provide 125 hot spots with data for six months for families of students in need of internet access.

Food was one of the biggest concerns, with such a high level of poverty among the students. The school system provided meals at various pick-up locations. The school board increased the school nutrition budget by $4.1 million over the year. "Costs are not just up in school nutrition," Ron Collier, the system's chief financial officer, said, "but for masks, super cleaning, counseling, and preparing for what we do if a student or school personnel comes down with COVID-19. All of that is in the planning phases."

"We've given out more food in seven months than we did in all of 2019," said Pastor Horace Holmes of World Changers Church–Macon, who is also a board member of the Middle Georgia Community Food Bank. The Food Bank has held food-distribution events all over Middle Georgia. In Macon–Bibb County, it works in collaboration with the city's three Rotary Clubs, the Community Church of God, Healing Experiences Ministries, Bibb Mount Zion, St. Paul AME World Changers, and Kingdom Life Church. Pastor Jason McClendon of Community Church of God has held ten food giveaways at his church, and he calculated they have given away forty-seven tons of beef, chicken, hot dogs, kids' packs, vegetables, canned goods, and bologna, along with household items such as paper towels, hand sanitizer, and dish washing and laundry detergent.

Sheriff's deputies had to be called in to guide traffic for a food-distribution event at Pastor McClendon's church on July 29 as a line of cars wrapped around the block. World Changers, Navicent Health, and the Middle Georgia Food Bank had another food-distribution event on July 31, and the line of cars wrapped around a huge parking lot. Community Church of God has also tested 20,000 residents for COVID-19. "There's no infrastructure in place for mass testing. Our community is just ravaged," Pastor McClendon said.

The Bibb County School System is one of 181 school systems in the State of Georgia. Over the summer, school districts in this system, in particular those in Middle Georgia, have been inconsistent regarding starting dates for the fall and whether they should return to face-to-face instruction. Most districts plan to start in early August, but the Bibb County School System has pushed its start date back to September 8, after Labor Day. "By pushing the time back," added Collier, "we can make more educated decisions."

A third of the system's students, 7,500, have registered for online instruction. "We're using this time," Collier noted, "to work through all the issues we could face and preparing staff and students. The key is to move, respond, and be flexible." The Bibb County School System has 24,110 students in thirty-seven facilities. The Houston County School System, with 28,150 students, has delayed its opening until August 6, just two days later than originally planned. It reports that 77 percent of parents have decided to send their children to face-to-face classes; 15.4 percent choose to have their children get digital instruction; and 38.7 percent plan to have their children ride a school bus.

In the South, you know something is serious when it affects the Church of Gridiron Philosophy. The Georgia High School Association, which governs high school sports, announced on July 20 that it is delaying the start of the football season by two weeks because of COVID. Workouts with pads aren't allowed until August 1. That is just as well. Middle Georgia has experienced a heat wave with temperatures in the high nineties and topping 100 degrees some days. The normal summer pattern of heat followed by an afternoon thundershower, followed by high humidity, hasn't changed much with one exception: the after-noon showers have been rare.

Bibb County schools originally considered three options. One is full face-to-face instruction; another is a hybrid model where one group of students would attend in-person classes on Mondays and Tuesdays and the other group on Thursdays and Fridays, with digital instruction on the days students are not in classes and deep cleaning of facilities on Wednesdays. The third option is digital-only learning. After announcing the three options, the school board went into executive session and decided to eliminate the hybrid option for being "too disruptive." But there was another reason. At the same school board meeting, a Bibb County health official told the board that the community is already in the "high-risk" category that will mandate digital-only learning.

Parents and teachers have been leery of resuming face-to-face instruction. Bibb County surveyed employees to identify any personnel at risk, but Superintendent Curtis Jones admitted that some personnel didn't feel comfortable with the survey because "they didn't trust the system."

The county also surveyed parents. Dr. Jones wrote in his blog, "Our survey of parents showed that many parents are interested in a virtual option—even if we are able to return to school in person. We are working on a plan or option that will allow parents to choose to do so if they feel like they are not ready to send their child back to the school setting just yet."

Macon–Bibb County has a high number of private schools, most formed after the *Brown v. Board of Education* Supreme Court decision of 1954 and with tuition averaging $15,000 annually. Most are planning to open in August.

Stratford Academy, established in 1960, will welcome students to campus on August 19, and face masks are required for all students from the third to twelfth grade. Temperatures will be taken daily, and social distancing will be practiced. According to the school's website, "Lunchroom service . . . will be utilizing a pre-order online system, and food will be served in pre-packaged containers and will be consumed either in the lunchroom on a rotating schedule to limit mixing, inside the classroom, or in our outdoor spaces."

Mount de Sales Academy, a Catholic private school established in 1876, will open its campus on August 12. First Presbyterian Day School, founded in 1970, the same year the public schools integrated, will open for face-to-face instruction on August 13. There are several other private academies in the area, but the other major ones are Windsor, Central Fellowship Christian, Tattnail Square, and two Montessori schools.

There are also two state-sponsored charter schools. One is the Academy for Classical Education, K–12, first chartered by the Bibb County School System in 2013 but in 2019 becoming a state-chartered school. There is no tuition, but the school uses a weighted lottery system to select students and is at the north end of the county. It begins classes on August 3. One of the differences between being chartered by the local school board and being chartered by the State Charter Schools Commission of Georgia—other than funding and control—is that the state schools can accept out-of-county students.

The other charter is Cirrus Academy, opened in 2016, located in an urban area of the county, with a predominately African American student body. The school specializes in a STEAM (science, technology, engineering, arts, mathematics) curriculum. When the school opens on August 10, it will be virtual. Of all the private and charter schools, only Mount de Sales will provide limited transportation for its students living in Warner Robins.

The racial breakdown of the public-school student population, according to the Georgia Department of Education, is more Black than white, with a few Hispanic and Asian students, except for the Academy for Classical Education, which has 264 Black, 1,240 white, and 206 Hispanic and Asian students.

Many school systems around the state decided to open only with virtual instruction, including the largest systems in the state: Atlanta (54,946 students), Fulton County (94,000 students), Gwinnett County (180,000 students), and Cobb County (112,000 students).

The Richmond County School System (34,691 students) will open with virtual and face-to-face instruction but gave parents until July 27 to sign up for virtual instruction. That system has also moved its start date back to September 8. The Muscogee County School System (32,944 students) will open for digital instruction only on August 17, and the Savannah-Chatham County School System (38,100 students) will begin virtual-only classes on August 19.

The Cobb County School System's superintendent of schools, Chris Ragsdale, said during the system's July board meeting, "I know we need to get back to face-to-face instruction. That is why we tried to offer parents two options—in person and virtual—to start the school year. Unfortunately, public-health guidance does not make that possible."

On May 3, the Georgia Department of Public Health had reported a seven-day average of 667.6 COVID cases. A month later the seven-day average jumped to 782.7. By July 2, the seven-day average soared to 3,269, and the state began setting new records almost daily. By July 31, the average was 3,615.4, with a one-day high of 4,836 confirmed cases. The highest rate of confirmed COVID cases is in the 18–29 age bracket with 45,323 cases and 28 deaths. There have been 2,039 cases in children not yet a year old and 12,290 cases in school-age children. Fortunately, there has been only one death in that age group. By July 31, the state was averaging almost 45 deaths daily over a seven-day period. Health-care workers throughout the state have also been hit hard, with 11,301 of them contracting COVID and more than 50 of them dying.

On Friday, July 17, Dr. Kathleen Toomey, the Georgia Department of Public Health commissioner, said the state is experiencing widespread community transmission of COVID-19.

Middle Georgia's largest hospital, Navicent Health, a 637-bed level-one trauma center, has been on diversion during periods in July. In a written statement, the hospital acknowledged it was "currently at capacity" but added that the situation wasn't due to COVID. Navicent had to send patients as far away as Rome, Georgia, 150 miles from Macon. That was confirmed by Chuck Hufstetler, a Republican state senator who is also a full-time assistant anesthesiologist in Rome. In a video stream, Hufstetler said, "We were the closest ICU [intensive-care unit] bed open. Macon is a long way from Rome, so there's a lot of ICUs filled up right now." On July 31, Houston Medical Center's ICU/CCU (critical-care unit), medical/surgery unit, and ER were, according to the Georgia Hospital Resource Report, "saturated." Six hospitals in the state were either on total diversion or at COVID-19 saturation.

Exactly how many COVID patients are being treated by Navicent is unknown because the hospital decided not to release that information over the objections of local media outlets, including the *Telegraph*, the area's daily newspaper. The *Telegraph*, owned by McClatchy, the second-largest local media company in the nation, has been in unchartered waters.

McClatchy filed for Chapter 11 bankruptcy protection in February. The company was up for grabs and ended up in the hands of Chatham Asset Management, a hedge fund based in New Jersey, ending 160 years of McClatchy family ownership. Even with diminished ranks, though, the local newspaper has managed to provide daily COVID-19 updates and has reported on the mask controversy between Governor Brian Kemp and Mayor Keisha Lance Bottoms of Atlanta.

The political pressure to open the school year with face-to-face instruction is tremendous. On top of the pressure from President Donald Trump, Secretary of Education Betsy DeVos has threatened to withhold funds from schools that don't open. White House Press Secretary Kayleigh McEnany said during a briefing, "The president has said unmistakably that he wants schools to open. And when he says open, he means open in full, kids being able to attend each and every day at their school. The science should not stand in the way of this."

The pressure also comes from Kemp, who during a press conference on July 17 played down the risks of opening schools with face-to-face instruction. "I personally think once kids start going back—it's not going to be easy, there are going to be challenges, but every new school year has a challenge. We're going to have cases that break out in schools, either with personnel or perhaps students, just like you do with a stomach bug or a flu or anything else. Our schools know how to handle those situations."

The trouble is that COVID-19 is not a stomach bug or flu, and in the spring our schools were not prepared to handle the outbreak when it occurred. At that same July 17 press conference, Kemp also blamed the media for scaring parents. "When newspapers and the media only write about one side of the story, and they're not writing about really the lack of risk—I mean everybody's having risk. People that have been working in grocery stores through all this, people that have been in critical infrastructure jobs go to work every day with risk, our law enforcement—protecting peaceful demonstrators, going after those that were disruptive—they face risk every day from the coronavirus. We have to be very smart about how we do this."

On July 21, the Macon–Bibb County Commission voted to require masks in public and backed up its decision with penalties. Mayor Robert Reichert had already issued an executive order "encouraging" mask use. But on July 27 the commission received a letter from him saying, "After receipt of numerous emails advocating for both sides of this legislation, and deliberate and protracted thought and reflection, it is with deep respect and commitment that I hereby VETO the Emergency Ordinance calling for masks to be mandated in public spaces, as passed by the Commission on July 21st."

Interesting side note: During the July 21 meeting, commissioners also voted five to four to remove two Confederate monuments located prominently downtown. On July 28, Martin Bell, the leader of the Military Order of the Stars and Bars, filed an eleven-page lawsuit in Bibb Superior Court to halt the moving of the monuments. The lawsuit states that the commissioners who voted to move the memorials are carrying out a "racially-motivated action designed for political purposes to placate the mob mentalities current in American society."

All of this is playing out before the August 11 runoff election that will decide the mayor's race, two commission seats, and a school board position.

Students, their parents, and school personnel are waiting for the other COVID shoe to drop. If the area stays in the red zone with hospital beds at capacity, it is thought that opening campuses will only lead to disaster. While younger folks could probably survive a match with COVID, the same can't be said for those who teach, clean, and administer their schools, not to mention their families.

26

WHAT WILL "NORMAL" MEAN AFTER COVID-19?

McKeesport

I n a year filled with disappointing cancellations, the one that may have stung the most here in McKeesport is the cancellation of International Village.

The three-day food and music festival was created in 1960 as part of an Old Home Week celebration to lure people downtown. The first International Village was a modest affair, with food vendors representing ten of the nationalities that immigrated to western Pennsylvania in the late nineteenth and early twentieth centuries: Greek, Polish, Ukrainian, Serbian, Hungarian, Italian, Croatian, Romanian, Irish, and Jewish.

Old Home Week didn't return in 1961, but International Village did, now representing fifteen nationalities. The event shifted to Renziehausen Park, which could better accommodate parking and crowds. Folk dancing and ethnic music became a big part of the event. By 1965, the *Pittsburgh Press* reported that International Village was "drawing enough attention to challenge the city's steel mills as its hallmark," with an estimated 60,000 visitors over three days.

Even after the collapse of Pittsburgh's steel industry and the resulting economic decline of McKeesport in the 1980s, International Village remained a point of pride. A few years ago, the city expanded the event again, adding craft booths, vendors, carnival games for kids, and demonstrations by the McKeesport Senior High School robotics club, the McKeesport Police K-9 unit, and others. If Memorial Day marks the unofficial beginning of summer, for generations of McKeesport schoolchildren (including me), International Village has marked its unofficial end.

International Village had always been there throughout the hard times—until the COVID-19 pandemic. With Pennsylvania officials prohibiting all outdoor gatherings of more than 250 people, McKeesport officials considered staging a very small event, with no entertainment and take-out food only. But in June, Mayor Michael Cherepko of McKeesport announced International Village would be canceled after the church groups who form the backbone of the festival said they didn't want to participate. "The vast majority of them weren't interested in having the village this year in any way, shape, or form," he said. "They're concerned about COVID-19 and concerned about having volunteers at their booths."

For about ten years, our community nonprofit news website Tube City Online offered livestreaming coverage of International Village. Our planning each year included lining up sponsors to pay for the webcast, repairing broken equipment, and scrounging replacements. It may be a blessing that this year's festival has been canceled because the stress of keeping our other operations online during the pandemic is wearing all of us a bit thin. Our freelance writers are struggling to find different ways to report the same story again and again—things are canceled, people are stuck at home, the number of COVID-19 cases continues rising. At our internet radio station, a popular Wednesday night rock show hosted by Eric and Judy Wisniewski, *The Electric Crush*, dropped live in-studio performances by local and touring bands. Another host who does a bluegrass show was forced to self-isolate for fourteen days after being exposed to the virus.

Some municipalities have resumed in-person public meetings, but most are still holding them electronically, which—as more than one of our writers has lamented—makes follow-up questions difficult, if not impossible. Many of those questions lately have revolved around the planned reopening of local schools in a few weeks. Several districts have announced that all classes will be conducted over the internet, at least for the first nine weeks of the school year. As of now, McKeesport Area School District is giving parents the option of sending their kids either to school or having them take classes online.

Almost every parent, teacher, and school bus driver I know think that holding in-person classes is going to be difficult while the pandemic continues to rage and while so many people—for political and ideological reasons—refuse to wear face masks or practice social distancing. The parents and teachers I talked with also agree that once the virus hits any school, it will race through classrooms, and children will bring it home to their parents and grandparents. All of the usual maladies—from chicken pox and norovirus to mononucleosis and lice—already wreak havoc on elementary and high schools. It is inconceivable that COVID-19 won't do the same.

Yet here in Pennsylvania and across the country, we have pressed forward. In late July, the Pennsylvania Interscholastic Athletic Association, which sanctions school sports, announced the fall schedule would continue as planned. On the one hand, this decision was predictable. In western Pennsylvania, high school football is our second-largest religion after Roman Catholicism. This region, after all, produced Mike Ditka, Dan Marino, Tony Dorsett, Joe Namath, Joe Montana, Johnny

Unitas, George Blanda, and scores of other high-profile college and professional football players and coaches. On Friday nights in September and October, Pittsburgh TV stations lead their 11:00 p.m. newscasts with high school football highlights and send their helicopters to cover games.

Proponents of resuming in-person school activities cite the need for kids to socialize with one another and the communal benefits of learning together as a group. Football fans argue that if students don't play this fall, they won't be recruited by universities for scholarships. For many poor families in the Monongahela Valley, sports scholarships remain one of the two avenues to a college degree that doesn't involve going into tens of thousands of dollars of debt. (The other is to enlist in the armed services.)

The Pennsylvania Interscholastic Athletic Association reportedly reconsidered the decision to begin fall athletics after Governor Tom Wolf recommended that schools postpone all contact sports until January. Wolf's recommendation—not an order, a recommendation—set off a new wave of vitriol on social media and talk radio about "government tyranny" and "hysteria." On Twitter, Paul Zeise, a sports columnist for the *Pittsburgh Post-Gazette* and talk-show host on KDKA-FM, railed, "'Flatten the curve to save hospitals!!!' had become 'lock everyone up and shut everything down until there are zero cases of COVID-19!!'" Another KDKA-FM host, Colin Dunlap, said people who wanted to cancel fall sports are "scared to death of their own shadow."

The COVID-19 deniers are extremely vocal and strident, but they also seem to be in the minority. One friend who has a nine-year-old stepdaughter is not optimistic about the prospect of sending her and her fellow pupils back to classrooms. "By the third week in September, most open schools will be closed again due to outbreaks, and sports will be canceled," he predicted on Facebook. "Hopefully it won't result in too many dead kids. But does this really surprise anyone in a nation that has pretty much decided that school shootings are a way of life and children's lives are expendable?"

For much of the twentieth century in places such as McKeesport, manufacturing jobs paid wages that were high enough to allow one parent to stay home. These days, most parents here need to go back to work, which means they need to do something with their kids. Ready or not, that "something" means going back to classrooms. In poor communities like ours, where 74 percent of students are eligible for free school lunches (compared to 44 percent on average across Pennsylvania), the hot breakfast and lunch served in the cafeterias might be the healthiest two meals those kids get each day.

The situation is further complicated by America's privatized, often sketchy infrastructure. Tube City Online has a hard time getting a reliable internet signal for our International Village broadcasts each year because the two largest broadband providers in the Pittsburgh area—Comcast and Verizon—don't prioritize service to low-income communities such as McKeesport.

So even if a parent is able to stay home with their school-age child during the period of online-only classes, many families lack the high-speed broadband necessary to support applications such as Zoom and Google Classrooms. In the school shutdown during the spring, school districts were distributing 4G Wi-Fi hot spots to families and turning up the signals on their own Wi-Fi networks to provide some access, but it was a patchwork effort at best.

The pandemic has exposed the weak foundation of the current American way of life in places such as McKeesport, including utilities that function more for the benefit of shareholders than of customers; school districts that are overwhelmed trying to plug gaps in the social services network; and families who are always one or two paychecks away from calamity. It has also provided evidence that the concept of collective action—necessary for a functional democracy—has been undermined by years of rhetoric that prioritizes individual needs and wants over the common good.

Yes, I am tired of wearing face masks, too. I want to have big, noisy, crowded events such as International Village again. (I would be content just having a date night with my wife that involves us leaving the house.) And although I don't have kids in school, I understand how important (and fun) hometown high school and college sports are.

I want to get back to our normal routines. But as Americans continue to stumble through this pandemic, we really need to think hard about what we consider normal. Much of what we accept isn't tolerated in other industrialized countries. If our "normal" wasn't so good in the first place, should we really be trying to return to it?

27

SOUTH TEXAS IS A BAD ALGORITHM RIGHT NOW

McAllen

The out-of-control COVID-19 crisis in South Texas is a deadly numbers game gone frighteningly wrong.

It has resulted in more than 1,400 deaths and 44,000 coronavirus cases in the region. The positivity rate has far surpassed the statewide recommendation of keeping it at 10 percent, and bodies are stacking up in refrigerated trucks parked outside hospitals and alongside the interstate. Resources are starting to trickle into the region, but they could be too little, too late.

In the Rio Grande Valley, the situation is inflamed by fighting among various communities over Coronavirus Aid, Relief, and Economic Security (CARES) Act disbursement funds from county and state officials, slow testing and tracking methods, and two questionable recovery field hospitals supported by federal money given to two companies that culled favor with the Trump administration—one a nonprofit that runs migrant detention facilities for children and the other a for-profit that builds border walls. In Hidalgo County, one of the nation's worst hot spots for coronavirus, Judge Richard Cortez has likened the pandemic to a "tsunami" that has quadrupled in cases since June 2020.

A month ago, the county had only a dozen or so health investigators to conduct contact tracing for more than 7,000 active cases, the Hidalgo County Health Authority told me. More were added with resources provided by Governor Greg Abbott. But many people here are asymptomatic and completely unaware of the contagion they carry and bring to their families, coworkers, and those they pass by on the streets.

Up to this point, July 21 was the deadliest day in the county's history of this virus: 49 people died from the novel coronavirus; 339 new cases were identified; there were 7,286 active cases that day, and 1,080 were hospitalized, including 257 in intensive-care units, the county reported.

My husband was one of the lucky ones who walked out of an area hospital that day after spending ten days hospitalized for COVID-19. During this time, he received two life-saving doses of plasma donated from other coronavirus survivors. One batch came from a New York donor, we were told.

He may have caught coronavirus at a June 29 news conference where the head of the county Health Authority left early to take an urgent phone call in which he learned that he had COVID-19. Since his release, my husband has remained self-isolated on oxygen. We have been told that he could test positive for up to ninety days.

Imagine my family's dismay when my three adult children and I received early-morning phone calls on Sunday, August 2, from different state-funded contact tracers to alert us all that we "may have been exposed to coronavirus."

My husband had tested positive twenty-one days earlier and been hospitalized for that period. According to Centers for Disease Control guidelines, we should have been informed within three days of his diagnosis so we could mitigate community spread. Of course, we knew he had COVID-19, and we all self-isolated and monitored ourselves for symptoms in our McAllen home. He had been isolated in a wing of the house since he first began feeling feverish on July 1, despite getting negative results on two COVID-19 tests. How many people could he have infected if he had relied on the faulty tests? How many other families or friends of those infected went weeks before learning they had "been exposed to coronavirus"?

More resources are repeatedly requested by hospital administrators and three local county judges, who met for a roundtable discussion with U.S. senator John Cornyn on August 11 at the Regional Academic Health Center of the University of Texas Rio Grande Valley in Harlingen. President Guy Bailey said that the university's School of Medicine is running four COVID-19 testing facilities in South Texas. The university was also funded by the state to conduct contact tracing and hired 191 contact tracers to locate and inform individuals that they have been in contact with someone with coronavirus in South Texas.

"If there was ever a time to be grateful for a School of Medicine, this is it," Bailey said. "I couldn't be prouder of what our School of Medicine has done to adapt and work with this crisis." Indeed, it is a point of pride, but as Dr. John Krouse, dean of the School of Medicine, told the group, "Testing without contact tracing is ineffective."

And that is basically what happened here in Hidalgo County for several weeks. Krouse said that the university is testing about 1,200 people per day and that 35 percent are positive—that is one in every three people tested, far more than the state-recommended goal of a 10 percent positivity rate. Krouse said tests now "have a twenty-four-hour turnaround."

But just a few weeks earlier, test results were taking upward of seven to ten days, and that time lag led to higher infection rates and community spread, Cortez said. "It's a disaster, and we cannot continue this way," he told Senator Cornyn on August 11. "We need rapid, rapid testing."

My eldest son and I waited seven days to learn we were negative after testing on July 16. We self-isolated, but it was scary to imagine how many people circulated in the community spreading the germs unchecked before they got results.

With news media from all over the world reporting on what is happening in the United States, it is clear that infections in South Texas are a bad algorithm that is repeating and replicating with uncontrolled speed. Cornyn said the Rio Grande Valley has been sent $530 million to help hospitals, public schools, public transportation, airports, and even public housing as part of CARES Act funds.

Although there is no doubt that this money will help, it seems as if it is coming much, much too late. Most hospitals have been at capacity for several weeks. The death and infection counts are rising daily, and each time we think we have reached our shock maximum, the next day brings even worse news.

There are also serious questions about how many millions of dollars are being spent on two step-down facilities that have been virtually unused because they are set up for low-acuity patients, even while hundreds are in ICUs, not ready for these convalescent facilities—one at the converted McAllen Convention Center, the other in Harlingen at a converted conference facility. The Texas Division of Emergency Management issued a contract for the Harlingen field hospital to a for-profit company that builds border wall segments throughout the Southwest. The McAllen facility is being run by a nonprofit that operates controversial migrant-detention facilities for children, two of which have been shut down.

As I reported for *Border Report*, BCFS Health and Human Services converted the McAllen Convention Center into a

250-bed capacity facility for recovering COVID-19 patients. But as of August 11, only eight patients had been sent to the facility for free care, which was paid for with CARES Act funds. The converted Casa de Amistad conference center in Harlingen is being run by SLSCO, a general contracting and construction-management firm that has received more than half a billion dollars in federal government contracts to build segments of border wall throughout Texas and southern California. The facility had not helped a single patient as of August 11.

Local hospital administrators told me that the lower-level acute care available at these facilities is not what most patients need: they need high-level intensive care, which the facilities are not licensed to provide.

So, are the recovery facilities a good use of federal funds? I put the question to Senator Cornyn at a news conference on August 11 immediately following the roundtable discussion, and he responded: "The big concern with the spike in cases was that it would overrun the hospital facilities, hospital ICU beds, the number of ventilators and the like, and so we worked to bend that curve. The possibility that there would need to be additional surge facilities built is what those facilities are for, and the fact that they are not widely needed is actually good news. But they are there if they are needed."

Yes, but how many families will they help if they remain virtually empty?

I submitted several requests with the state for information on how much these contracts are worth and the names of other companies that put in bids and for how much, but the information was not provided. My daily requests to the Texas Division of Emergency Management have largely gone unacknowledged and unanswered. I find it curious that no other companies seem to be getting big-dollar border contracts, even during a pandemic.

28

IN RURAL VIRGINIA,
A TALE OF TWO
CONGRESSIONAL DISTRICTS

Bowling Green

Virginia is an irregularly shaped state spanning both sides of the Chesapeake Bay and sliced into segments by rivers and mountains. One of the original thirteen colonies, Virginia once claimed land from the Atlantic Ocean to the Mississippi River. Kentucky was sliced off in 1792, and West Virginia was split off in 1863 in the midst of the Civil War, a war that produced wounds that have still not healed.

Because of geography, rapid population growth along the Interstate 95 and 64 corridors, and a good bit of gerrymandering, the state's eleven Congressional Districts have developed unusual shapes over the years. The First and Seventh Congressional Districts—where I have lived, worked on newspapers, and voted since 1987—run roughly north and south and parallel one another. And they make pretty good specimens if you are trying to get a sense of what's going on at ground level in this strange and monumental election season.

Not that figuring what is going on is easy. For one thing, so much is different this time around. Gone, thanks to COVID-19, are opportunities for candidates to meet tens of thousands of voters at the Hanover Tomato Festival and the State Fair of

Virginia in Caroline County. Gone, too, are many smaller county fairs as well as the food, beverage, and music festivals. COVID-19 is not the only difference this time around. There is also the rapidly changing face of the media, which dictates different strategies for the candidates and tosses into elections an element of the unknown.

Although the First and Seventh Districts have a lot in common, they also have exhibited some differences over the years.

Virginia's First District, sometimes billed as "America's First" because it included Jamestown for more than a century, includes Caroline and Hanover Counties, where I wrote for two weekly newspapers until their demise in 2018. It has sent Republicans to Congress since 1977, usually by comfortable margins. This is still rural, small-town Virginia, although proximity to rapidly growing metropolitan areas has brought suburbs and demographic changes.

This year's First District race pits a longshot Democratic nominee, Qasim Rashid, against Rob Wittman, the Republican who has represented the district since 2007.

Wittman, who is sixty-one, was first elected in 2007 in a special election after the incumbent died. He was reelected in 2008 and has been reelected every two years since then. Wittman worked for twenty years with the Virginia Department of Health as an environmental health specialist and later for the Division of Shellfish Sanitation. Regarded as somewhat moderate compared to current Republicans, Wittman commutes to Washington, DC, from his home in Montross, near George Washington's birthplace, experiencing the same highway gridlock as many of his constituents. He has been a champion of the local seafood industry, is strong on veterans' affairs, and is pushing for greater broadband access in rural communities, which is in tune with many of the voters in his district.

The thirty-eight-year-old Qasim Rashid of Garrisonville was born in Rawalpindi, Pakistan. He earned a bachelor's degree from the University of Illinois at Chicago and a JD from the University of Richmond School of Law. He has worked as a human rights lawyer and written several books, including *The Wrong Kind of Muslim*, which *Kirkus Reviews* called "a heartfelt memoir of Muslim-on-Muslim discrimination and oppression" in his native Pakistan. Rashid won the Democratic nomination for Congress in the June 23 primary, narrowly defeating Vangie Williams, who was the Democratic nominee in 2018 and gave Wittman his strongest challenge to date.

Virginia's Seventh District has also been considered a GOP sure bet for decades. It is less rural and arguably more cosmopolitan than the First. It sent Republicans to Congress from 1971 to 2016, yet in 2020 it is regarded as one of the nation's key battleground districts.

First-term congresswoman Abigail Spanberger, a forty-one-year-old Democrat from Glen Allen, seeks reelection. A former teacher and CIA officer, Spanberger flipped this once-Republican stronghold in 2018, defeating the two-term Republican incumbent, Dave Brat, by fewer than 6,800 votes. But this didn't all happen all at once. Attitudes within the district and the geography of the district itself had changed.

Republican Eric Cantor had been elected to Congress in the Seventh District in 2000 and rapidly climbed up the ladder. He was chosen to be the House minority whip in 2009 and then moved up to House majority leader in 2011. For years, Cantor easily bested the sacrificial lambs that the Democrats put up in his district. Then it all imploded when he lost his own party's nomination in the 2014 primary, becoming the first sitting House majority leader in history to lose his congressional seat.

Cantor lost to a political neophyte—Dave Brat, an economics professor at Randolph-Macon College in Hanover County and a darling of the Tea Party and several conservative radio talk show hosts who portrayed Cantor as someone who spent too much time in the nation's capital and too little time tending to the concerns of his constituents.

In a *Washington Post* interview in 2016, Cantor said, "It turned into an anyone-but-Cantor vote. But it was also a little bit of canary in the coal mine." Cantor did not elaborate on what message the dead canary was sending, but after his defeat in the primary, he resigned his seat, and Brat was elected to finish his term and then won reelection in 2014 and again in 2016.

That year in the presidential election, Donald Trump won the Seventh District with 51 percent to Hillary Clinton's 44 percent. But in 2018, the Seventh District again confounded the pundits when another political newcomer, Spanberger, won with 50 percent of the vote to Brat's 48.

Voter dissatisfaction with Brat and two years of Trump played a role in this turnover, but so did redistricting. In 2014, a panel of federal judges had ruled that Virginia's congressional map violated the Fourteenth Amendment of the U.S. Constitution by packing Black voters into the Third Congressional District. The court-ordered redistricting moved Hanover County, which is 86.7 percent white and solidly Republican, from the Seventh to the already conservative First District, which affected the 2016 and 2018 congressional elections in both districts. Spanberger began her well-financed campaign for reelection in 2020 by launching local television ads long before she even knew who she was running against.

Meanwhile, the pandemic played a role in the selection of Spanberger's opponent. A much-delayed Republican nominating convention finally took place on July 18, where a state legislator, Nick Freitas of Culpeper, who is forty-one, defeated five other candidates. Freitas, born in California, is a former army Green Beret with two tours in Iraq. He had been elected to the state House of Delegates in 2015, winning reelection twice. In 2018, he unsuccessfully sought the Republican nomination to challenge U.S. senator Tim Kaine. His campaign started running TV ads in the district on August 12 that emphasized his family's dedication to service, starting with his father, a police officer, and his mother, a nurse, and on his own decision to enlist in the army when he was just out of high school, three months after the terrorist attacks on September 11, 2001.

One certainty is that these two races—Wittman versus Rashid in the First District, Spanberger versus Freitas in the Seventh—will be vastly different from past campaigns. The ongoing pandemic and uncertainties about mail-in ballots are factors, as is the rapidly changing nature of media.

Just a decade ago, local media were much healthier than they are now, according to Dr. Stephen J. Farnsworth, director of the Center for Leadership and Media Studies at the University of Mary Washington, in Fredericksburg. That poor health has had an effect on politics.

"Medium-sized papers were able to invest the resources necessary to cover at least some statewide matters themselves," Farnsworth said, "and even local weeklies would have some stories about the world beyond one's home communities. With all the cutbacks required in the financially challenged environment of local news, there is much less attention to regional or statewide politics, and that makes it very hard for challengers, and even incumbents, to receive much attention." But incumbents are better known, so "they benefit from an environment where politics generates less media attention."

One result: candidates do more on the web "and hope that a significant number of voters notice their efforts," Farnsworth said. COVID-19 has accelerated that trend. "Candidates really have to be online almost exclusively during the pandemic," Farnsworth said.

That shift, in turn, has raised a challenge: "The biggest problem with social media is misinformation," Farnsworth said. "Individual politicians and/or their partisan supporters have decided that deceit really pays off in politics. So there is a lot of false information out there. There has always been a misinformation problem in political discourse, but social media outlets allow lies to move faster and to be distributed more widely than ever before."

To help understand how things have changed from as little as four years ago, particularly in the First District, I also went to Matt Rowe, the First District Democratic chairman. In 2016, Rowe, then thirty-five, was the Democrats' nominee for Congress in the First District. This was also the first congressional election after a court-ordered redistricting, under which the Seventh became more competitive and the First even more Republican. "The political makeup definitely changed," Rowe said.

On top of that, it was a presidential election year, so voter turnout was higher than in off years. He lost decisively. "I'll be honest; it was going to be very uphill to begin with. I did not know how the Trump factor would affect the election," Rowe said in reference to a strong showing by the Trump–Pence ticket in rural Virginia. "It's not unfair. You play the hand you are dealt."

But "in 2020 it is completely different," Rowe said. "Social media and Zoom can be used to provide content that will stand out. Rashid ran for state Senate last year. Often you get folks that come in—they don't have name recognition. Qasim has a quarter million followers on Twitter. He is a perfect candidate in some ways."

Rowe added, "One of drawbacks, though, is if you are good at speaking to a crowd, and there are no crowds. It's hard to imagine how this could be any more different from 2016."

Qasim Rashid has a young but seasoned campaign manager, Ayodele Okeowo, who has worked hard to confront the challenges of 2020. Okeowo said this is his fifth political campaign and his fourth as campaign manager. He was the director of the presidential campaign of Pete Buttigieg in the southeastern United States.

"The objective of any campaign is to get to the voters, and it is extremely difficult now to get before the voters and express ourselves," Okeowo said. "Digital and virtual communications offer opportunities, but even that is difficult in areas where broadband access is limited, as it is in rural Virginia."

"It's trial and error. Without major events to go to, it is difficult to get our message across. It is not a one-size-fits-all solution." Okeowo mentioned the series of debates taking place between Rashid and the Republican incumbent, Wittman. Small gatherings of nine or ten people are also in the works.

The first of those encounters took place on August 20 at a Criminal Justice Forum and Debate at the Rappahannock Regional Criminal Justice Academy in Spotsylvania County. Appearing before an audience that was mainly law officers or retired officers, both candidates said they do not support "defunding" the police. Their approaches to preventing police brutality and overreach are quite different, however. Rashid said he supported national standards. Wittman argued for state and local control.

In the Seventh District, Deborah Caprio of Spotsylvania County was a grassroots volunteer in Spanberger's campaign in

2018 and has been involved in the campaign's early stages this year, though she misses the person-to-person contact. "We used to get training and meet at a campaign office two or three days a week," Caprio said. "There is no campaign office now."

In an August 16 email to volunteers, Spanberger acknowledged the changes: "I know what you're thinking: not another Zoom. Believe me, I understand. Everything we do these days is virtual: committee meetings, caucus calls, town halls, meet and greets, phone banking—you name it, we're executing it online! Both my Congressional office and our campaign team are adapting to this challenging climate in every way we can."

29

A LOCAL ELECTION, SCHOOL REOPENINGS, AND THE PANDEMIC

Macon

Macon–Bibb County will have a new mayor come January 1, 2021. The nonpartisan race wasn't even close in the August 11 runoff that pit attorney and school board member Lester Miller against businessman Cliffard Whitby, with Miller taking 59 percent of the vote. There are 104,558 registered voters in the county, but only 38,520—36.8 percent—voted, a bit less than the 39 percent that voted in the 2013 mayoral election.

Miller touted his campaign as a broad coalition of citizens, while Whitby depended on a cadre of Black ministers from large and small congregations to support him. That cadre wasn't enough for Whitby, and it was visible evidence that the days of powerful preachers being able to guide their flocks—at least in Macon–Bibb County—are over. Black registered voters outnumber white voters in the county by 12,729, and yet Whitby could attract only 15,716 votes to Miller's 22,840. Whitby won the precincts considered majority Black but not by the expected margins. Miller won the majority-white precincts by a wide margin.

Reverend James Bumpus, PhD, who was head of the Macon–Bibb County Office of Small Business Affairs until 2018 and interim pastor at New Fellowship Missionary Baptist Church, said he is "heartbroken" by Whitby's loss. "The math favored us [the Black community], but we were unable to mobilize our community," said Bumpus, who expressed his concern that disillusionment and apathy among Black voters might have dampened turnout. "They don't believe the opportunity is there, even when state officials tell them the opportunity is there. When it comes to politics, there is a sense of unbelievability that there could be Black people in the highest decision-making roles." Historically, many Black legislators in the state House and Senate expressed concerns that consolidation of the Macon city and Bibb County governments might dilute Black voting strength as part of an overall Republican strategy.

This election was shaped by a force that none of the candidates in the runoff—for mayor, county commission, or school board—could have controlled or predicted: COVID-19. Certainly, the pandemic should receive part of the blame for lower turnout. Most houses of worship in the area were still meeting virtually, if at all. Standard ways of campaigning were tossed aside as candidates participated in Zoom debates and virtual town halls. The usual down-home glad-handing was nowhere to be found.

The local newspaper, the *Telegraph*, which used to cover all of Middle Georgia and is now owned by Chatham Asset Management (purchasing it from McClatchy), is but a shadow of its former self. In its heyday, when daily circulation topped 100,000, the newspaper had four political reporters, four editorial writers, and a newsroom with more than fifty reporters, plus others stationed in bureaus in Atlanta, Milledgeville, Houston, and Laurens Counties. Now there are four reporters—total.

In the past, the newspaper's editorial board took seriously its responsibility for informing the communities about political candidates. The newspaper sponsored community forums, interviewed and researched candidates' backgrounds, and invited members of the community to take part in the deliberations. All of that is ancient history now. The newspaper abandoned its editorial voice in February 2018; the mix of local and national columnists is drastically reduced; and letters to the editor are mostly abandoned.

Another great impact on turnout was the timing of the election. Instead of holding nonpartisan municipal elections in November to coincide with the presidential calendar when turnout is heaviest, lawmakers originally scheduled primary and nonpartisan elections for March—nine months before the offices would be vacated.

The primary and nonpartisan election of 2020 was originally slated for March 24. The date was postponed to May 19 and then again to June 9, all courtesy of COVID-19. Unlike in past elections, in this one there were plenty of new faces on the ballot to draw voters out because three commissioners retired, and another ran for mayor. Eight of nine commission seats were contested, along with the mayor's office, four of eight school board seats, and the district attorney's office. But the runoff attracted 1,600 fewer voters than the June 9 general primary.

Macon's first African American mayor, C. Jack Ellis, served two consecutive terms, from 1999 to 2007. After consolidation in 2012, each county district's racial mix was affected. When Ellis ran for mayor again in 2013, he was defeated in a runoff by incumbent mayor Robert Reichert, who still holds the office. Ellis ran for tax commissioner in 2016 and lost by 4,777 votes. It will be interesting to see if another African American runs for mayor any time soon; Reverend Bumpus can't see another candidate on the horizon, even though there are two long-serving African American commissioners. Three other major cities in Georgia—Atlanta, Savannah, and Augusta—have Black mayors.

The COVID-19 pandemic has been wreaking havoc in Georgia. Since the pandemic began, 5,576 Georgians have died from COVID-19. Schools are opening as COVID-19 hot spots continue to pop up throughout the state. Atlanta is identified nationally as one of the top-ten hot spots in the country. A White House report leaked to the *Atlanta Journal-Constitution* said that Georgia had the highest rate of new COVID-19 cases in a seven-day period in mid-August. The report riled up Governor Brian Kemp—who quickly blamed the media rather than admit his missteps.

In an op-ed published on August 23 in the *Atlanta Journal-Constitution*, Kemp wrote, "Georgia is making progress in the fight against COVID-19, but you wouldn't know it from reading the state's flagship newspaper. . . . The editorialized front page is crawling with sensational 'news' that undermines confidence in state agencies and school leaders." Kemp also charged the *Constitution's* editorial board with printing "a list of baseless grievances coupled with a clickbait headline." Kemp continued, "During this crisis, the *AJC* has turned into a tabloid rag—appealing to supermarket shoppers waiting in line, six feet from their neighbor. Since the paper of record refuses to live up to their mantra of 'compelling, credible and complete' coverage, I'll do it for them." He then gave his take on the still high but falling statistics.

Kemp forgot the old axiom, "Never argue with someone who buys ink by the barrel," but he did decide to end his feud with Mayor Keisha Lance Bottoms of Atlanta and dropped his lawsuit against Atlanta over Bottoms's mandatory-mask order. Kemp also lifted his restrictions against local governments instituting their own mask mandates. He did insert a caveat that counties or cities could mandate masks only if COVID cases reached 100 cases per 100,000 people over a fourteen-day period. It was an empty requirement: only two of the state's 159 counties were below that threshold.

When schools opened in Paulding County, north of Atlanta, on August 3, COVID came to school, too. North Paulding High School was the scene of the viral video showing kids crowded in a hallway, most without masks. The school district called mask wearing a "personal choice." The student who shot the scene and posted it on social media was suspended but then later reinstated after appearances on national television. By the end of the first week of school, fifty-four teachers, staff, and students had tested positive for the virus. The COVID rate in the county was 193 per 100,000 as of August 29. The district closed the school for five days to give it a deep cleaning and reopened using a hybrid model where students would have face-to-face instruction only two days a week.

Cherokee County shut down face-to-face instruction in three of its six high schools. More than 1,100 of its 31,000 students who were getting face-to-face instruction have been in quarantine since August 28, along with forty-nine teachers and staff.

In Macon–Bibb County, there were 4,354 confirmed cases with 88 deaths as of August 20. By August 23, the county had 937 cases per 100,000, with 5,388 confirmed cases and 118 deaths. The Bibb County School System announced on August 13 that schools would open virtually on September 8. Although the opening date had been announced, pushed back from an August opening, school officials delayed making the final call for digital-only instruction, hoping COVID-19 would subside. It didn't, and the system began distributing 13,000 computers and tablets for student use for the first eight weeks of school. The district also canceled all fall sports and later allowed a diminished schedule of football games with limited attendance.

How successful digital-only learning will be in Macon-Bibb is unknown. Information technology departments in other state school systems have been swamped, and the coupling of the high rate of poverty in Macon-Bibb and the low level of computer knowledge has made for a challenging situation. Many of the district's parents have to work and face a grim choice: provide food and shelter or assist in their children's education. Students are allowed to receive virtual instruction with their cameras off owing to the worry of possible bullying because of family situations ranging from homelessness to poverty.

In Houston County, just south of Macon-Bibb, less than a week after schools reopened, each of the thirteen schools there saw at least one case of COVID. Monroe County, Macon-Bibb's northern neighbor, opened its middle and high schools virtually and decided on a mixture of face-to-face and digital learning for elementary students. Twiggs County, east of Macon-Bibb, canceled its 2020 football season and opened its schools virtually on August 17.

Middle Georgia is also home to Middle Georgia State University, Mercer University, Wesleyan College, Fort Valley State University, and Central Georgia Technical College. Middle Georgia State has five campuses in the region; Central Georgia Tech has eleven campuses and centers. All campuses opened with face-to-face instruction in one form or another, but students and faculty are required to wear masks indoors, and classrooms have been retrofitted to allow social distancing. Mercer University canceled its fall sports programs but will play a limited football schedule. Fort Valley, a member of the southern Intercollegiate Athletic Association, has canceled all fall sports.

In Georgia, football isn't a sport; it's a religion. The University of Georgia will play a ten-game season starting September 26. It announced that Sanford Stadium, which holds 92,746 fans, will be limited to 25 percent of capacity: 23,000. Georgia is a member of the hallowed Southeastern Conference, known for its football prowess. Its game against its bitter rival, the University of Florida, will be played in Jacksonville on November 7. The contest is nicknamed the "World's Largest Outdoor Cocktail Party." How that party will play out in the Age of COVID is unknown. Schools in Florida returned to face-to-face instruction because they had to after the state's education commissioner, Richard Corcoran, issued an edict requiring school districts to reopen five days a week. However, Corcoran's order was shot down on August 24, albeit temporarily, by Judge Charles Dodson of Leon County Circuit Court. The judge wrote that Governor Ron DeSantis, Education Commissioner Corcoran, and the Florida Department of Education had "arbitrarily prioritized reopening schools statewide in August over safety and the advice of health experts." Florida has been a COVID hot spot since Memorial Day, forcing the cancellation of the Republican National Convention in Jacksonville.

The University of Georgia started classes on August 20. The university is known for its social scene, and downtown Athens presents many opportunities for student face-to-face contact. Fortunately, Athens–Clarke County has had a mandatory-mask ordinance since the beginning of July, but the area had a COVID rate of 420 per 100,000 on August 29, and with the influx of almost 39,000 students, "Go, You Hairy DAWG," will have an entirely different meaning by the end of the semester.

30

WILL WESTERN PENNSYLVANIA BECOME A STRING OF GHOST TOWNS?

McKeesport

With everything else that has happened during America's *annus horribilis* of 2020, it is easy to overlook the fact that it is a U.S. census year.

Just as COVID-19 has wreaked havoc on businesses, schools, and sports teams, so, too, it has affected the census. A lockdown was imposed in Pennsylvania while the U.S. Census Bureau was mailing 2020 forms. In years past, households that failed to return their forms were visited in person by enumerators, but many of the temporary workers hired to perform the task in 2020 reportedly dropped out of training due to the pandemic, leaving the bureau with only 220,000 of the 300,000 canvassers it needs.

Already under fire for trying to politicize the count by attempting to include a question on U.S. citizenship, the Trump administration ordered the U.S. Census Bureau to end the data-collection process a month earlier than officials requested, on September 30 instead of October 31.

In an editorial on August 2, the *Washington Post* suggested the 2020 census is likely to miss between 10 and 15 percent of the population in some parts of the country, especially in communities with a high percentage of residents who are poor, Black, and renters rather than homeowners.

McKeesport fits all three categories, as do nearby Mononga-hela Valley communities such as Duquesne and East Pittsburgh. Their response rates to the census are indeed dismal—49 per-cent in McKeesport, 48 percent across the river in Duquesne, and 47 percent in East Pittsburgh, compared to 68 percent for all Pennsylvania residents.

There are historic reasons why some populations don't com-plete the census. Poor people are often transient. People who rent rather than own homes may receive the form at one address but move to a new location without completing it in either place. Black families who have suffered at the hands of public officials, including police, are liable to be suspicious of any attempt by a government agency to pry into their personal lives.

Regardless of the causes, the end result will be the same: those neighborhoods that need the most state and federal support for education, housing, health care, and public transit are also the most likely to lose that assistance if the 2020 census shows their population has shrunk dramatically.

Black residents also are more likely to vote for Democratic candidates in elections, and since the census helps determine the boundaries of state House and Senate districts as well as Con-gressional Districts, they're certain to be disenfranchised.

In the end, it is hard not to conclude—as the *Post* did—that the Trump administration is deliberately trying to undercount places such as McKeesport for ideological and political reasons.

Even without an intentional undercount, the 2020 census is expected to show that McKeesport's population has shrunk, as it has in every census since 1950. From a World War II high of 55,355 to 19,000 today, the city has lost roughly two-thirds of its residents.

The outward migration began during the post–World War II boom years, when workers moved their families to new suburbs with names such as "Pleasant Hills" to escape the pollution and noise of the steel mills where they earned their paychecks.

During the years of the civil rights movement, Black steelworkers, until then forced into low-paying jobs in the mills, fought for better-paying positions and the right to purchase homes in previously all-white neighborhoods. That's when white flight took hold; to this day, despite fair-housing laws, some of the townships close to McKeesport remain between 97 and 99 percent white. The collapse of the American steel industry in the 1980s accelerated the outward migration—this time not to nearby suburbs but to the southern United States as families left the Rust Belt in search of work.

McKeesport's population loss isn't as dramatic as that of nearby Braddock, home of Andrew Carnegie's first steel mill and of Lieutenant Governor John Fetterman. That borough has plummeted from 20,000 residents to just 2,000. In fact, all of western Pennsylvania is declining in population, some communities more quickly than others.

According to the political consultant Chris Nicholas, writing in *Catalyst*, the magazine of the Pennsylvania Chamber of Business and Industry, only two counties in the state's western half have increased their population in recent years—Butler, north of Pittsburgh, and Centre, home to Pennsylvania State University. Of Pennsylvania's six media markets, Nicholas noted, only two—Harrisburg and Philadelphia—have grown, while the Pittsburgh market overall has shrunk by 2 percent. Philadelphia was the only Pennsylvania media market that Hillary Clinton won in 2016.

Although Pennsylvania's overall population has increased slightly since 2010, the state is almost certainly going to lose one of its eighteen congressional seats following the 2020 census, and it seems likely the seat will be taken from western Pennsylvania.

Speculation on why the Pittsburgh region continues to shrink usually focuses on "lack of jobs," but that really isn't the case. In fact, until the pandemic the Pittsburgh region had the opposite problem: we had more jobs than workers to fill them.

In Beaver County, just north of Pittsburgh, Shell Oil is building a massive petrochemical plant. The company was reluctant to locate in western Pennsylvania for fear that it wouldn't be able to hire enough people from the shrinking local labor force. U.S. Steel, which remains an important industrial employer here, has had problems finding qualified workers for its three remaining mills near McKeesport. UPMC Health System, now the region's largest employer, is offering signing bonuses of up to $10,000 for registered nurses.

Our problem also isn't a lack of affordability: according to *Kiplinger's Personal Finance*, in February 2020 the median home price in the Pittsburgh area was $152,000 versus $220,000 in Philly.

And finally, it's not a lack of recreational, educational, or cultural opportunities—Pittsburgh has three professional sports teams, a symphony, an opera, and several major public and private universities.

I started to wonder instead whether the Pittsburgh region continues to lose population because we've made ourselves unwelcoming. Although we western Pennsylvania residents pride ourselves on our friendliness, and natives who move away often express regrets and want to return, people who are new to the area can receive a cold reception.

A coworker who grew up in Ohio purchased a house in Braddock in the 1990s after graduating from college in Pittsburgh. Thirty years later she still hears, "You're not from around here." I heard the same thing last week from a woman in Monessen, another former Mon Valley steelmaking town. She's lived there for roughly fifty years, she said, but is still considered an "outsider."

It is a theme that has popped up in political advertising in 2020. Emily Skopov, a Democratic candidate running for the Pennsylvania General Assembly in a district north of Pittsburgh, was targeted by a Republican PAC: its advertisements alleged that Skopov, who grew up in New York and later worked in TV production in Los Angeles, would bring "Beverly Hills" and "California" values to the district.

The effects of this nativism are worse, naturally, for immigrants and Black people. Michael Santiago, a photojournalist who was a member of a *Pittsburgh Post-Gazette* team that won a Pulitzer Prize in 2019 for its coverage of a shooting rampage at a synagogue, told the alt-weekly *Pittsburgh City Paper* that he intends to leave the region altogether. Santiago, who is Black and was born in the Dominican Republic, told *City Paper* that even as other cities were tearing down Confederate flags and monuments, some Pittsburghers continued to embrace racism and xenophobia. "It is disheartening, knowing what Pittsburgh is like and wanting to see some of that change," Santiago said.

The *GQ* columnist Damon Young, who grew up in Pittsburgh and created the Very Smart Brothas (VSB) website (now part of G/O Media's The Root), has made similar observations. Young—who once ran a youth program here in McKeesport—notes that the Pittsburgh area lacks neighborhoods or even bars and restaurants where middle-class Black residents can relax and feel safe.

"Whatever the national disparities are in income, wealth, health, and education, Pittsburgh is decidedly worse," he wrote in a blog post at VSB on February 22, 2019. "Black nightlife here is a joke, the Black middle class is a whisper[, and] Black political capital is a rumor."

Pennsylvania was not a part of the Confederacy, but based on the number of Confederate battle flags around Pittsburgh, you could be forgiven for not knowing this fact. I once asked a Black colleague new to the area what his first impressions were. "Northern Alabama," he said quickly.

In the 2016 election, Allegheny County, where McKeesport is located, went for Clinton by 56 to 40 percent, but the greater Pittsburgh media market as a whole went for Trump by almost the opposite margin, according to Chris Nicholas. If yard signs, flags, and other merchandise are reliable indicators, President Trump still has many enthusiastic supporters in the outer suburbs. In August, my wife spotted a roadside stand selling Trump souvenirs on Route 51, a half hour south of McKeesport, and a full-fledged "Trump Store" opened in Pittsburgh's North Hills.

My own progressive and creative friends for the most part either have moved from places such as McKeesport into the city of Pittsburgh (which is politically becoming a "blue" dot in a sea of "red") or have fled western Pennsylvania entirely.

I suspect we've created a climate in western Pennsylvania that chases away our own young people—especially if they're Black, creative, or liberal—while also repelling newcomers from staying in the region.

That's deadly to our future. What's even more troubling is that the more we lean into these nativist positions, the faster our young, creative, and Black people will leave the area. The tendency is destined to become a feedback loop.

After World War II, while the suburbs around McKeesport were booming, the prairie communities of the United States and Canada became ghost towns when their youth moved away in search of better opportunities. I'm afraid that western Pennsylvania is now heading that way, not for economic reasons but for cultural and ideological ones.

If the trend persists (and I think it will), I don't know if it will matter if housing continues to be affordable, jobs remain plentiful, and universities and professional sports teams are still just a few minutes away in Pittsburgh. At some point, the population decline of McKeesport—and of western Pennsylvania overall—is going to become a nosedive from which we will never surface.

31

WHERE ARE THE CAMPAIGN SIGNS AND THE *POLITIQUERAS*?

McAllen

The Rio Grande Valley in deep South Texas embraces local political campaigns with gusto unlike any community I have ever lived in. Most candidates for office—from constables to sheriffs to judges to congressional hopefuls—come from gigantic extended families. They typically have hundreds of cousins and friends who rally and block-walk for them in the weeks preceding an election. They post colorful and bilingual campaign posters throughout their districts and convince homeowners to put smaller versions of them up in their front yards. On Election Day, they sit outside voting offices under tents in every weather climate—from near triple-digit heat to freezing temperatures—wearing T-shirts bearing their candidate's likeness or slogan, tooting horns, waving banners, yelling, and trying to snatch that last vote before someone goes in to cast a ballot.

I've often admired the tireless energy and devotion to the American electoral system here, just a few miles north of the border with Mexico. I've also marveled at how it all operates under the watchful eyes of *politiqueras*—paid campaign operatives who carefully craft and structure the region's political scene. They are much more than mere employees. They are part of the

Mexican American culture here. They are the ones largely in charge. They are the king- and queenmakers who determine who will run for office—a decision often made by considering the size of the family and fan base—and they get the votes from *la gente* to make it happen.

But COVID-19 has struck this region hard, and the energy that normally pulses through the political landscape—which should have been especially stoked by the upcoming presidential election—has been substantially diminished. There is now one month until early voting begins on October 13 in Hidalgo County, and it almost feels as if there is no upcoming election whatsoever. McAllen and South Texas are struggling, and the campaigns appear to be as well. The roads that are usually overwhelmed with colossal political billboardlike signs are now almost completely devoid of the expensive advertisements, customarily placed atop one another with lumps of sandbags holding them down against the Gulf of Mexico winds. A few political operatives told me they substantially cut back on the number of signs they ordered this election season in Hidalgo County. They have instead restructured their social media campaigns and purchased large TV ad buys.

On Monday, Judge Richard Cortez of Hidalgo County lifted a shelter-in-place order that had been in effect since March 25 because of the overwhelming number of coronavirus infections that have crippled this region. An overnight curfew remains, and there are still refrigerated trucks full of bodies on the roadways. But, overall, new infections and deaths are decreasing.

At the time of this writing, Hidalgo County has the second-highest death rate from COVID-19 in the entire Lone Star State, with more than 1,400 fatalities and 29,400 coronavirus cases in a population of just a little more than 860,000. The carnage has many residents scared, and it has affected the normally jubilant campaigning. Block-walking by major candidates, such as Representative Vicente Gonzalez, a Democrat from McAllen running for his third term in Congress, won't happen, his senior campaign adviser, Martha Hinojosa, told me. They have instead diverted their funds to social media. But will online ads reach the low-income colonias where so many families live, most of them without internet service?

Hinojosa said almost everyone has a cellphone, and the campaign is using geofencing-like marketing to text and call anyone within the area who has a mobile device. TV ads, especially those on the Spanish-language stations, have been acquired with the hopes of reaching the Hispanic community that dominates this region. This year's swag includes hand sanitizer and masks with Gonzalez's name on it. The campaign hopes to cover the mouths and noses of as many people as possible, Hinojosa said.

They call it a "contactless campaign," and Hinojosa—who is related to former congressman Rubén Hinojosa, a Democrat who held the seat from 1997 to 2017 and whom Gonzalez replaced—said she initially doubted whether it could work. "At first, I thought it was not doable. I thought there was no way. We are always used to contacting people and having that in-person relationship," she said. "But I think it's worked out great so far because we have adapted. We don't have the physical contact, but we definitely have a lot of outlets."

Gonzalez has reused his popular slogan from his first run for office: "*Vicente con la gente!*" (Vicente for the people). He won in 2016 largely by investing more than $2 million of his own funds from his successful McAllen law firm. The rhyming phrase still catches one's ear, and Hinojosa said Gonzalez's wife, Lorena, a soft-spoken former schoolteacher, came up with it.

The Hinojosa clan are representative of the organized, well-oiled political machines that have dominated this region for decades. Nearly all are Democrats; although some of the wealthier families have more conservative views, they register as Democrats so they can hold an office of importance in deep South Texas. Names such as "Palacios" and "Guerra," families whose members have held several elected offices in the town of Edinburg and Hidalgo County, are well known. J. E. "Eddie" Guerra has been sheriff of Hidalgo County since 2014 and is up for reelection. His cousin, state representative R. D. "Bobby" Guerra, a former broadcast journalist, has represented House District 41 since 2012 and is competing for another term against Republican John Guerra, an ob-gyn who is not related. Not much has been written about John Guerra or other lesser-known opponents. And with COVID still dominating the daily news cycle, even remarkable reporting about political races goes largely unnoticed.

In neighboring Cameron County on the Gulf Coast, Vanessa Tijerina—the Republican challenger to longtime state senator Eddie Lucio Jr., a Democrat who has held office since 1991—is not being endorsed by the Texas Republican Party after Tijerina was arrested numerous time this summer, including for allegedly driving while intoxicated with children in her vehicle, the *San Antonio Express-News* reported on September 4. But the news of her arrests and how they might affect her challenge have largely been ignored. Lucio's son, state representative Eddie Lucio III, is forty-one years old and has represented the Texas Thirty-Eighth District since 2007, when he first took office at age twenty-nine. He also is in a reelection bid that is being run mostly on social media, where supporters can check off a box to request a campaign sign or to volunteer with the campaign.

But with contactless campaigns being operated via social media, the biggest question has remained: Where are the *politiqueras* this season? It's true that their outspokenness has taken a back seat since they were tied to several voter fraud schemes at the turn of the twenty-first century. In its 2013 report *To Congress on the Activities and Operation of the Activities and Operations of the Public Integrity Section*, the Justice Department found that more political officials were convicted of corruption in South Texas than in any other region of the country. But the *politiqueras* are still usually a force. They are rumored to control the many vans rented to transport the elderly and low-income voters to the polls on Election Day. They are especially effective and influential in the poorest of communities, and they always promise that their candidate will deliver people from poverty.

Hinojosa is one of the best-known campaigners in South Texas and, in addition to Gonzalez's campaign, is also running the reelection campaign for the mayor of the town of Donna. She told me she has never actually met a *politiquera*. But then she laughed and said some might suspect her of being one because of her involvement in so many campaigns. She said Gonzalez forbids the hiring of *politiqueras*.

Last Friday, la Unión del Pueblo Entero (LUPE, Union of All the People), a well-known nonprofit group that helps low-income communities in the Rio Grande Valley, launched its 2020 general election Get Out the Vote campaign specifically targeted at colonias. Its campaign is designed "to shift power and resources away from the small set of hands who have deepened the crisis by squandering public resources and put decision-making power back where it belongs: with the people," the organization said in a news release.

"The people have the power, don't forget it, to change the course of history. Right now, with these elections they can make this system work for real," said LUPE member and Get Out the Vote canvasser Tomás Martinez. The pitch sounded a lot like what the *politiqueras* promise.

LUPE officials claim current officeholders have squandered federal Coronavirus Aid, Relief, and Economic Security Act funds and have failed to give to the poor and needy; they have instead hoarded funds for themselves and big businesses.

"Together, we have the power to win representation that will govern by, for, and with the people so that we can recover from the pandemic with dignity and direct the resources we pitch in together to the things that make our communities thrive," said the LUPE vote coordinator Daniel Diaz.

That is quite a charge in today's fearful COVID environment. I wondered if LUPE has already reserved a fleet of rental vehicles for November 3.

32

A CONFEDERATE SOLDIER MOVES ON

Bowling Green

A few hundred yards from my driveway is a historical marker denoting the location of the Caroline Friends Meeting House, established by Quakers in the early 1700s at what is now known as Golansville. The marker notes that on March 12, 1739, members of this congregation joined with fellow Quakers in nearby Hanover County and issued a call to end slaveholding. It took another 126 years and a bloody civil war to accomplish that goal. Residents of Caroline County—and the nation—are still divided over the legacy of that war and the constitutional promise of equal rights for all regardless of race, sex, or religion.

Throughout the history of rural Virginia, churches have played an important role as gathering places for worship, fellowship, and the exchange of local news and as launching pads for social change. To at least some degree, that remains true today. One recent example of this was the involvement of local pastors and their congregations in deciding the fate of a 114-year-old Confederate monument on the grounds of the historic Caroline County Courthouse in Bowling Green.

Local clergy were at the forefront of the movement to remove this generic Confederate soldier from his perch high on a stone obelisk. Biblical scripture peppered the rhetoric of many of those who made presentations at two public hearings. The church people were opposed, meanwhile, by a number of prominent local historians, historical preservationists, Civil War buffs, and descendants of the soldiers.

The soldier has stood in front of the courthouse for more than a century. The stone fighter and the column he stands atop were placed there by the United Daughters of the Confederacy, a group formed in 1894 out of concern for the historical legacy of the Confederacy, deemed "neo-Confederate" by the Southern Poverty Law Center, and (still) dedicated to retaining the memory of all of the men from Caroline County who served the Army of the Confederacy. The monument's dedication took place in 1906, three years after the Wright Brothers' first flight in Kitty Hawk, three years before a group of activists, including W. E. B. Du Bois and Ida B. Wells, founded the NAACP, and more than four decades after Lee surrendered to Grant at Appomattox.

A brief account of the dedication in 1906 that ran in the nearby *Northumberland County Echo* said this: "When near four thousand people, mostly citizens of Caroline, assembled in Bowling Green on the 25th of July to witness the unveiling of the Confederate Monument, and spent the entire day quietly and without drinking, swearing, and fussing, we remarked that it was quite different to what we had witnessed in other towns."

Generations of Caroline County residents, Black and white, Hispanic and Native American, have passed by the monument without explicit protest—until this year, a year marked by a pandemic, political turmoil, and widespread and sometimes violent Black Lives Matter demonstrations against police brutality.

On August 25, 2020, 114 years and one month after the monument was dedicated, the Caroline County Board of Supervisors

decided the statue's fate. There were no nightly vigils with hundreds of protestors, as there had been earlier this summer at the
Robert E. Lee monument and other Confederate statues in
Richmond. An initial demonstration in early July calling for the
statue's removal attracted fewer than a dozen people, mostly
local clergy. In mid-July, Lydell Fortune, a trustee at St. John's
Baptist Church in Woodford and a member of the Germanna
Community College Board, presented the supervisors with a
petition containing more than 2,500 names calling for the statue
to go. Another resident, Pamela Smith, presented a petition containing 808 names calling for the statue to stay. (Smith pointed
out at the August public hearing that all the names on her list
were of documented residents of the county. Fortune's petition
was conducted online, and my examination found that most of
the names on that list were of people from out of state.)

Reacting to the issue, the supervisors first held a public hearing on August 11 and defeated by a four-to-two vote a motion to
put the question of the statue on the November 3 ballot in a non-
binding referendum. At a second public hearing on August 25,
fifteen letters were read into the record—ten in favor of keeping
the statue and five opposed. But of the nearly three dozen residents registered to speak at the meeting, more than two-thirds
were in favor of removing the statue.

Most, though not all, of those asking for the statue's removal
were Black, but it is worth noting that most of those defending
the statue, all of them white, also had longer histories in the area,
while those seeking its removal were relative newcomers.

Why now?

In 2020, though passions ran high during the lengthy public
hearing, COVID-19 restrictions on social distancing prevented
the sort of packed-house atmosphere that has characterized previous discussions of hot topics. All in all, the episode has

underlined the sort of low-key, measured approach Caroline County residents tend to take to solving problems.

In his letter to the Caroline County Board of Supervisors, the Reverend Marvin Fields of Dawn explained that it was the well-documented cases of police brutality against Black citizens this year that have led to protests over Confederate symbols.

"Now when I walk past that statue, I look at it different," he said. "What were they fighting for? They were fighting to uphold slavery. This is not a political issue. This is a moral issue."

Herbert Collins, a retired Smithsonian acquisitions officer, Caroline County native, and descendant of the county's early Quaker settlers, defended the Confederate monument because, he said, it represents the common soldiers, many of whom had little choice but to fight for Virginia. "Our history is not perfect," he said. "We cannot change history by tearing down statues."

But Stanley O. Jones argued that the point of these Confederate statues, still standing a century and a half after the end of the Confederacy, "is to disenfranchise and alienate African Americans. . . . We need to take advantage of the time and help heal and bring us together," he said.

On the other side, a former county librarian, Kay Brooks, wrote that history is "a big part of what draws people to our county," and "there is nothing distinguishing the race, affiliation, or time in history of the dignified soldier standing atop the tribute. It is simply a recognition of the sacrifice men have made to protect our home."

The Reverend Duane T. Fields Sr., however, writing on behalf of the NAACP, did not see the statue as benign. "If we are ever to heal," he wrote, "then it must begin with removing the Confederate monument from the lawn of the county courthouse and offering it for display in a privately held space or institution."

Calling for unity on the topic, the Reverend Cynthia Golden, a former Caroline County schoolteacher, quoted biblical scripture and Abraham Lincoln: "A house divided against itself cannot stand."

Toward the end of the meeting, the board chairman, Jeff Sili, a prominent county Republican, pushed for a compromise of a sort: "The one thing I can say everyone agrees upon is that this piece of history be preserved. We simply do not agree about its location. I believe we can move past that."

At the end of the nearly four-hour session, the supervisors voted unanimously to remove the statue and locate it somewhere more appropriate. A final decision on disposition will follow a thirty-day period to receive proposals and cost estimates.

One of many clergymen involved in the debate over the monument was the Reverend Duane Fields Sr., who was born in Queens, New York, and came to Caroline County as a teenager. Fields is married to an ordained minister, the Reverend Sheree Fields, and is the son of the Reverend Marvin Fields of Second Mount Zion Baptist Church in Dawn, Virginia. The younger Fields was installed as pastor of Oxford Mount Zion Baptist Church in Ruther Glen, Virginia, twenty years ago and ministers to a congregation of six hundred people.

"In the rural South, I believe the church is the hub for everything," Fields said. He has witnessed family tragedies and community controversies in his twenty years at the pulpit, but he rates the controversy over the county's Confederate monument as "the most divisive topic that we have dealt with. There hadn't been a social issue as important as this."

Nearby Greenlawn Cemetery, which contains many graves of Civil War soldiers, has submitted a proposal that it take the statue. The Caroline County Historical Society has endorsed that choice.

Maybe the removal of one Confederate statue here in quiet, rural, tradition-loving Virginia is some kind of political tea leaf. Or maybe it isn't. The tea leaves here have been exceedingly difficult to read in this strange political season.

As we near the end of this *Columbia Journalism Review/ Delacorte Review* series, I look back at my earlier columns. It is clear that I did not anticipate what 2020 would bring us. In that, I am not alone. Most of us expected 2020 to be mainly about the presidential and congressional elections. Back in January, who could have predicted a worldwide pandemic? Or the dramatic Black Lives Matter response to the deaths of George Floyd, Breonna Taylor, and many others at the hands of police officers? Or the death of a U.S. Supreme Court justice just six weeks before Election Day?

In January 2020, Virginia's unemployment rate was 2.7 percent, and the economic picture was rosy. Almost overnight, that rate soared to double digits; as of July, it was around 8 percent. Governor Ralph Northam, a neurosurgeon, was loudly criticized for closing down the state at the beginning of the pandemic and then for dragging his feet on reopening Virginia for business. After we saw what happened to states that were too eager to ease restrictions, those voices became quieter.

Because Caroline County is rural and sparsely populated, we have avoided staggering COVID-19 statistics in the first year of the pandemic. Earlier last week, the total cases in this county of 31,000 topped three hundred. Then on September 18, we recorded our largest spike in cases: twenty-three in one day. The spike was attributed to an outbreak in the Caroline Detention Center, a former regional women's jail leased by the county to the federal Immigration and Customs Enforcement agency. This facility currently houses 163 federal detainees and employs a number of county residents. The spike could have a significant impact on future COVID-19 statistics. Meanwhile, many events that discourage social distancing were canceled this year. The nearby Kings Dominion amusement park never opened, and the State Fair of Virginia, which would have drawn tens of thousands of people to Caroline's Meadow Event Park this week, did not take place. More people are wearing masks this fall than in May and June.

This is an election year, and, in fact, early voting in Virginia opened up Friday. But there is little tangible evidence of that. I drove around Bowling Green Wednesday and saw dozens of lawn signs for the town council election and one for incumbent congressman Rob Wittman, but none for either Trump or Biden. Puzzled by this absence, I drove the streets of Belmont and Ladysmith Village but saw no political signs there either. The usual attack ads for one particularly hot congressional race and for a U.S. Senate seat—Democrat Mark Warner versus Republican Daniel Glade—saturate TV in the Richmond area, but they are the only harbingers of November 3.

It is almost as if we can't wait for the election—and the rest of 2020 for that matter—to be over.

33

MACON–BIBB COUNTY AND THE UNRELENTING SHOCK OF COVID-19

Macon

The Cotton Brothers were a fairly well-known gospel singing group in the late 1950s and 1960s, starting with "Remember Me" in 1961, "Be There Directly" in '64, and "Life's Too Short" in '65. The brothers grew up in Marshallville, about thirty-five miles south of Macon. Their parents, Floyd and Helen, were sharecroppers. The family eventually called Macon home. There were several iterations of the Cotton Brothers, understandable since the family had ten brothers and six sisters. The Brothers' a cappella style was compared to that of the Mighty Clouds of Joy. Bishop John Cotton, one of the lead vocalists for the group, also had a call to the ministry and was pastor at Greater Overcoming Church of God in Macon for forty-six years, where the Brothers performed regularly, packing the sanctuary.

Bishop Cotton died at age seventy-five in 2014. Tommy Cotton, who also sang lead, passed away in 2017 at age seventy-nine. But 2020 has been particularly devastating for the Cotton family. Louis passed on July 6, 2020, at sixty-eight; Alfred (A. C.) at seventy-five on July 27; Jessie on August 11 at seventy-two; and Eddie Lee, only sixty-three, entered the gates of heaven on August 17. A. C., Jessie, and Eddie Lee were victims of

COVID-19, according to a deputy coroner, and the three brothers may have contracted the virus at Louis's graveside service on July 11. The back-to-back deaths of the Cotton brothers are just three of the 157 COVID-19 deaths in Macon–Bibb County as of September 21, 2020.

This election year wasn't supposed to be this way. At the dawn of 2020, the race for president was at the top of everyone's mind. Who would get the Democratic nomination? And then there was President Donald J. Trump's impeachment trial, which began on January 16 and concluded with his acquittal by the Senate on February 5. All that seems so long ago and far away now.

On January 21, the Centers for Disease Control announced the first case of COVID-19 in the United States in Washington State. The next day in Davos, Switzerland, Trump, commenting on COVID-19, told CNBC, "We have it totally under control." The president was informed of the virus's danger on January 28, according to Bob Woodward's book *Rage*. Yet at his State of the Union Address on February 4, he barely mentioned the virus. At a rally in New Hampshire on February 10, he told supporters, "By April, you know, in theory, when it gets a little warmer, [the coronavirus] miraculously goes away." He didn't know then that COVID-19 had already claimed the life of fifty-seven-year-old Patricia Dowd of California, nor did anyone else. Dowd's autopsy wasn't performed until April.

On March 17, the U.S. death toll hit 100. A month later, COVID-19 deaths exceeded the number of U.S. military lost in the Korean War. By the end of April, the virus had claimed 65,832 lives—more than were lost in Vietnam.

On February 29, Andrew Jerome Mitchell, sixty-four, a retired janitor, was laid to rest in Albany, Georgia, about 105 miles southwest of Macon. A couple hundred mourners attended his funeral at the Martin Luther King Funeral Home. It was the first superspreader event of COVID in the state, an unlikely distinction for a county of only 88,000 people. The night of the funeral, one of the attendees was admitted to Phoebe Putney Memorial Hospital and would become the state's first victim of COVID-19. A week after Mitchell's homegoing, Johnny Carter's service was held at Gethsemane Worship Center. He was seventy.

The first twenty-three COVID-19 patients admitted to Phoebe Putney had attended at least one of the funerals, according to the *New York Times* on March 30, 2020. The eulogist at Mitchell's funeral, Chief Apostle Izell Williams Jr., pastor of New Direction Christian Church Ministries, died of COVID-19 on March 22 at the age of fifty-eight. That same day, local Dougherty County authorities issued a stay-at-home order, and Governor Brian Kemp did the same on April 2, after ordering the closure of schools the previous day. It soon became apparent to everyone that COVID-19 was a real and present danger. As of September 22, Dougherty County has lost 182 residents to COVID-19.

The first death in Macon–Bibb County was reported on April 1. Schools closed, everyone was ordered to shelter-in-place, church services were canceled, and political campaigns, of which there were many, shut down. The thriving downtown hub filled with bars and restaurants became ghostlike. Everyday life—from spring sports to graduations to working at home to constant handwashing and social distancing—sent everyone reeling into an alternate universe. Hospital visitations were curtailed, particularly in the emergency room. COVID-19 wards were opened, and temporary facilities were built as the number of intensive-care beds dwindled. When local hospitals couldn't accept more patients, they diverted them hundreds of miles away to hospitals that had available beds. In mid-April, Pruitt Health, a local nursing home, became a hot spot and reported that sixty-eight patients and eight staff members had tested positive for COVID-19.

Facing the fall, the Bibb County School System—after vacillating about whether to reopen schools with face-to-face instruction—decided to postpone opening until September 8, hoping the virus would abate by then. It didn't, and the system opted in mid-August to have virtual instruction only, at least until the end of October. Houston County schools, south of Macon-Bibb, opened, but not without issues. One of the schools in the Houston County School System, Perry High School, suspended its football season until the end of September because one of its players tested positive for COVID-19. Several other district schools also had at least one student or staff member who tested positive.

In a note to parents on September 21, Dr. Curtis Jones, superintendent of the Bibb County School System, attempted to explain why the system was instructing virtually rather than face-to-face, while surrounding counties had opened their schoolhouse doors:

> When I look at the surrounding counties of Baldwin, Crawford, Hancock, Houston, Jasper, Jones, Monroe, Peach, Putnam, Twiggs, Washington and Wilkinson, it becomes clear that Bibb County is one of the counties most severely hit by COVID-19. Based on data from last week from the North Central Health District, those thirteen counties have experienced almost 16,000 cases of COVID-19. What may not be well known is that almost 6,000 of those . . . in fact, were all in Bibb. The closest county to us had 3,100. Another county had 2,000. But we are by far more affected. The same is true of the number of deaths that have occurred. In those same thirteen counties, [there have been] 465 total deaths; 158 of them were in Bibb County. No other county

is in triple digits. In fact, the next highest number is 74. We are being affected more than others. So, when people ask me why we aren't like others, the answer is because the numbers indicate that we have just been more severely hit.

All the while, the local newspaper, the *Telegraph*, is in flux. Gone are the days when council and commission meetings were covered by the local paper. The same goes for coverage of school board meetings and Robins Air Force Base, the largest industrial complex in the state. To its credit, the *Telegraph* has presented the daily COVID-19 numbers; however, for much of the pandemic, the local hospital has refused to release hospitalization statistics concerning COVID-19, with little pushback from the newspaper and other media outlets.

The *Telegraph* is owned by McClatchy, based in Sacramento, California. The company owned twenty-nine other papers, including the *Charlotte Observer*, the *Kansas City Star*, the *Miami Herald*, and the *Sacramento Bee*, when it filed for bankruptcy in January 2020. Chatham Asset Management, a hedge fund, won the bid for the company when the federal bankruptcy judge Michael E. Wiles approved the $312 million sale. What a twist of ironic fate. When McClatchy bought Knight Ridder Newspapers in 2006, it paid $4.5 billion. CEO Craig Forman, who was paid $2.87 million in 2018, including a $5,000 monthly housing stipend, was out, and for the first time in 163 years the newspaper chain will not be headed by a member of the McClatchy family because Kevin McClatchy, chairman of the board, has stepped aside, along with his three cousins.

Macon–Bibb County is a high-poverty area. The concentrated poverty rate in Macon rose from 30.3 percent to 44.7 percent between 2010 and 2016, according to *24/7 Wall Street*. The increase—14.4 percentage points—was the largest of any metro area in Georgia, and Macon's concentrated poverty rate went from the eleventh highest in the nation to the third highest. The area had an 8.1 percent unemployment rate at the end of July 2020, while the state, according to the U.S. Department of Labor Statistics, had an unemployment rate of 7.1.

The Bibb County School System says its students are the most impoverished in the nation. All the system's students receive free or reduced lunch, so when the system decided to open virtually, it was imperative that students receive meals. The system created two options: students or parents could pick up breakfast and lunch meals at twenty-five school locations or pick up meals from designated buses along the students' bus routes. The system distributed more than 13,000 tablets and laptops to students and deployed Wi-Fi-enabled buses in areas with low internet connectivity.

The Middle Georgia Food Bank partnered with several churches to distribute food throughout the area. Thousands of pounds of food were given to families. Many of the food giveaways were held in conjunction with COVID-19 testing. The United Way of Central Georgia and the Community Foundation of Central Georgia established the Central Georgia COVID-19 Response & Recovery Fund and dispensed almost $700,000 in funding to not-for-profit organizations to help them serve people during this time of crisis.

Even as the death toll mounted, and the state became a COVID-19 hot spot, with Macon–Bibb and Houston Counties near the eye of the flame, there were voices of doubt following President Trump's lead, calling the pandemic a hoax or a crisis inspired by the media and Democrats. The Georgia mask controversy flared in July when Mayor Keisha Lance Bottoms of Atlanta implemented more stringent restrictions than were allowed by Kemp's executive order. Masks became a political statement across the nation, more so here in the South. A mandatory-mask ordinance was instituted by the Macon–Bibb County Commission in July but was vetoed by Mayor Robert Reichert because he said the law violated the governor's order.

Some residents became rather salty when asked to wear masks in grocery stores or other essential businesses. Some stores and restaurants displayed notices that stated: "The operator of this location does NOT consent to enforcing face covering orders on this property."

As the city slowly reawakens, what has begun to feel normal is abnormal. Even though some restaurants have opened their dining areas, fear lingers because many patrons just won't adhere to precautions. Many people choose drive-through, curbside, and home delivery rather than dine-in service. Civic clubs such as the Rotary, Kiwanis, and Exchange Clubs have been meeting virtually; others have hybrid meetings, a combination of in-person and Zoom. Some clubs aren't meeting at all, and there are worries that some clubs will not survive the pandemic.

Aside from businesses that might not reopen, other closings happened out of sight and mind. Many houses of worship won't survive the virus. While tithes and offerings actually increased in some churches that had the ability to worship virtually, those that were not as technically savvy may be down for the count.

Adding to the maelstrom caused by COVID were national protests in cities across the country after George Floyd's murder in Minneapolis, the killings of Breonna Taylor in Lexington, Kentucky, and, closer to Macon, of Ahmaud Arbery in Brunswick, Georgia, and Rayshard Brooks in Atlanta. Demonstrations also morphed into efforts to remove Confederate memorials. In Macon-Bibb, demonstrations have been peaceful, and the Macon–Bibb County Commission approved plans to remove the statue of a Confederate soldier that sits in a prominent area of downtown and another memorial to "women of the

South," placed by the United Daughters of the Confederacy across the street from the Government Center.

Boat parades supporting President Trump were held in late August and early September on three lakes: Lake Lanier, north of Atlanta; Lake Oconee, about an hour's drive northeast of Macon; and Lake Thurmond, which sits on the Georgia–South Carolina border (the lake is named for Senator Strom Thurmond on the South Carolina side but is called Clarks Hill Lake in Georgia). The Great American Boat Parade held on Lake Lanier alone drew an estimated 3,100 boats.

Mother Nature participated in this atmosphere of unrest by unleashing repeated storms to batter the Gulf Coast, their remnants affecting inland areas. The eye of Hurricane Sally passed directly over Macon-Bibb after it made landfall on September 16. Fortunately, it mostly delivered rain, dropping seven to nine inches on the area.

Voters, many dealing with grief, fear, and unemployment—for themselves, friends, or loved ones—were further shocked by the loss of Justice Ruth Bader Ginsburg on September 18.

Through it all, the virus has surged on as Georgia is once again in the red zone, according to the White House Coronavirus Task Force. And yet the state turns its attention to November. Since the June primary debacle, the county that saw the longest lines has opened thirty additional precincts and one large precinct where the Atlanta Hawks usually play. In Bibb County, more ballot drop boxes have been distributed. More than one million voters in Georgia have requested absentee ballots.

There have been a high number of political ads, mostly concerning the two Senate races. Some polls indicate neck-and-neck races for the presidential and both Senate races—raising predictions that Georgia may turn blue for the first time in thirty years.

34

WILL THE SONS OF STEELWORKERS SEE TRUMP'S COVID-19 BEHAVIOR AS STRONG OR RECKLESS?

McKeesport

Pittsburgh's beer is still called Iron City, Pittsburgh's football team is still called the Steelers, and here in McKeesport we remain proud of our smokestack heritage—even if manufacturing plays only a tiny part in the region's economy.

At one point, 10,000 people labored in McKeesport to make such products as steel pipes. Two remaining mini-mills now employ only a few hundred people. Across all of western Pennsylvania, according to the University of Pittsburgh economist Chris Briem, the percentage of jobs in manufacturing fell to an all-time low in 2019.

But while blast furnaces and rolling mills are gone from McKeesport, Duquesne, and Homestead, toughness and a strong work ethic remain our region's brand. Just down the river from McKeesport, in Braddock, Pennsylvania, a huge statue of Joe Magarac stands at the entrance of U.S. Steel's Edgar Thomson Works, one of the Monongahela Valley's last fully integrated steel plants.

Magarac is a Pittsburgh folk legend, a Paul Bunyan–like character who was larger than life and stronger than Superman and who protected other millworkers from harm. The story goes that Magarac was born in a mountain of iron ore and died when he leaped into a ladle of molten steel to make the steel stronger. The Mon Valley, too, was the setting for Michael Cimino's film *The Deer Hunter* (1978), about young steelworkers who return from the Vietnam War trying to hide their emotional trauma under layers of macho posturing.

It stands to reason, then, that many Pittsburghers—especially white men—would embrace toughness as a virtue, and it's also no surprise that many around here took a liking to tough-talking Donald Trump. In 2016, Hillary Clinton won McKeesport, Duquesne, Clairton, and other cities with large Black populations, but Trump ran the table in the surrounding, mostly white boroughs and townships, many of them populated by the children and grandchildren of retired steelworkers.

In 2020, although Biden–Harris signs are sprouting in front yards, Trump signs and flags still predominate. Many of them bear one of two mottos—"NO MORE BULLSHIT" or "FUCK YOUR FEELINGS"—that seem more appropriate to a tough-talking 1970s steelworkers' bar than to a twenty-first-century presidential election campaign.

To be sure, Biden is more popular here than Hillary Clinton, but it would be hard to be less popular in western Pennsylvania than she was. In the 1990s, Pittsburgh billionaire philanthropist Richard Mellon Scaife funded many of the Arkansas Project investigations into the personal lives of Bill and Hillary Clinton, and the findings were splashed across the front pages of his regional chain of newspapers, including the *Greensburg Tribune-Review*, the *Pittsburgh Tribune-Review*, and, later, the *McKeesport Daily News*.

Indeed, the roots of the QAnon conspiracies can be found in those stories, which suggested prominent officials had been murdered to conceal Clinton administration secrets. The byline on many of them was that of *Tribune-Review* reporter Christopher Ruddy, today the CEO of Newsmax Media and a close confidant of Trump. In other words, from the beginning the odds were against Hillary Clinton in western Pennsylvania, but she did herself no favors during her campaign when she became the first Democratic presidential nominee in memory not to visit the Mon Valley.

Donald Trump did. He came to Monessen, Westmoreland County, the site of a long-closed Wheeling-Pittsburgh Steel mill, where he told his audience it was "time to declare our economic independence once again."

"The legacy of Pennsylvania steelworkers lives in the bridges, railways, and skyscrapers that make up our great American landscape," Trump told employees of a recycling plant that operates on a portion of Wheeling-Pitt's old Monessen works. "But our workers' loyalty was repaid with betrayal," he said, arguing that trade deals with China and Mexico negotiated during the Clinton administration were responsible for the Pittsburgh region's loss of manufacturing employment.

Trump promised his Monessen audience that he would put "American-produced steel back into the backbone of our country" and create "massive numbers of jobs."

Although the city of Monessen voted for Clinton in 2016, Westmoreland County went for Trump by more than 56,000 votes, and Trump won Washington County on the opposite side of the Monongahela River by 24,505 votes. In fact, Trump swept all of western Pennsylvania outside of Allegheny County on his way to winning Pennsylvania—and its twenty electoral votes—by about 68,000 votes.

Joe Biden seems determined not to repeat Clinton's mistake of ignoring the old steel towns. Following the first presidential debate on September 29, he and his wife, Jill, staged a whistle-stop train tour through Ohio and Pennsylvania, making two stops in Westmoreland County before ending in Johnstown, another former steel town that fell on hard times in the 1970s and 1980s. The Biden campaign has also opened a field office in McKeesport this week.

Biden, like Clinton in 2016, is expected to win Philadelphia and its suburbs. That means western Pennsylvania is likely to be the deciding region once again, and pundits and political reporters are stalking the valleys around Pittsburgh.

In September, Nina Lakhani of the *Guardian* visited Beaver County, north of the city, where she talked to many lifelong registered Democrats who said they were sticking with Trump. "He's the lesser of two evils, and he cares for working people, that's the bottom line," one woman told Lakhani. The woman bristled at the implication that a vote for Trump is a vote for racism. "We don't see that here," she said.

Much has been written, of course, about Trump's appeal to white supremacists, nativists, and nationalists, but less has been written about how Trump's hypermacho behavior is appealing to men and some women.

At first glance, Trump, who loves luxury and was born into wealth, would seem to have little in common with a Mon Valley steelworker. But consider Trump's love of golf. Western Pennsylvania—birthplace of Arnold Palmer—loves it, too. Pennsylvania reportedly has more golf courses per capita than any other state. There are nearly seventy in the Pittsburgh region alone, including one in North Braddock, literally within sight of the Edgar Thomson steel plant.

Trump has been mocked for preferring his steaks charbroiled, but that's reminiscent of the style called "Pittsburgh rare"— blackened to a crisp on the outside. And throughout his career, Trump has surrounded himself with fashion models, many of whom could have served as pin-up girls inside a steelworker's locker.

So it shouldn't stretch anyone's imagination to see why any man who embraces Pittsburgh's legacy of macho behavior would aspire to Donald Trump's lifestyle—and connect with him on a visceral level. On September 20, hundreds of Trump supporters, almost all of them white, many of them men driving customized pickup trucks and motorcycles, staged a parade down U.S. Route 30 in nearby North Huntingdon Township. Some of them said they have little or no interest in politics. But they like Donald Trump.

The following weekend, the *Washington Post* covered a boat parade on Lake Erie near Sandusky, Ohio, home to Cedar Point amusement park and a popular vacation spot for Pittsburghers. Participants in the "masculinity-oozing" event, reported the *Post*, "live by the rules [Trump] lives by: that concepts such as white male privilege or structural racism and sexism are to be scoffed at" and that "liberals are crybabies and snowflakes."

(Not coincidentally, these hypermasculine—some would say "toxic"—attitudes overlap nicely with overt Republican hostility to issues such as LGBTQ rights, the Black Lives Matter movement, and women's reproductive health.)

Following Biden's whistle-stop in Johnstown, Andrew Seidman of the *Philadelphia Inquirer* visited the area, where he spoke with James Bender of nearby Loretto, who was flying two Trump flags from his house. Both have Trump in macho poses. In one, the president is depicted standing on top of a tank. The other has Trump's face superimposed on Sylvester Stallone's Rambo. Bender was dismissive of rules imposed by Pennsylvania's Democratic governor, Tom Wolf, that require people to wear face masks in public. "That," Bender said, "ain't never happening."

Trump has been one of the nation's biggest skeptics about the ability of face masks to stop the spread of the coronavirus. During the chaotic first presidential debate, he mocked Biden for wearing "the biggest face mask I've ever seen."

Opponents of face masks have given me a number of not very convincing theories why they can't or shouldn't wear them. But any boy who grew up in the Mon Valley knows the real reason: men don't want to wear face masks because it implies they're vulnerable. It's not macho. By mocking Biden's face mask, Trump was implying that his opponent is a sissy. On Tuesday, October 5, 2020, Fox News commentator Tomi Lahren, a close Trump ally, tweeted a video of Biden wearing a face mask and added, "Might as well carry a purse with that mask, Joe."

Yet by this point Trump's masculinity had almost literally turned toxic. Trump and more than a dozen of his closest allies as well as several members of the White House press corps tested positive for COVID-19. Even after Trump was hospitalized and medicated, some of his surrogates continued to insist that the president would somehow cure himself of the deadly disease merely by acting tough.

Senator Kelly Loeffler of Georgia tweeted a pro-wrestling video that was edited to show Trump body-slamming a coronavirus molecule. Representative Matt Gaetz of Florida tweeted, "President Trump won't have to recover from COVID. COVID will have to recover from President Trump."

On the day of his release, Trump urged followers, "Don't be afraid of COVID"—as if only cowards would succumb to a disease that by this point had killed 210,000 Americans. After arriving back at the White House following three days at Walter Reed National Military Medical Center, he wasted no time publicly removing his face mask despite the fact that he was still struggling with the symptoms of COVID-19 and was still infectious to the people around him.

Trump's behavior, in other words, went from tough to reckless.

Mon Valley steelworkers were tough and courageous, but that doesn't mean they were reckless. When the mills were organized by the steelworkers' union in the 1930s, laborers wanted better pay, protection from abusive mill management, and paid vacations. They also demanded safer working conditions.

The Joe Magarac legend was first recorded around the same time by a writer for *Scribner's Magazine* who claimed he heard it from eastern European immigrant workers in the steel mills in the Mon Valley.

But just as Trump's self-proclaimed business prowess is largely a creation of his fourteen years starring in NBC's series *The Apprentice*, the Magarac folk tale was also made up. Scholars have been unable to find any evidence that the Magarac story is based on a real person.

The name "Magarac," in fact, is derived from *маэга* or *mazga*, the Croatian word for "mule." The implication of the story was thus that only a jackass would kill himself to help the steel mill. Now that Trump has contracted COVID-19, it remains to be seen if his western Pennsylvania supporters will still see him as strong and tough for flouting safety rules—or as merely a reckless jackass.

35

COUNTING ON NEXT YEAR
BEING MUCH BETTER

McAllen

I t has truly been a year full of fear in South Texas, particularly in Hidalgo County, which has had the second-highest number of coronavirus-related deaths out of the 254 Texas counties. But the coronavirus pandemic is just one in a series of catastrophic events to strike this often forgotten and isolated part of the country. This year has also included a census boondoggle, which could have lasting repercussions well after the November 3 election.

At the beginning of 2020, this region, like many American cities, was preparing for the upcoming decennial census count. Local congressional representatives touted the importance of the count, saying that every thousand households missed in the count could cost the region $150 million in federal resources. *Counting for Dollars 2020,* a study by the George Washington Institute of Public Policy, found that a population undercount of just one percent could cost the state at least $300 million annually. But just as the census count was kicking off in March, the coronavirus pandemic struck. Our region went into lockdown, and precautionary measures staved off a significant spread of the deadly novel virus. In May, however, Governor Greg Abbott ordered that the state begin to reopen in phases, and that's when the virus came roiling into our homes and workplaces.

Although Hidalgo County has only 860,000 residents (according to the latest population estimate), there have been more than 33,300 coronavirus cases in the county and 1,850 deaths, second only to Harris County, which includes the Houston area. On July 17, the *Wall Street Journal* reported that Houston was averaging 2 deaths per 100,000 people; Texas overall had 3 deaths per 100,000. Hidalgo County had 17 deaths per 100,000 people.

Hospitals and medical staff have been overwhelmed and have lacked the resources needed to treat the high number of cases. Medical authorities attribute the higher levels here to comorbidities and existing conditions, such as hypertension, diabetes, and obesity, which complicate and make the virus more difficult to fight and treat.

Many of these conditions are a product of the abject poverty that so many Rio Grande Valley residents live in—one-third of them to be exact. The median income is just $37,582, according to 2018 census data. That translates into poor diets for many who are unable to afford healthier foods. Many people work multiple jobs and do not have the time or the means to exercise.

That is why the federal monies tied to the 2020 census count are so important, and yet it is almost certain that many people here will not be counted. There are several reasons why. For example, undocumented residents fear filling out the census questionnaire. And although census officials have assured the public that no information will be shared with other government agencies, many families here don't believe that. Why should they after the Trump administration tried to get a citizenship question put on the census in the summer of 2019? Although the U.S.

Supreme Court blocked the question, the administration's intent was clear, and many undocumented families became scared.

Aware of their concerns and the real dollars at stake, leaders in the Rio Grande Valley banded together and formed coalitions and task forces aimed at getting into communities and stressing the importance and confidentiality of filling out the census. But when COVID-19 hit, all plans were lost, as one city leader told me. It didn't take long for census officials to extend the count through October 31. But then, in what seemed like an obvious move to undercount low-income regions that need the extra time the most, the Trump administration declared that the count would stop a month earlier instead, in September.

A federal judge ordered that the count must continue through the end of October, but by the time the ruling came out, the damage had already been done because all of the salaried census workers in the Rio Grande Valley had been let go, the former spokeswoman told me. Remaining on the ground are hourly door knockers, but there is no local organizational leadership structure to steer this ship.

In a last-ditch effort to reach residents, the Census Bureau has begun mailing out the nine-question forms to PO boxes, which is something the bureau originally said it would not do in order to maintain count accuracy. Area nonprofits have also begun helping officials by block-walking in some of the poorest colonias, or neighborhoods, despite real fears of catching the virus, which remains quite prevalent here.

U.S. representatives Vicente Gonzalez and Henry Cuellar, Democrats who represent South Texas, have called on the Trump administration to extend the count through the end of 2020. Gonzalez said that although the Constitution mandates a census be held every ten years, there is no rule that decides when the count must stop. But the census spokeswoman told me that for census officials to have time enough to compile all of the gathered data and to present it to Congress by the December 31 deadline, they must end the count by the end of October.

Cities have begun holding day-long census telethons, staffing the phone banks with area mayors and local celebrities and offering cash and prizes to those who call in their information. It seems as if all forms of Hail Marys have been thrown in these past few weeks to try and identify everyone who lives here.

Aside from federal funding, the census count also is tied to the number of congressional seats for each state. The 2010 census resulted in an addition of four House seats for Texas. The state is expected to gain four again or even as many as six, but that will happen only if everyone is counted.

Additional representation in Congress is essential for this part of the state. Our current lawmakers represent constituents who live hours away and hundreds of miles from each other and who have very different needs and interests. These constituents range from undocumented migrants to cattle ranchers who advocate for a border wall and more border security and everything in between. Cuellar, for instance, represents the Twenty-Eighth Congressional District, which includes the region from the western town of Laredo to Mission, which is next door to McAllen, and even a part of San Antonio. Gonzalez represents the Fifteenth Congressional District, which spans from McAllen north through ranchlands to San Antonio. Additional voices in Congress could force officials to acknowledge the real economic hardships, deaths, and financial losses due to the continued border restrictions on land ports.

Beginning on March 20, 2020, the land ports between the United States and Mexico were closed to all but "essential" workers. The Trump administration invoked a little-known public-health code, Title 42, to close the borders to thwart the spread of coronavirus. This resulted in border crossers being forbidden to cross—from families visiting loved ones across the Rio Grande to shoppers coming to border communities to asylum seekers. Local border cities are losing millions of dollars, and they don't know how they will make it up. The McAllen-Hidalgo-Reynosa International Bridge reported a loss of more than $2 million as of July.

Mayor Jim Darling of McAllen told me it's not fair because whereas land ports remain closed to Mexican nationals trying to enter the United States, airports are not. "We don't understand the government's policy of letting Mexican nationals fly into any city," he said, "but they cannot cross the bridge."

U.S. senator John Cornyn, a Republican, led a bipartisan delegation that included Cuellar and Gonzalez and that sent a letter to Acting Homeland Secretary Chad Wolf asking for a plan to reopen the land ports of entry. The letter demanded the administration "develop and publicly articulate a detailed plan, including benchmarks that must be reached, for land ports of entry along the southwest border to return to normal operations."

The demand sounded tough on paper, and I expected Cornyn, who is seeking his fourth term this upcoming election, to tout it during his first debate with his opponent, air force veteran M. J. Hegar, this past Friday. But, surprisingly, the issue never came up. In fact, neither candidate discussed South Texas at all during the hour-long debate, except for a brief mention of the asylum seekers who have been forced to remain in Mexico during the pandemic and during their U.S. immigration hearings. The border wall, the high rates of COVID deaths here, and the reopening of the border never came up.

I was in Austin covering the debate for Nexstar Media and was selected to appear on a live after-debate panel. In the moments before the program began, I felt I had little to talk about and was struggling with what to say. But then Hegar was interviewed by a KXAN reporter and declared that she had wanted to talk about many other things, "including immigration." If immigration were so important to her, I believe she could have found a way to work it into the conversation, I said on air.

Likewise, immigration and the border wall never came up during the first presidential debate between Donald Trump and Joe Biden. The absence of discussion only amplified how little folks know or seem to care about this South Texas border region.

And, unfortunately, if the number of people who really live here isn't accurately reflected in the 2020 census count, this area will receive less funding in the future and less representation in Washington, DC. The poverty will continue, and the high obesity rates will increase, continuing to lead to more COVID-19 fatalities. For now, the census count limps along here, and early voting has begun.

36

ELECTION DAY APPROACHES

Who could have known?

Who could have predicted that a year whose story would surely have been seen through the lens of a presidential campaign would have unfolded as it did? Who could have anticipated a virus that by a week before Election Day 2020 would kill more than 225,000 Americans and infect 8.7 million; that a video capturing a Minneapolis officer killing a Black man by pressing a knee into his neck would unleash across the nation rage and protest that transcended race and class; that the American economy would come to virtual standstill for tens of millions of people who suddenly found themselves out of work and out of money; that wearing a mask and keeping one's distance from others to avoid contracting and spreading a deadly disease would become political statements, litmus tests for whose side you were on?

Who could have anticipated that the general fears that so many of us accept as part of our lives would be overwhelmed by fears more dire and terrifying?

Our reporters' stories of four American towns began in February 2020, less than a week after the third presidential impeachment trial in the nation's history ended in an acquittal. The following week, President Trump attended an election rally in New Hampshire. Federal prosecutors called for a prison term of seven to nine years for the president's longtime friend and associate Roger Stone after his conviction for impeding a congressional investigation. The Justice Department sued local and state governments in California, New Jersey, and Washington State in an escalation of the administration's battle against so-called sanctuary cities. Pete Buttigieg was suddenly the Democratic candidate to beat after his apparent narrow win in the Iowa caucus. Unemployment stood at 3.5 percent. And the Chinese city of Wuhan was on lockdown as a virus that had first appeared as a suspected flu in December was racing through the city. Meanwhile, the first laboratory-confirmed case of coronavirus in the United States was reported to the Centers for Disease Control on January 20.

At the end of October, the nation was set to choose a president in a week, and there was great uncertainty as to how this election would play out. Would it end on Election Night, or would it take weeks or longer to know the winner? Would voters decide, or would the courts? Four journalists have told their stories of their towns from February to November. Here they describe where they found their communities—and themselves— as Election Day neared.

GREG GLASSNER, BOWLING GREEN

I turn seventy-six on Election Day. That puts me in the same age ballpark as Donald Trump and Joe Biden. I know I do not have the same physical and mental stamina I did at age sixty-six or fifty-six, so I admire that two men my age are willing to

tackle a four-year commitment to what may be the most challenging job in the nation. But I also question their sanity.

That thought and others were on my mind as I voted on October 20 at the Caroline County Registrar's Office in Bowling
Green. Virginia loosened the restrictions on early voting this
year, and an estimated 25 percent of the electorate voted early in
person or by mail.

The ubiquitous yard signs that were missing back in September
have eventually sprung up along the roadside like mushrooms
after a heavy rain. Perhaps COVID-19 delayed their distribution.

I am not sure how much impact these signs have on voters; it
appears that most folks have already made up their minds. Opinion among Caroline County residents is divided on the issues as
they head into the polls in the first presidential election in a century where there is no local newspaper to report on it.

As of Election Day, Caroline County's 31,000 residents have
experienced only 402 total cases of COVID-19 and six deaths
between April 1 and October 21 owing in part to its rural location and low population density. Even wearing masks in public
places caught on eventually.

The county had been poised in January for a very good year.
That outlook was gutted by COVID-19, but the fallout here was
less severe than in other locales. Unemployment rose from 3.3
percent in February to 10.9 percent over the summer and settled
at 6.6 percent by November 2020. Several planned commercial
developments were still a "go," however, so it was not all gloom
and doom here.

In 2016, Caroline was one of a handful of pivot counties in
the state that gave Trump a 5 percent win over Hillary Clinton
in Virginia—after handing Barack Obama a 12 percent win in
2008 and an 8 percent win in 2012. My crystal ball is no more

reliable than others'. Still, I see Biden taking Caroline County and Virginia this year, but not by a landslide.

Few Republicans will switch to Biden, in my view, but a number of independents who went for Trump in 2016 are feeling buyer's remorse. In Caroline County, I also see incumbent Democratic U.S. senator Mark Warner and Republican First District congressman Rob Wittman ahead. Campaign spending in the neighboring Seventh Congressional District race between Democratic incumbent Abigail Spanberger and challenger Nick Freitas has outstripped spending on the presidential race in all of Virginia. That race is a toss-up.

SANDRA SANCHEZ, McALLEN

Early voting surpassed all previous records in Hidalgo County, the largest county in the Rio Grande Valley, despite the area having one of the worst COVID-19 infection and deaths rates in the nation.

As of October 25, 140,499 early votes had been cast, 8,000 more than for all of the early voting period in Hidalgo County during the 2016 presidential election, according to Hidalgo County officials. The total number of registered voters to date is the largest ever set in the county.

Early voting began October 13, a week earlier than usual, to allow for more voters to safely access the polls and to help minimize the spread of the deadly virus, which has killed 1,924 people and sickened more than 35,000 in this county of 860,000 people.

Months ago, most voters had adamantly rejected the idea of voting in person because of the lockdown and the spiraling death rates from coronavirus. But on the day early voting began, lines snaked around parking lots of voting sites, and thousands of people gave up their lunch hours and dinner hours to wait to cast their ballots.

Drive-through voting is available at a few sites to anyone who pulls up and honks. One poll worker told me you don't have to have an excuse: just pull up, hit your horn, "and I'll come out and take your vote."

At other polling sites, voters are given long sterilized Q-tips on sticks to touch the electronic poll screens. Drivers' licenses are doused in antibacterial liquid as they sit in a tray before election workers will handle them. Most are returned wet and sticky, but poll workers say it is necessary.

Signs for either Trump/Pence or Biden/Harris have started to pop up in front yards throughout the region as Election Day approaches. Billboards and palm trees are also decorated. This is the most outwardly politically active this region has been since March. And it is a testament to the strong feelings voters have toward their choice for president that they are willing to risk contracting the virus to venture out to vote.

This area has long been a Democratic stronghold, and Biden is expected to easily win here, but Texas turning blue is a very long shot. Either way, the election process has prevailed because with more than 7.8 million Texans—46 percent of registered voters—casting their ballots early, it is obvious that for this election, at least, Texas voters are engaged and participating, and that is a big win.

CHARLES RICHARDSON, MACON

Please, let it be over.

The year 2020 will not be soon forgotten. We have been sheltering, mostly in place, since March as COVID-19 has ravaged through our communities. A shudder went through me when the Trump campaign announced it was planning a rally at our Middle Georgia Regional Airport on October 16, and I imagined all those maskless people flocking to see Donald Trump.

Before the rally, Professor Joshua Weitz of Georgia Tech told Georgia Public Broadcasting/Macon that those planning to attend had to assume there was an almost certain risk that someone there would have COVID-19. But the rally didn't disappoint its organizers: thousands attended, and although the campaign took temperatures and offered masks, few wore them or practiced social distancing.

Meanwhile, not far from the rally, a red-and-white billboard on Interstate 75 South read, "Trump COVID superspreader event," with a huge arrow pointing in the direction of the airport.

It was frightening to think that COVID-19 would be racing its way back to communities in a state that even by this point barely had a handle on the pandemic. In Macon–Bibb County, there were 209 cases per 100,000 in the two weeks before the rally, and not a single surrounding county had a rate lower than 100 cases.

These fears do not stop with the pandemic. How will the end of this year play out? If Republicans lose, will all hell break loose? Will the Proud Boys and groups of their ilk wreak havoc, or will they continue to "stand by"? Will the president concede and bow out gracefully, or will he encourage insurrection? Will he use unfounded claims of voter fraud to fan the flames of his discontent?

I fear that if Trump loses, some of his followers will try to start a second civil war, with his encouragement.

And there is another question I've asked myself and others: What will we do if Trump wins? I've thought about my options:

Canada, Mexico, or some island in the Caribbean? America, no matter how flawed, will not be the same America I grew up loving. I know people who are loyal to Trump. I will never speak to them again.

The long early-voting lines are encouraging, even in the face of voter suppression. It's hard to believe that Macon–Bibb County, with a population of only 156,000, has more drop-box locations for absentee ballots than Harris County, home to Houston, with a population of 4.5 million.

Long lines at the polls, mainly in minority neighborhoods, are the rule, and our new voting system has been found lacking. I am praying for a landslide, but even with an overwhelming victory by Democrats, the time between November 4 and January 20 will be fraught with danger for our republic.

JASON TOGYER, McKEESPORT

On some days in 2020, I have been afraid to check my email or text messages. Besides COVID-19 and the bitter presidential campaign, in June my dad passed away of esophageal cancer at age seventy-five. He had otherwise been healthy, as far as we knew. It turned out he hid the illness from us until shortly before his death.

We'll never know how he developed the cancer. He was only an occasional smoker and a social drinker. I suspect his illness was related to breathing silica dust while working in a steel foundry in McKeesport, but I also believe it was related to the near constant ulcers and heartburn he suffered in his thirties and forties, brought on in part by repeated stretches of unemployment as Pittsburgh's steel industry collapsed. (He eventually and fortunately had a second, lengthy career as a schoolteacher.)

I wonder how the emotional strain of our current pandemic, the resultant economic downturn, and the possibility of President Trump contesting the election results will affect people's health in the future. According to the Centers for Disease Control and other researchers, depression and anxiety disorders have increased substantially since April 2020.

Sometimes I worry that my own anxiety is leading to paranoia. My wife sent away for an absentee ballot to vote in the presidential election. It turned out to be one of nearly 29,000 Allegheny County ballots that were incorrectly printed by Midwest Direct, a Cleveland vendor. On Friday night, two Republican candidates sued the county, asking for my wife's ballot and others to be set aside and challenged.

Tens of thousands of absentee ballots printed by Midwest Direct for neighboring Westmoreland County went missing or were sent late. According to the *New York Times* on October 16, 2020, the company had until then been flying a "TRUMP 2020" flag at its headquarters. Is it all coincidence? Or is it part of a concerted effort by Republicans to undermine the vote in swing-state Pennsylvania?

As a child, I lived through the demise of heavy industry in western Pennsylvania and years of double-digit unemployment, including Dad's repeated layoffs. As a newspaper reporter, I covered countless tragedies, from fires, accidents, and homicides to the crash of Flight 93 in Somerset County on September 11, 2001. But none of it really prepared me for the endless, grinding, daily stress of 2020.

POSTSCRIPT:
JANUARY 20, 2021

McALLEN

On an unusually chilly and gray day in South Texas, one week before his presidency ended and the first time he was seen in public after a deadly mob attacked the U.S. Capitol, Donald Trump arrived at a stretch of border wall south of a very Texas-sounding town, Alamo.

Wearing a dark coat, Trump emerged from his vehicle caravan slightly before 2:00 p.m. CST on January 12, 2021. He had flown on Air Force One to Harlingen and then helicoptered to the nearby city of McAllen because the scene at the border wall wasn't fit for Marine One to land there. There was still an active construction site, a mammoth steel structure that had recently been built amid the rugged and dirt-swept terrain to keep people out of the United States.

With purposeful steps and a wide grin, Trump strode up to the thirty-foot-tall steel-bollard wall and admired it as his top remaining leaders at the Department of Homeland Security gave him adoring handshakes and applause. This particular half-mile section had been painted jet black just for his visit, which was to commemorate the 450th mile built during his presidency

"We worked long and hard to get it done, and they said we couldn't get it done. It's one of the longest infrastructure projects in the history of our country," Trump told a select crowd of about a hundred, mostly agents and officers with the U.S. Border Patrol and U.S. Customs and Border Protection. "We can't let the next administration even think of taking it down. That can't happen."

But it might just happen.

On his first day in office, President Joe Biden stopped the construction of sections of the border wall by issuing an executive order that revoked the emergency order issued by Trump that had allowed him to transfer billions of dollars from military funds into the building of a wall along the southwestern border with Mexico.

The border wall was without a doubt Trump's signature project—one that he had campaigned on in 2016 with the promise that Mexico would pay for it. But Mexico didn't. U.S. taxpayers did, and they still are, according to the $1.375 billion that Congress appropriated in the fiscal year 2021 budget even after Trump lost the election to Biden.

"This is a real success story," Trump continued. "When I took office, we inherited a broken, dysfunctional, and open border. Everybody was pouring in at will." He went on to accuse "free speech of being under assault like never before," and he rebuffed any notion that the Twenty-Fifth Amendment would be used to remove him from office.

In the end, he wasn't removed, but he never finished building the wall either. With his presidency ended, the future of his "big, beautiful wall" is uncertain, and miles-wide gaps remain between sections. Biden pledged not to build "another foot of wall," but he started to use the term *smart border controls*, which many expect to mean that the underground sensors, forty-foot-tall floodlights, infrared cameras, and other means of virtual spying will stay in place in border communities from the Gulf of Mexico in South Texas to the Pacific Ocean in California.

I found it curious that so many lamented the eight-foot-tall barbed-wire fencing and "militarization" of the inauguration on January 20 without bringing up the fact that an even more extensive militarization is found in border communities because of the border wall.

This doesn't seem to bother the majority of Americans. Whether the already rusting miles of border wall built during Trump's term in office will stay or we will spend additional billions in taxpayer funds to remove it is left to be seen.

—Sandra Sanchez

MACON

Can an entire community breathe a sigh of relief? That's what I observed in Middle Georgia in the second week of January 2021: a collective sigh that came from all political divisions.

Erin Keller, for one, stood happily before the downtown Macon Rotary Club on Wednesday, January 20, as a member donating to the club and bragging about the community. Keller, one of the youngest members of the local Rotary Club, said, "Today we made history. The first woman, the first African American woman, and the first Asian woman to be elected vice president of the United States." Explaining that daughters can now grow up to be anything, Keller said, "For my grandmothers when they were alive, this wasn't even in their wildest dreams. It was not a dream. It was unimaginable."

Even from voters who weren't as happy, there were still sighs of relief. Why? Voter fatigue. While the rest of the country

exhaled after the presidential election, in the Peach State we kept
going, enduring back-to-back-to-back-to-back campaign ads for
another two months. Regular advertisers disappeared from our
screens, even during the Christmas rush, as almost $1 billion was
spent by four candidates for the runoff that would decide control of the U.S. Senate. So soon after almost 5 million voted in
the November 3 election, more than 4.5 million voters returned
to the Georgia polls on January 5 in another record to vote for
either Republican senators David Perdue and Kelly Loeffler or
Democrats Jon Ossoff and Reverend Raphael Warnock.

Of Georgia's 159 counties, Warnock and Ossoff won only
thirty, and Macon–Bibb County was one of them. In the statewide vote count, however, Ossoff beat Perdue by 55,232 votes, and
Warnock bested Loeffler by 93,550, far above Joseph Biden's
11,779 margin over Donald Trump. Though the Georgia results
in the presidential election were clear, as the three recounts con-
sistently confirmed, Trump continued his "Stop the Steal"
campaign. The day before the January 5 runoff, he attempted to
involve Macon–Bibb County in his self-made controversy. He
claimed, according to the almost daily newspaper the *Telegraph*
(published six days a week), that he had "23,000 votes and Biden
had around 17,000 votes at 9:11 p.m." Trump said, "The vote
count switched a few minutes later, with Biden in the lead with
12,000 additional votes and Trump at 17,000 votes." Mike
Kaplan, the chair of the Macon–Bibb County Board of Elections, said of Trump's accusation, "Mr. Trump is sadly misin-
formed and must be getting his information and his news from
social media because what he said happened never happened."
Biden won the county by 16,883 votes.

Trump is widely believed to have depressed the Republican
turnout in the January 5 runoff. On the previous Saturday, January 2, came the release of the hour-long phone call Trump made

to Georgia's secretary of state, Brad Raffensperger, a fellow Republican, whom he both threatened and practically begged to find 11,780 votes that would give him a one-point win, even though the vote count had already been certified. On Monday, January 4, Trump held an evening rally in Dalton, Georgia, where instead of vigorously campaigning for Loeffler and Perdue, he continued to rant about voter fraud. Perdue, who had outpolled Trump in November, received almost 2,500 fewer votes in the runoff. As for Loeffler, if you add the totals of her Republican rival, Representative Doug Collins, to her own in the November 3 "jungle" primary, she received almost 58,000 fewer votes in the runoff.

The fatigue in this part of the country was palpable, and it was not just from the elections. The shadow of COVID-19 was everywhere. Dr. Patrice Walker, the chief medical officer for Navicent Health, the largest health system outside of Atlanta, said, "We've had high admissions rates and have added additional intensive care units in nontraditional spaces. It's not just a bed," she said. "Health-care workers get sick, too. Staffing is a struggle. It's been rough." The vaccine had a slow rollout as 2020 passed into 2021, not because people were hesitant to take it, though some were, including health-care workers, but because supplies of the vaccine were still spotty or nonexistent.

As the virus continued to rage, politics were quiet, but an undercurrent of fear lingered. Although some people were waking from the lie-induced fog and allegiance to Trump, others were still loyal. But the event that shook residents from their comfort in the win or despair in the loss was the unimaginable invasion of the U.S. Capitol on January 6, apparently instigated by Trump. "I listened to the oath differently this time," said Emily Hopkins, another young member of the Rotary Club, particularly the part where it says, 'I will support and defend the

Constitution of the United States against all enemies, foreign and domestic.' I heard the domestic part differently. I hope this is the darkness before the light."

Although this episode has ended, and the past four years may fade in our memories, what we all have experienced can't be wiped clean so quickly. It's a national scar. We now know the depth Trump's loyalists will go to in order to remain relevant in an ever-changing, multicultural society. Trump may not be in office now, but the struggle is not over.

—Charles E. Richardson

BOWLING GREEN

The residents of Caroline County Virginia survived their first presidential election in a century without the services of the local weekly newspaper, the *Caroline Progress*, which had withered on the vine for years and finally ceased publication on March 28, 2018. *Survived* is the key word here. Many miss the *Progress*, but with only 31,000 residents and few local businesses to advertise in the county, no replacement has proven viable.

The local aspects of the 2020 election, at least, went largely unnoticed by the bulk of the population. Those with an interest in politics made do with the daily but circulation-limited *Fredericksburg Free Lance-Star*, with regional and national TV, and with a very flawed and loosely disorganized network of social media outlets. The results at the polls in November were a mirror image of 2016. Donald Trump again carried Caroline County by a slim margin, but Virginia as a whole went for Joe Biden largely because of ample majorities in northern Virginia and other urban and suburban pockets. I had assumed from conversations with friends and neighbors and from local social media posts that Trump support had waned locally, but I was wrong. Caroline County had been named a pivot county in 2016 when Trump defeated Hillary Clinton by 5.02 percent of the vote. In 2020, he won by 4.17 percent, the difference easily explained by 1.59 percent of the vote going for the Libertarian ticket.

The incumbent First District congressman, Rob Wittman, who ran as an affable and reasonable Republican, easily defeated his Democrat challenger. Despite his moderate campaign rhetoric, Wittman jumped aboard the Trump bandwagon again, disputing the fairness of the election, thus irritating many of his constituents and prompting a flurry of letters to the editor and social media posts that went on and on.

Rural in character and habit, Caroline County had survived the early months of the pandemic with few reported cases and only a handful of hospitalizations and deaths. Unfortunately, widespread complacence and a tradition of large family holiday gatherings had their effect, and infections exploded in November and December. There were 402 total cases in Caroline County as of October 21. By January 23, 2021, this number had more than tripled to 1,429. Whether a local newspaper would have had any impact on this rapid spread is uncertain, but it could have disseminated information and evidence in a systematic and responsible manner. Facebook and other social media posts urging mask wearing and social distancing simply prompted all too predictable kneejerk responses from the antimaskers and disbelievers, and there were many of them around here.

A shining light was the excellent and energetic reporting on COVID-19, local hospitals, and the Rappahannock Area Health District by a veteran *Free Lance-Star* reporter, Cathy Dyson, who turned the pandemic into a full-time beat. So far, Caroline County's rural isolation has also slowed distribution of the

278 & POSTSCRIPT: JANUARY 20, 2021

vaccine. As of January 23, 2021, only 960 doses had been given, and only 107 residents had been fully vaccinated.

Even though the Biden–Harris ticket failed to carry Caroline County, it had many ardent supporters here, and some of them would likely have made the short drive to Washington, DC, to celebrate the inauguration had it not been for the pandemic and the January 6 storming of the U.S. Capitol. Spectators stayed home on January 20. As it was, the only local residents in attendance were likely in the National Guard. Members of the Fredericksburg-based 229th Brigade Engineer Battalion were among the first 1,000 Virginia guardsmen dispatched to assist in security. (That announcement came from A. A. "Cotton" Puryear, the chief of public affairs for the Virginia National Guard. Cotton was my freelance sports editor twenty years ago when I was editor of the *Madison County Eagle*, the only one of the six newspapers I worked for in a forty-year career that still exists.)

A year ago, when we started this series, I was asked for one photo that summed up Caroline County and its county seat, Bowling Green. I submitted a shot of the historic county courthouse with the ubiquitous Confederate monument in the foreground, a lone and nameless soldier on a high pedestal. As I wrote in chapter 1, "In some respects, change comes slowly to Caroline County and its residents, many of whose families have lived here for generations."

Still, change sometimes does come. As a result of the 2020 Black Lives Matter movement and polite but serious pressure from the Black community here, the county supervisors voted to remove the monument, a decision that did not please all. The statue now resides in a nearby cemetery where there are Civil War graves.

—Greg Glassner

McKEESPORT

While the eyes of the nation were fixed on various Republican Party challenges to and fraud conspiracies regarding the results of the 2020 presidential election, we had our own drama here in western Pennsylvania.

Our Democratic state senator Jim Brewster, a well-liked former mayor of McKeesport, was seeking his third full term in 2020. He faced a formidable challenge from a family law attorney in neighboring Westmoreland County, Nicole Ziccarelli, a Republican who garnered more than $2 million in support from the state party as well as the help of top-flight advertising experts.

Brewster had begun his reelection campaign stressing bipartisanship—he's one of the most conservative Democrats in the Pennsylvania State Senate, with widespread support from law enforcement and gun-rights groups.

Nevertheless, in direct-mail flyers and ads on cable television, Republicans portrayed Brewster as an out-of-touch, tax-and-spend liberal. It didn't hurt that Ziccarelli was an engaging speaker with a strong social media following and deep roots in the same communities where Brewster had built his base. On Election Night, she led by about 1,500 votes.

But Pennsylvania wasn't allowed to count mail-in and absentee ballots until after Election Day, and those ballots, when counted, broke about three-to-one for Democrats, giving Brewster the narrowest of leads—fewer than one hundred votes. State law requires that absentee ballots be signed and dated. Republicans alleged that election officials in Pittsburgh violated Ziccarelli's civil rights by counting absentee ballots that voters had failed to date but had been given a machine-stamped date instead. Excluding those ballots—more than 2,300—would have given Ziccarelli a victory.

A county judge rejected the Republican argument, as did a split Pennsylvania Supreme Court. Ziccarelli challenged their decision in U.S. District Court in Pittsburgh, using one of the same attorneys (and some of the same arguments) as Trump's campaign. Indeed, one of Brewster's colleagues, Jay Costa Jr., the Pennsylvania Senate minority leader, called the legal maneuvers "Trumpian."

The federal judge—a Trump appointee—eventually upheld Brewster's reelection, calling the Ziccarelli camp's arguments "novel" but invalid. Still, the dispute made national and international news when Pennsylvania Republicans refused to allow Brewster to take his oath of office. Pennsylvania's colorful lieutenant governor, John Fetterman, himself a former mayor in nearby Braddock, was removed as the Senate's presiding officer after he demanded that Brewster be seated.

On several occasions, Republican senators from adjoining districts flatly stated that absentee votes for Brewster were fraudulent and demanded that only "legal votes" be counted, literally adopting Trump's language. At one point, the majority leader suggested the state Senate would seat Ziccarelli if Republicans disagreed with the reasoning behind the federal judge's decision—in essence, making the state Senate both a legislative and a judicial branch.

Some of those same senators who alleged Brewster's reelection was fraudulent and refused to seat him will now need to work with him on regional development and transportation projects. I can't help but wonder just how successful those collaborations will be.

At *Tube City Almanac*, we played the dispute down the middle. I felt Ziccarelli had a valid point—state law clearly directs voters to both sign and date their ballots. However, past court decisions have usually erred on the side of enfranchising voters who make simple clerical mistakes.

That didn't matter to some readers, though, who claimed that Brewster had somehow "cheated" or that I was writing "propaganda" for the Democratic Party. ("How much is Brewster paying you?" one woman demanded.)

As we were writing almost daily stories about the dispute, a McKeesport police officer was shot—but thankfully only wounded. The wide-scale manhunt for the suspect included my own neighborhood and triggered protests from some residents and civil rights groups, which we also covered.

Those two months following the election left me worn out and frustrated about both the limitations of local journalism in the coming years and the deepening divisions in American democracy. By the second week of January, I was exhausted. Tube City Online is a nonprofit website run by volunteers, and I don't draw any salary (not even from Jim Brewster). I finally wrote to my board members, "I don't know if I can do this anymore. I'm worn out. I need help." They heard my message, and we're trying to come up with a path to sustainability that will preserve my own sanity.

I hope having Trump out of office will turn down the temperature on some of the political rhetoric. But Donald Trump Jr. is rumored to be considering a run in Pennsylvania for U.S. senator Pat Toomey's seat in 2022. (Lieutenant Governor Fetterman announced his own campaign for the Democratic nomination for the same seat.) Last week, someone on our street put up a flag that says, "TRUMP, THE SEQUEL: MAKE LIBERALS CRY AGAIN." So my optimism is—as they say—tempered by reality on the ground.

—Jason Togyer

This project began with a conversation in September 2019 between Kyle Pope, the editor and publisher of *Columbia Journalism Review*, and me. It was the kind of conversation that takes place in newsrooms large and small all the time (or did before COVID-19, when everything moved to Zoom): a reporter or editor runs into a colleague (our offices at the Columbia Journalism School are down the hall from each other) and says something along the lines of "Wouldn't it be interesting to . . . ?"

In this instance, the question revolved, as so many questions then did, around Donald Trump. In the months after his surprising victory over Hillary Clinton in 2016 (surprising to everyone, even, reportedly, Trump himself), the question among journalists was retrospective: How did we not see that coming? In September 2019, as Trump prepared to seek reelection and the Democrats began searching for someone who might defeat him, the question turned to the future: If we missed the story last time by not seeing what was taking place across the country, how could we best report the mood of the nation as the months, weeks, and days toward Election Day 2020 counted down? Or put more simply: How do we not blow it again?

This would necessitate a completely different way of covering an election year—a break from the familiar formula of polling, events, talking-heads analysis. It would mean looking at America not from New York or Washington but from the places New York and Washington know only as flyover cities and perhaps campaign bus stops.

Kyle suggested that if this were to be a journalism story, it would mean confronting the great crisis of the hollowing out of local newspapers. How is the story of a place at a moment in time told if the newspapers where those stories were once told are gone or vastly diminished?

With that suggestion, we set about searching for places from which to tell the story. We settled on four as an ideal number: enough to give a range but not too many to clutter the narrative we were envisioning. The search was aided considerably by a remarkably comprehensive report from the Hussman School of Media and Journalism at the University of North Carolina, Chapel Hill, titled *News Deserts and Ghost Newspapers: Will Local News Survive?* (at https://www.usnewsdeserts.com/). The report, overseen by Penelope Muse Abernathy, the Knight Chair in Journalism and Digital Media Economics, offered a detailed breakdown of where U.S. newspapers had gone out of business or where the staff had been so reduced as to render the community a "news desert." There was no shortage of potential locations; there were, in fact, hundreds of such towns across the country. We searched for months—first culling through the dispiriting list of the news deserts, then doing deep dives into those potential communities.

But because the journalism story we wanted to tell would be a narrative and therefore a series of dispatches propelled by the drama of an uncertain outcome, it was essential that we avoid communities that were either deep red or deep blue. We began with the towns themselves, all the while looking for a geographic spread. We cross-referenced the state of the towns' journalism with census data as well as with voting records for the past few presidential elections: Had there been changes? Were the votes close? Had a community, say, voted twice for Barack Obama but then switched to Trump? What were the demographics? Who lived there now as opposed to fifteen or twenty years ago? What had changed among those who lived in that particular place, and how did the changes affect the local politics?

It was one thing to find a town; it was quite another to find a journalist who lived there and worked or had worked there and whose knowledge was deep. There was something more: Would this journalist, already a seasoned pro or perhaps retired, be willing to try a very different way of telling her or his town's story?

Our search led us to the towns covered in this book and to the journalists whose stories you have read.

One of the most thrilling—and unnerving—experiences journalists encounter is watching a story change before their eyes. We begin one place, with a question that propels our inquiry, our reporting. Then, without warning, the story can begin to change—sometimes because what we are learning compels us to pivot in our thinking, sometimes because circumstances refuse to remain as we first encountered them. No one could have predicted what 2020 would bring to journalism, to America, and to the world.

It takes wise journalists to adapt on the fly, to toss aside whatever preconceived notions they have brought to their stories, to their reporting. Lucky for us, we found four journalists who knew just what to do when the world turned on its head.

—Michael Shapiro

INDEX

INDEX ∞ 287

43–48; in Iowa Democratic
caucuses, 4

campaign operatives. *See
politiqueras*
Cantor, Eric, 205–6
Caprio, Deborah, 209–10
CARES. *See* Coronavirus Aid,
Relief, and Economic
Security Act
Caroline County, Virginia: on Joe
Biden, 45, 47, 266; as Bowling
Green, 11; business closures and,
72; Buttigieg and, 43–48; citizens
and land of, 13–14; on H.
Clinton, 41, 265, 277; on
Confederate statues, 233–35, 278;
COVID-19 cases in, 71–74,
97–101, 124–27, 238–39, 265, 277;
COVID-19 election story on,
127–28, 207, 265; Democrats in,
11, 14, 41–45; elections in, 203–7,
265, 276–78; guns, dogs, and
football in, 11, 13; horses in, 16–17;
local story coverage for, 71–75,
173–79; masks in, 98, 239, 265; on
newspaper loss, 14–15; Northam
and, 73, 98, 101–2, 125–26, 129,
238; for Obama, 11, 14, 41–42, 265;
racial segregation in, 18; on
Sanders, 44–47; train stations of,
15–16; for D. J. Trump, 11, 14,
41–42, 265, 276–77;
unemployment in, 17–18, 265
Caroline Progress: churches and, 69,
71, 173; COVID-19 on, 70; loss
of, 173, 276; for ninety-nine

years, 11, 14, 42, 69, 173; staff of,
74, 177–78
Carter, Johnny, 243
Chapman, Jim, 121–23
Chatham Asset Management, 188,
212, 245
Chauvin, Derek, 5–6
Cherepko, Michael, 192
Christiansen, Clayton, 2–3
churches: of Bowling Green, 15;
and *Caroline Progress*, 69, 71, 173;
on Confederate statues, 233–35,
237; COVID-19 and, 77–78, 82,
125, 129, 131, 182, 192, 243,
246–47; journalists and, 87; of
Laredo, 39; of Macon, 21–22, 24,
50, 77–78, 182, 241; of
McKeesport, 30–31, 58–59,
140–41, 192; newspapers for, 1,
87, 140–41, 179; in Virginia, 129,
153, 233–34
Cisneros, Jessica, 66
Civil Rights Act of 1964, 152
classified advertising: loss of, 3,
53–54, 139, 174–75, 177; readers
reading, 9; as unsustainable, 3
Clinton, Bill, 41, 250
Clinton, Hillary, 206; Allegheny
County for, 224, 251; Blacks for,
32–33; Caroline County on, 41,
265, 277; McKeesport for, 32;
Pennsylvania Blacks for, 250;
Philadelphia for, 221; race legacy
on D. J. Trump or, 32–33; for
status quo, 31; surprise loss by,
282; without western
Pennsylvania, 251–52

COLUMBIA JOURNALISM REVIEW BOOKS

Second Read: Writers Look Back at Classic Works of Reportage, edited by James Marcus and the Staff of the Columbia Journalism Review

The Story so Far: What We Know About the Business of Digital Journalism, Bill Grueskin, Ava Seave, and Lucas Graves

The Best Business Writing 2012, edited by Dean Starkman, Martha M. Hamilton, Ryan Chittum, and Felix Salmon

The Art of Making Magazines: On Being an Editor and Other Views from the Industry, edited by Victor S. Navasky and Evan Cornog

The Best Business Writing 2013, edited by Dean Starkman, Martha M. Hamilton, Ryan Chittum, and Felix Salmon

The Watchdog That Didn't Bark: The Financial Crisis and the Disappearance of Investigative Journalism, Dean Starkman

Beyond News: The Future of Journalism, Mitchell Stephens

The New Censorship: Inside the Global Battle for Media Freedom, Joel Simon

The Best Business Writing 2014, edited by Dean Starkman, Martha M. Hamilton, and Ryan Chittum

Engaged Journalism: Connecting with Digitally Empowered News Audiences, Jake Batsell

The Best Business Writing 2015, edited by Dean Starkman, Martha M. Hamilton, and Ryan Chittum

Journalism After Snowden: The Future of the Free Press in the Surveillance State, edited by Emily Bell and Taylor Owen, with Smitha Khorana and Jennifer R. Henrichsen

Journalism Under Fire: Protecting the Future of Investigative Reporting, Stephen Gillers

Printed and bound by CPI Group (UK) Ltd, Croydon, CR0 4YY

03/05/2023

03215920-0001